NELSON'S ANNUAL
Youth Ministry
SOURCEBOOK

2007 EDITION

NELSON'S ANNUAL
Youth Ministry
SOURCEBOOK

2007 EDITION

NELSON REFERENCE & ELECTRONIC
A Division of Thomas Nelson Publishers
Since 1798
www.thomasnelson.com

Book design and composition by Kristy L. Morell, Smyrna, Tennessee

ISBN 1-4185-0896-9

ISBN-13 9781418508968

Printed in the United States of America.
1 2 3 – 07 06

Contents

Feature Articles

Introduction

In case no one's mentioned this to you lately, you're a gift from God. You may not always feel it, your students may never say it, their parents may not know it, but you are a gift from God in service to teenagers. Yours is not the most sought after position in most churches. But, those of us called to this service know its secret. There is no better place to be! We use our vacation for camp, our home for sleepovers, our cars to teach driving skills, and our cell phones for midnight calls. Oops, are those the things we love? If you read that list and didn't cringe, you love serving teens. They are full of passion. They care deeply in spite of what adults perceive. They desperately need you to love and teach them, and to simply pay attention to them.

The world pays a great deal of attention to them. Just check out TV, radio, movies, and advertising. The world pays attention, but not in the way we would like. It has all the resources, money, and technology that we could ever dream of having. How can it be possible that an evening of reading scripture and prayer can compete with the world?

Here's the good news: Research tells is that regardless of all the world offers, parents are the greatest influence in the lives of their children. Here's even better news: The influence of the world is strong but God's love is stronger. Young people need you to deliver that love to them. They need adults who will speak truth, who will be models of the faith, and accept them as they are.

You are that person! You are a gift to your students from God. He can and will work for them through your life of faith. But if you are burned out, you cannot serve your students. Care first for your spiritual life; this is not selfish, it is the first step in ministering to your students. Draw near to God and your ministry will overflow from this. By taking care of your walk with the Lord, you are teaching more to your students than any lesson ever could. Spend time with Jesus Christ. Be in love with Him!

In such love, take the lessons in this book and make them your own. Each one is broken down into several parts including *Scripture, Memory Verse, Focus, Discovery, Life Application* and *Making It Personal.* Objectives, supply lists and explanations are also provided.

Focus gets the attention of your students. It is intended to help them be fully present with you and with one another by introducing a topic or concept that makes them think and even make them laugh! Adjust this section as you see fit for your group. The *Focus* section helps everyone make the transition from the activities of the day to what the Lord has prepared that evening.

Discovery is the core of the lesson. But this is not a time for a mini-sermon from the youth leader—teens get lectures all the time. *Discovery* assumes they have a brain and can use it. It encourages them to ask questions and seek answers for themselves.

Life Application reveals what the topic means for Christians in general and for your youth group specifically. It is the communal aspect of each lesson.

Making It Personal focuses on the individual. For example, it is good to say Christians should care for the poor but what are you going to do about it? This section does away with generalities and forces young people to come face to face with God while grappling with life and faith.

That is the simple road map of each lesson in this book. If you find blank spaces on the map, fill them in with your experiences in the faith. Nothing here is sacred. Change a lesson to tell your own story. This book is simply a place to begin. You have more to offer your students than any book does. It is doubtful that your students will remember these lessons years from now but they will remember how much you loved them and how you loved the Lord and His Word.

May you be blessed by God and by your service to him until your cup overflows for all to enjoy.

—*Amy Jacober*

Contributors

Ruben Alvarez is a youth ministry veteran working as an Area Director for Young Life's Capernaum in San Jose, California. He is the husband of Renee and father of three beautiful girls. He is a minister who not only works with special needs adolescents but has Cerebral Palsy himself.

Alicia Claxton is a freelance writer living near Nashville, Tennessee. She serves as a student ministry volunteer at ClearView Baptist Church and writes small-group Bible studies and student ministry material for churches across the country.

Adam Cozens is a May 2006 graduate of Azusa Pacific University in Azusa, California. He graduated with a Communications degree with a media emphasis and a Youth Ministry minor.

Kyle Cravens is a full-time Coordinator for Centrifuge, a student camp sponsored by LifeWay Christian Resources, and he teaches the 8th grade students in Sunday school. He is married with a two-year-old son and lives in Franklin, Tennessee.

Joyce DelRosario is an urban veteran and a graduate of Princeton Theological Seminary. She is an Area Director for Young Life. She is particularly interested in ministry to and with Asian American adolescents.

Ben Donley is the Assistant Pastor at Agape Christian Church in Pasadena, California and is the President/Executive Director of Agape Life Change, Inc, a non-profit organization that provides life coaching, affordable housing, and living-wage jobs to the poor. He is married to an amazing singer named Stephanie and is the son of Pat and Paula.

Matthew Freeman is a recent graduate of Azusa Pacific University with a B.A. in Biblical Studies and Theology. He is living in Nashville, Tennessee, and pursuing ministerial opportunities.

Chuck Hunt holds an M.Div. from Fuller Theological Seminary and has worked with middle school, high school, and college students for more than a decade.

Amy Jacober is Assistant Professor of Practical Theology and Youth Ministry at Azusa Pacific University. She is a graduate of Southwestern Baptist Theological Seminary and Fuller Theological Seminary. She serves on the Mission Wide Committee for Young Life Capernaum.

Christine Kern teaches at Azusa Pacific University. She has a Ph.D. in English from the University of Wisconsin.

Sharon Koh is the Director of Young Adult and College Ministries at Evergreen Baptist Church of Los Angeles, California. She is a graduate of Fuller Theological Seminary.

Justin Little is a recent graduate of Azusa Pacific University. His heart is for marginalized communities and he desires to serve in areas of social justice.

Terry Linhart, a 20-year veteran of youth ministry, is Professor of Youth Ministry and Dean of the School of Religion and Philosophy at Bethel College in Indiana. His doctorate is from Purdue, where he studied the curricular nature of short-term service projects. He and his wife, Kelly, are youth ministry volunteers and are proud parents of Lauren, Jayson, and Sean.

Keith McDorman is from Southern California and is a student at Azusa Pacific University. He is addicted to puns.

Dennis Ockholm is Professor of Theology at Azusa Pacific University. He is ordained in the Presbyterian Church (USA) and has been an Oblate of the Order of St. Benedict for a couple of decades. Dennis is finishing a book on Benedictine spirituality for Brazos Press.

Raymond Peacock is Lt. Colonial (Western Territory) in the Salvation Army.

Will Penner is the Executive Editor of *The Journal of Student Ministries,* the President of DevelopMinistries, and a popular speaker at youth leader training events and youth retreats, camps, and conferences. He and his wife are the volunteer youth pastors at Westview United Methodist Church in Fairview, Tennessee. Will is completing his Ph.D. in Education and Human Development at Vanderbilt University.

Carina Proano recently graduated with a bachelor's degree in Youth Ministry from Azusa Pacific University. She is the Associate Youth Director at Sierra Madre Congregational Church in Sierra Madre, California.

Whitney Prosperi has contributed to numerous devotionals and teen magazines, including a devotional used in the Song of Solomon teen conferences. Formerly a girls' minister, she now develops curriculum and Bible studies for teen girls. She has been a conference consultant for the music group Point of Grace, and was a contributor to their latest book. *Lifestyle,* a Bible study for teen girls, is in stores now and her newest book, *Girls Ministry 101,* will come out in August 2006.

David Upchurch serves young married adults on the Maturity and Ministry staff at Champion Forest Baptist Church. He has been in ministry since 1990 and worked with students for over 15 years in churches of various styles and sizes in Texas and Georgia. David is married to Kendra, his high school sweetheart, and they have three children. David has a Communications degree from Baylor University and a Master of Divinity degree from Southwestern Baptist Theological Seminary.

Joe Usher is a student at Azusa Pacific University.

2007 Calendar

January 1	**New Year's Day**
January 6	**Epiphany**
January 7	
January 14	
January 15	**Martin Luther King, Jr. Day**
January 21	**Sanctity of Human Life Sunday**
January 26	**Australia Day**
January 28	
February 1-28	**Black History Month**
February 1	**National Freedom Day**
February 2	**Groundhog Day**
February 4	**Super Bowl Sunday**
February 11	
February 12	**Lincoln's Birthday**
February 14	**Valentine's Day**
February 18	**Chinese New Year**
February 19	**President's Day**
February 21	**Ash Wednesday**
February 22	**Washington's Birthday**
February 25	**First Sunday of Lent;**
	30 Hour Famine—World Vision
March 4	**Second Sunday of Lent; Purim**
March 11	**Third Sunday of Lent;**
	Daylight Saving Time Begins
March 17	**St. Patrick's Day**
March 18	**Fourth Sunday of Lent**
March 21	**Spring Begins**
March 25	**Fifth Sunday of Lent**

April 1	Palm Sunday
April 3	Passover Begins
April 5	Maundy Thursday
April 6	Good Friday
April 8	Easter Sunday
April 9	Easter Monday
April 15	Holocaust Remembrance Day
April 22	Earth Day
April 25	Administrative Professionals' Day
April 29	
May 3	National Day of Prayer
May 5	Cinco de Mayo
May 6	
May 13	Mother's Day
May 17	Ascension Day
May 19	Armed Forces Day
May 20	
May 23	Shavuot
May 27	Pentecost
May 28	Memorial Day
June 3	Trinity Sunday
June 10	
June 14	Flag Day
June 17	Father's Day
June 21	Summer Begins
June 24	
July 1	Canada Day
July 2	Canada Day Observed
July 4	Independence Day
July 8	
July 15	
July 22	Parent's Day

November 12	**Veterans' Day Observed**
November 18	
November 22	**Thanksgiving Day**
November 25	
December 2	**First Sunday of Advent**
December 5	**Hanukkah Begins**
December 7	**Pearl Harbor Remembrance Day**
December 9	**Second Sunday of Advent**
December 10	**Human Rights Day**
December 16	**Third Sunday of Advent**
December 22	**Winter Begins**
December 23	**Fourth Sunday of Advent**
December 24	**Christmas Eve**
December 25	**Christmas Day**
December 26	**Boxing Day (Canada); Kwanzaa Begins**
December 30	
December 31	**New Year's Eve**

Weekly Suggestions for 52 Weeks

Forerunners of Our Faith

by Amy Jocober

In this lesson, students will:
- ✔ Learn that following Jesus can be lonely
- ✔ Understand that God is with us always
- ✔ Recognize that we are surrounded by a great community of believers
- ✔ Take comfort in the lives that have gone before

Stuff you'll need:
- ❏ Blindfolds
- ❏ Large sheet of paper or dry erase board
- ❏ Markers

Memory Verses

And Jesus came up and spoke to them saying, "All authority has been given to Me in heaven and on earth. Go therefore and make disciples of all the nations, baptizing them in the name of the Father and the Son and the Holy Spirit, teaching them to observe all that I commanded you; and lo, I am with you always, even to the end of the age." —Matthew 28:18–20

Scripture

Hebrews 12:1–3

Lesson in a Sentence

We are neither the first nor the last people to follow Jesus Christ.

The Big Picture

Each new generation of Christians faces new challenges. Each believer follows a host of others and is part of a community of believers around the world. We are not alone. Teenagers may think their group is the only one trying to follow Jesus. It can be disheartening and confusing when you feel left out of the majority. It is encouraging to know that others too have struggled, survived, and even thrived in the faith. The stories of those who have gone before show us the shoulders on which we stand. There is strength in numbers and God has provided for us a great cloud of witnesses!

Focus

Option 1

Create a Sherpa walk with your students. On a mountain trail, the sherpa is the guide, the one who sets the pace and makes certain all of the people are on track. The Sherpa however must have the cooperation of those following. If they mess around or don't pay attention the consequences can be as minimal as bumping into the person in front of him or her or it could mean sliding down the mountain to ones death.

There are two ways to do this activity. Take your pick and feel free to alter them as you prefer.

Have your group break into partners. One partner is the Sherpa, the other will be blindfolded and depend on their Sherpa. The Sherpa may not touch their partner or use words to lead. Set a distant location as the goal. For example: The end of the block or down the stairs and to the front lawn of the church. Choose a location that will take ten to fifteen minutes to complete. Once the team has reached the goal, switch roles and come back.

OR

Blindfold teams of six to fifteen people with one Sherpa leading the group on a walk. The Sherpa will talk loud enough for only the first few people to hear. The directions must be passed down the line in order for teammates to not be lost or hurt. If your walk is going to be complicated, allow the team to hold hands.

Option 2

Invite a few pillars of your church community to share their faith journey with your group. This can be a great opportunity to connect elders of your church with the youth group. Ask them to share how they learned of Jesus and who in their life was a mentor along the way.

Point out to your students that no matter who you are, we all have had others pour into our lives. As Christians, we are not alone and we stand on the shoulders of generations who have come before.

Discovery

Break into three groups. Have each group read Hebrews 12:1-3. Each group reads all three verses but focus their attention on only one. Questions will focus their attention. After each group has had a chance to look at the passage and the questions, bring them back together to share their findings.

Group 1:
Hebrews 12:1
What does "cloud of witnesses" mean?
Describe the race the passage mentions.

Group 2:
Hebrews 12:2
What does it mean to fix your eyes on Jesus? How can we do this?
What did Jesus endure to sit at the right hand of the throne of God?

Group 3:
Hebrews 12:3
How does Jesus' enduring hostility help us to not grow weary and lose heart?

For the whole group:
How does a race tie into persecution?
Isn't it a little crazy to think that just because Jesus endured hostility 2,000 years ago that we are somehow not supposed to grow weary or get discouraged?

Push your students to wrestle with this. We have the Holy Spirit and other believers to help us through difficult times but we often do not recognize that we are not alone.

Teacher's Note:
Hebrews was written to Jewish believers who heard testimony of those who had known Jesus and were now undergoing persecution. Persecution still happens today all around the world. Some of your students may be feelings some pressures with regard to authentically following Jesus. While this is not the level of persecution that others around the world experience it can feel overwhelming during adolescence. Explain the context of persecution to your students as they consider these questions.

Life Application
We all struggle at times. We all need others to encourage us along the way.
Choose your favorite sports movie. Pick one that relates to a sport you know your students like:
Soccer—*Bend it like Beckham*
Football—*Remember the Titans*
Basketball—*Glory Road*
Hockey—*Miracle*
Boxing—*Cinderella Man*

Find a scene where the team is struggling to survive and the fans, their families, or their friends give the boost they need.

How does a clip like this relate to the passage we've just read?

What is the hardest part of life?

What makes it hard to follow Jesus?

Do you know anyone who is authentically seeking to follow Him?

Have you ever that when you get serious about following Jesus that life gets more difficult? Why would this be?

The film clip shows a team that has struggled, that has worked hard and when they really decided to go for it, they hurt and grew tired. They could have given up. In fact, in many cases they do, at least temporarily. It is not out of their own power that they are able to continue on. They need each other and they need their fans to keep them going. As Christians we're not that different. Most of us have the best of intentions but when we get serious about following Jesus, life changes. Your friends may reject you, family may mock or misunderstand you, you are left out of parties and other activities that are normal for other teens.

Making it Personal

Ask each student to consider:

Where do you struggle?

Where do you need encouragement?

Is there someone in your life you can ask for encouragement?

Just as they need encouragement, invite each of them to look for others who need encouragement.

Close in prayer asking the Holy Spirit to encourage each person in the throughout the week. Ask that they may encourage others in need.

Memory Verse Activity

Most often we look to this verse as admonition that we are to share our faith. Indeed this is true. Another truth however is clear in this verse: The Holy Spirit is with us each and every day until the end of the age.

Spend some time talking through this verse and what it means for us to have the Comforter, the Holy Spirit, with us as we walk through daily struggles.

Songs

Bethany Dillon's "Hero" *Music Inspired by The Chronicles of Narnia*

Connections:
- Romans 9:24–27
- Luke 3:18
- Acts 11:23–24

Extra Extra!!

Consider the history and tradition from which we come. You may want to introduce your students to a few notable people from church history reminding them that we come from centuries of others who struggled to continue in the faith. Check out a church history book from your pastor's library or do an internet search on such people as John Wycliffe, Thomas Cranmer, Martin Luther, John Calvin, or William Carey.

Forerunners of Our Faith

by Amy Jocober

Memory Verse

And Jesus came up and spoke to them saying, "All authority has been given to Me in heaven and on earth. Go therefore and make disciples of all the nations, baptizing them in the name of the Father and the Son and the Holy Spirit, teaching them to observe all that I commanded you; and lo, I am with you always, even to the end of the age."
—Matthew 28:18–20

Scripture

Hebrews 11:1–40

Lesson in a sentence

We are neither the first nor the last people to follow Jesus Christ.

Focus

Hand each student a strip of paper. On this paper, ask each person to write a trait for which they may be known. This can be anything from being a vegetarian to loving hockey. Encourage them to choose something that even an acquaintance might know. These can be funny or serious as long as it relates to the student who wrote it.

Distribute lined paper for your students to take a quiz. Collect the strips papers and read only the traits aloud. Have each student make a list of who they think belongs to each trait. Once you have read each strip, go back and read them again including the names and traits allowing your students to grade their papers. Give a small prize to the students who go the most answers correct.

How did each person know about the others?

Have you ever thought about how much who you are comes out in the life choices you make?

If you were going to go down in history, how would you want others to know you?

Think of a one or two sentence description of what others might say your life stands for.

Discovery

On a large sheet of paper or a large dry erase board make two columns with the headings shown below. On one side write the following names, leave the other blank. Read through Hebrews 11:1–40. As you come to each name, have your students call out what that person has done.

Name	What he/she/they did
Abel	
Enoch	
Noah	
Abraham	
Abraham, Sarah	
Abraham, Isaac, Jacob	
All previously named	
Isaac	
Jacob	
Joseph	
Moses' parents	
Moses	
The people of Israel	
Rahab	
Gideon, Barak, Samson, Jepthah,	
David, Samuel and the prophets	
Women	
Others	

Hebrews 11:2 states that the ancients were commended for serving and honoring God in a variety of ways. This passage is often referred to as the Hall of Faith. From these men and women of biblical times we can take our example of what it means to have faith and live it out.

Which of these examples sticks out to you?

Which example seems odd or out of place?

Does it make sense to the world to follow Jesus?

How can we find encouragement from those who have gone before?

Application

Ask your students to come up with their own definition of faith. Write these in a place that is easy for all to see. Re-read Hebrews 11:1. Faith here is defined as being sure of what we hope for and certain of what we do not see.

If the people listed are known to have a great deal of faith, what can we learn from them?

Do you think they were special and that this made them able to live in faith? Or, were they ordinary and their ability to live in faith is what has made them go down in history?

Can ordinary people like us live in extraordinary ways for God?

Ask your students what stories of people they have known have encouraged or inspired them.

Invite your students to dream of what the Lord may do in and through them that can only be accomplished by a leap of faith. Spend some time in prayer asking the Holy Spirit to work in your lives what He desires of you. How might you seek the Lord in order to fulfill what He is calling?

Connections:

Genesis 4:4
Genesis 5:21–24
Genesis 6:13–22
Genesis 12:1–7
Genesis 12:8 and 18:1, 9
Genesis 17–21
Genesis 22:17
Psalm 39:12
Exodus 3:6
Genesis 22:1–12
Genesis 27:27–29, 39–40
Genesis 50:24–25
Exodus 13:19
Exodus 1–2
Exodus 12:50–51
Exodus 14:21–31
Joshua 6:12–20
Joshua 2:1, 9–14, 6:22–25
Judges 4–5
1 Samuel 16:1–20
2 Samuel 7:11, 8:1–3
Daniel 6:22
2 Kings 20:17
Judges 15:8
1 Kings 17:22–23
Jeremiah 20:2
2 Chronicles 24:21
1 Kings 19:10
2 Kings 1:8
1 Kings 18:4

What Is That Pain in Your Eyes?

by Adam Cozens and Amy Jacober

In this lesson, students will:

✔ Understand that when the world turns against them, God is still by their side. They will also learn that anger is natural. Even those that do not show anger feel it like everyone else does. However, remaining angry will only hurt them personally and cause separation from others.

Stuff you'll need:

❑ Punching bag
❑ One stack of construction paper per student

Memory Verses

"Be angry and do not sin": do not let the sun go down on your wrath, nor give place to the devil. —Ephesians 4:26–27

Scripture

James 1:20

Lesson in a Sentence

Harboring anger only distances you from God and robs you of peace.

The Big Picture

Many things happen to us that we cannot understand. Some of these cause indescribable anger. When we embrace this anger, it weakens our spiritual lives. A believer must learn to let these things go and let God handle them. By releasing our anger to God, we find peace.

Focus

Have two of your youth leaders get into an argument over something stupid that your students can relate to. After they have argued for a minute, one of them storms out of the room, leaving the other one seething in anger. He or she describes how angry he or she is with the other person. Be sure the students experience something that is way out of proportion. Play it out like a skit. After the leader finishes venting, have another leader ask the students about their thoughts on what they saw. Have they ever experienced unreasonable anger. Have they ever been the focus of such anger?

Discovery

Read James 1:20
 What three things does this passage say we are to do?
 According to this passage, is anger acceptable?
 What does it mean to be slow to anger?

Read Ephesians 4:26–27
 How does this passage harmonize with the one in James?
 What does this passage say about remaining angry?
 What does it mean to give a place or a foothold to the devil?

Life Application

Present the following scenario to small groups of students to discuss. If necessary, write a scenario that fits your group better.

You are excited about your new car. You love the feeling of freedom that comes with owning a car and you enjoy driving people around town and having fun. Even though it is a used car, it is still your baby and you keep it looking good and running great.

One day, your buddy needs to run some errands and wants to borrow your car. You are nervous about letting someone else drive your prized possession, but you trust your friend and so let him take it out for a few hours. While he is gone with the car, your mom takes you to the store to pick up some dinner. There in the store's parking lot you see your car. You notice that the driver side seat belt is hanging out the door. You are enraged over this. How could your friend be so stupid as to let that happen! Your mind races as you think what you will do to him when you see him again. Your mom goes home as you wait for your friend to come back. He is surprised to see you, but doesn't appear nervous or scared. If anything, he is confused by the look on your face. You ask about the seatbelt.

"Oh, I didn't notice that. Sorry."

This enrages you. "Sorry?" Is that all you have to say?"

Instead of letting him drive home, you take him back despite not wanting to even look at him. You can't stand the thought of this careless person behind the wheel of your car. As you drive him home, he apologizes, but, you cant hear it. You can't think of anything except your anger. After you drop him off, you don't even say goodbye. You just drive home with music blaring as you think about all the time you wasted on friendship with that guy.

Making it Personal

In Psalm 4:4 it says, "Be angry, and do not sin. Meditate within your heart on your bed, and be still." This scripture says that while anger comes naturally, you are not to harbor it. While in your bed, search your heart for the anger of that day, and release it. Going to bed with anger will make your heart a breeding ground for stronger animosity. Never go to bed angry.

What Is That Pain in Your Eyes?

by Adam Cozens and Amy Jacober

Memory Verses

"Be angry and do not sin": do not let the sun go down on your wrath, nor give place to the devil. —Ephesians 4:26–27

Scripture

Proverbs 28:13

Lesson in a Sentence

Harboring anger only distances you from God and robs you of peace.

Focus

Obtain the book *Blue Like Jazz* by Donald Miller and read pages 116–118 to your students. The story tells of confession and forgiveness. In it, Christians confess their harsh and judgmental attitudes toward non-Christians. Ask your students what they think of this. Would it be hard for them to confess like this? If they were to do it, what would they confess?

Discovery

In small groups, read Proverbs 28:13. What does this verse mean?
Recall the memory verses for this week, Ephesians 4:26–27, and read it in context? Ephesians 4:25–32. How do these two verses work together?

The scripture says says to be angry and not sin, to not let unwholesome talk come out of your mouth and to forgive others? Is this literal or figurative?

Application

Forgiveness, confession, and anger without sin are against our cultural habits. Yet, this is exactly what these passages are saying. Spend some time with your students wrestling with these ideas. Are they realistic? Will this make a person into a doormat to others? How do Christians follow these rules when the world does not? Are we exempt from these rules since the world does not follow them? What is so compelling about anger?

What makes confession and forgiveness so hard in our lives?

Close with thoughts like these: Anger hurts everyone involved. At school tomorrow you will see old friends that you don't talk to anymore. Think about why this is. Did you grow apart or is there unresolved issues between you? Could it be anger? Can you talk with your old friend about this? It may not bring your friendship back to where it once was, or cause immediate improvement. But if you try to talk with them, you have done your part to reopen the door of your friendship and clear the air of anger.

How God's Commands
Transform Our Lives

By Matthew Freeman

In this lesson, students will:
- ✔ Learn that when we get to the place of darkness and chaos God is not interested in judging, but rather transforming our lives
- ✔ God's commands are intended to transform our lives
- ✔ Even the smallest of God's commands are important and transformative.

Stuff you'll need:
- ❏ Play-Doh
- ❏ Strips of paper

Memory Verse

I will give thanks to You, for I am fearfully and wonderfully made; Wonderful are Your works, And my soul knows it very well. —Psalm 139:14

Scripture

Genesis 1:1—2:3

Lesson in a Sentence

God uses obedience to transform lives and bring about blessing.

The Big Picture

God does not judge the chaos of Genesis 1:2, he simply goes about ordering it to take it from seething waters and utter darkness to teeming life and light. It is the same in our lives: When we get to the place of darkness God is not interested in judging, but rather transforming. He uses commands to transform creation. God deals with each day of creation before moving on to the next. Even the smallest of God's commands are important. If it feels like God has stopped working in your life, look back to see if He has spoken something into your heart that you have ignored. He has probably given you the direction you need.

Focus

Give each student a ball of Play-Doh and a strip of paper with one aspect of creation written on it. For example: bird, fish, human, tree, etc. Give them time to create the item with the Play-Doh.

Discovery

As students are working on their Play-Doh creations, give a second strip of paper with a fragment of Scripture written on it. The length of the scripture fragment will depend on the number of students in the group. Each group will get the full account of one day of creation. The students combine their scripture fragments and the read about their day of creation. When a formed Play-Doh item is mentioned, the students show off their creative work.

Once the students have read the scripture text and shown their Play-Doh creations, have them explore certain aspects of creation by asking them these questions:

Q: When God observes the chaos and darkness in Genesis 1:2, does he judge it or call it bad?
A: No, he simply goes about making it good.

Q: What does God do to the darkness and the chaos of water in this story?
A: He limits it.

Q: Why doesn't God just get rid of the darkness and chaotic waters?
A: There influences in our lives that we may think are negative, but we can't get rid of them. For example: a family situation, schoolmates, or a health issue. God uses these things to transform us and further his purpose.

Q: God specifically calls everything good, except for two items of creation. Which are these?
A: Heavens and humankind. The heavens merely compose the space that surrounds the goodness of creation. As for human beings, we are not good in and of ourselves. Our goodness is tied to our obedience to God, who alone is good.

Q: Can you observe any parallels in the days of creation? Are there any similarities between any of the days?
A: On days one, two, and three God brings about order, once the order is in place, he injects it with teeming life and overflowing blessing.

Q: What does God do each time He creates; before moving on to the next day?
A: He makes sure that it is good. He values each command He speaks into our lives and will wait for us to implement that command before continuing His work in us.

Q: What would happen if creation decided to ignore any of the commands of God?

A: What if creation said, "I don't like this idea of separation between the land and sea. I think we should live together in harmony. Besides, that command was in the Old Testament. It doesn't apply today." Each of God's commands is vital if our lives are to be full of life and light.

Life Application

The creation account in Genesis 1 shows that God is not interested in judging us when we take wrong turns and our lives end up in chaos and darkness. Instead, He is willing to get His hands dirty, transform our lives, and fill them with life and light through our obedience to His commands. How do Christians either fulfill such obedience or fall short?

Making it Personal

If we want God's creative power in our lives, we must listen to what God is commanding us to do. If we feel that God has stopped working in our lives, we need to look back and see if there is some command we have ignored. The chances are God has given us the direction we need.

Take a few moments and ask each person to ask God to show him or her a command that God had given to which he or she needs to return.

How God's Commands Transform Our Lives

By Matthew Freeman

Memory Verse

I will give thanks to You, for I am fearfully and wonderfully made; Wonderful are Your works, And my soul knows it very well. —Psalm 139:14

Scripture

Psalm 136

Lesson in a Sentence

God uses obedience to transform lives and bring about blessing.

Focus

This Psalm has a meaningful repetition in it, speaking of God's mercy. Read the first part of each verse and then have the students respond, "His mercy endures forever!" Read the first verse and stop them after the first verse a couple of times to encourage them to really shout out the blessing to God! Then start over and let them really get in to it.

Discovery

Q: In verses 1-9 why is the psalmist praising God?
A: For the amazing work He did in creation.

Q: What is the psalmist praising God for in verses 10–15?
A: Deliverance from oppressive, negative influences.

Q: What is the psalmist praising God for in verses 16–22?
A: Leading them to and preparing for them a safe land of rest.

Q: What is the psalmist praising God for in verses 23–26?
A: Caring for people in bad situations, lifting them out of them and giving them new life.

Life Application

What is the psalmist saying about God? God cares deeply about you, especially when your life is in the dumps. It is the very nature of God to deliver you from your situation and give you a new life. As we saw in the Genesis text, God does this through our obedience to His commands.

God has worked throughout history to bring about life and blessing and deliverance in His creation and in the lives of His people. Do a little research ahead of time and collect three or four stories of people who have been obedient to God and used in amazing ways in the process. Find one-page summaries of these people and pass out the stories to be read out loud by the students. After each story, discuss the subject's obedience and what God did because of this obedience.

Teacher's note

This is a great time to introduce your students to the lives of ministers and missionaries throughout history. A few of these are William Carey, Annie Armstrong, William Booth, and Aimee Semple McPherson.

Fear Can Be Good

by Amy Jacober

In this lesson, students will:
- ✔ Learn the difference between fear that communicates respect and fear that communicates terror
- ✔ Understand that fear can be useful and positive
- ✔ Consider how God uses fear to motivate us

Stuff you'll need:
- ❏ *The Lion, the Witch and the Wardrobe* video or DVD
- ❏ Strips of paper with the memory verse written on it
- ❏ Paper
- ❏ Pen

Memory Verse

You shall fear the Lord your God; you shall serve Him and cling to Him, and you shall swear by His name. —Deuteronomy 10:20

Scripture

Deuteronomy 6:4–25

Lesson in a Sentence

Fear of the Lord is about respect and awe not crippling terror.

The Big Picture

Fear of the Lord does not mean that we are to cower in a corner. It means we have a healthy reverence for the Lord and are in awe for who he is. Remember when you were a young child and the principal would enter your classroom? He or she seemed larger than life, students gasped, and everyone paid attention. Consider the ocean. It is beautiful and powerful yet, if taken for granted, it can be dangerous and overwhelming. How much more is God like this? We are in awe of Him. In the presence of His greatness, it seems as if the world stops and all is focused on Him. This is fear that stems from respect and a realization that we could never survive His presence were He not to will it.

Focus

Option 1
Trust Falls
Be certain you have enough students to do this activity. Find a picnic table or other stable structure that is two to three feet off of the ground. Your students line up shoulder to shoulder in two rows facing one another in a straight line coming out from the picnic table. Each places their arms out in front of them each almost touching the elbow of the person across from them. Ask one volunteer to stand on the table, back to the group and arms folded across their chest. When they are ready, the person on the structure yells, "Falling," and the group responds by yelling, "Fall on." It is easy to fall but not easy to do. It takes a great amount of trust. Give each student who would like a turn an opportunity to fall.
Caution:
If the group does not yell, "Fall on," with strength and confidence, the person falling would be wise to not trust it. Be certain your students are paying attention as this activity does have potential for injuries.

Ask:
> Were any of you afraid at all?
> Why?
> Can you think of any times when fear is a good thing?

Option 2
Show a clip from *The Lion, the Witch and the Wardrobe*—the scene when Aslan enters the camp and a hush falls across the crowd. This is the perfect picture of fear in the form of respect. Ask your students what they saw in the clip. How does it relate to their understanding of fear?

Discovery

This is Deuteronomy 6:4–25 presented as reader's theatre. It is best for the readers to practice before their presentation.

All: Hear O Israel: The Lord our God, the Lord is one!
A: You shall love the Lord your God with all your heart,
B: with all your soul
C: and with all your might.
D: And these words which I command you today shall be in your heart;

B: You shall teach them diligently to your children,
C: and shall talk of them when you sit in your house,
D: when you walk by the way,
E: when you lie down, and when you rise up.
All: You shall bind them as a sign on your hand, and they shall be frontlets between your eyes.
A & B: You shall write them on the doorposts of your house and on your gates.

C: And it shall be,
D & E: when the Lord your God brings you into the land of which He swore to your fathers, to Abraham, Isaac, and Jacob, to give you large and beautiful cities which you did not build,
A: Houses full of good things, which you did not fill,
B: hewn out wells which you did not dig,
C: vineyards and olive trees which you did not plant—when you have eaten and are full.
All: Then beware lest you forget the Lord who brought you out of the land Egypt,
D: from the house of bondage.

All: You shall fear the Lord your God and serve Him, and shall take oaths in His name.
E: You shall not go after other gods of the peoples who are all around you
All: For the Lord your God is a jealous God among you
A: Lest the anger of the Lord your God be aroused against you and destroy you from the face of the earth.
B: You shall not tempt the Lord your God as you tempted Him in Massah.
C: You shall diligently keep the commandments of the Lord your God,
D: His testimonies,
E: and His statutes which He has commanded you.
A: And you shall do what is right and good in the sight of the Lord,
B: that it may be well with you, and that you may go in and possess the good land of which the Lord swore to your fathers.
C: To cast out all your enemies from before you, as the Lord has spoken.

D: When your son asks you in time to come, saying "What is the meaning of the testimonies, the statutes, and the judgments which the Lord our God has commanded you?"
E: Then you shall say to your son

A: "We were slaves of Pharaoh in Egypt, and the Lord brought us out of Egypt with a mighty hand.

B: And the Lord showed signs and wonders before our eyes, great and severe, against Egypt, Pharaoh and all his household.

C: Then He brought us out from there, that He might bring us in, to give us the land of which He swore to our fathers.

D & E: And the Lord commanded us to observe all these statutes,

All: to fear the Lord our God,

A & B: for our good always, that He might preserve us alive, as it is this day.

C: Then it will be righteousness for us,

D: if we are careful to observe all these commandments before the Lord our God, as He commanded us."

[END]

Ask:

> What did you hear?
>
> Were there any repeated concepts, phrases or words?
>
> What commands are we to observe?

Life Application

This passage admonishes the people to not forget that they were set free from Egypt and to fear the Lord. Israel's time in Egypt was a time of slavery, hard work, and difficult conditions.

> What kind of fear does this bring to mind?
>
> How does this differ from the fear we are to have for God?
>
> In what ways does Fear of the Lord play out in our lives?
>
> Is this good or bad?

Make a list of the characteristics of God and write them on a dry erase board. These include such things as lover and comforter but also judge and protector.

> Which of these characteristics lead us to fear the Lord?

Think of a story from your own life when you had no respect for someone; when someone let you and others walk all over them. They may have been nice, you may have had nothing against them, but you did not respect them, you were not in awe of them. This might include a teacher who was a pushover in class, a boss who would not take a stand on anything, a friend who could be manipulated. These are all people who do not demand respect.

Teenagers know what it is for someone to demand respect. Ask for their stories of people that they fear in the respectful way.

Making it Personal

Write Deuteronomy 10:20 on a strip of paper for each student. Give this to them with a piece of paper and pen. Allow a few moments for them to read and meditate on the verse.

Play music to set the tone as you invite students to consider all you have covered in this lesson. Reading the verse will take just a few moments. Give five minutes for them to meditate on this passage. They may read it repeatedly, or simply ponder it. Encourage them to think about what this means for all people and what it means for them. After five minutes, invite them use the sheet of paper as a journal to record what they have been thinking or wondering.

Spiritual Discipline Option

The school year is just about to begin and this is a perfect time to remind your students to create space for God in their lives. You may purchase a journal for each student and invite them use it to interact with scripture for the entire school year. Let this session be the first of many journal entries. The weekly memory verses are great to use in this way, not only for memorization but also for reflection and application.

Fair Can Be Good

by Amy Jacober

Memory Verse

You shall fear the Lord your God; you shall serve Him and cling to Him, and you shall swear by His name. —Deuteronomy 10:20

Scripture

Nehemiah 5:1–11

Lesson in a Sentence

Fear of the Lord is a motivation to do right.

Focus

Break your students into four teams. Offer each team an assortment of items, wire, tape, wood blocks, aluminum foil, etc. The items are not important. The object of this game is to create the greatest structure from what they have. They can also use items from their backpacks or purses. Be certain to include tape for each group.

Give ten to fifteen minutes for each team to build their structure. You may want to set the tone by playing one of your students' favorite CD's.

Have your leaders judge each structure on creativity, use and stability. Offer prizes to the winning team.

Discovery

Have each team read Nehemiah 5:1–11. Give each a piece of poster board and ask them to draw a storyboard of the passage. Note: Storyboarding is one of the first stages of creating a movie. The story is depicted in pictures on a storyboard—setting, what the characters look like, etc. It is like a cartoon of the story shown frame by frame.

As the students create this storyboard, draw their attention to verse nine. What does it mean that these people to walk in the fear of the Lord? What is Nehemiah trying to encourage and admonish them to do?

Along with each storyboard, have each group create a one-sentence tag line to explain the main point of the passage.

TEACHER'S NOTE:

You may want to tell the students what is going with Israel the time of Nehemiah. The Jews have been in exile. Nehemiah was written when some of them returned from exile.

They had been away from their land for a long time and were restoring Jerusalem, the temple, and their spiritual lives.

Life Application

Nehemiah 5:1–11 is all about working and struggling together to get back on track.

What tied them together? It was their faith in God. Sometimes this faith was strong, sometimes it waned. Nehemiah was a prophet calling them back to what they were to be. He reminds them of whom they serve and their task. He connects helping the poor with fearing God. He connects obedience and good choices to the fear of God.

How do we today relate to the fear of God?

When have you been so in awe of God that you wanted to offer Him your best?

How can fearing God motivate us to live in ways that honor Him?

Think of all of the times you do something that does not honor the Lord. Confess these struggles and ask God to help you remember who He is as you live you life.

Getting Youth Involved in Good Works

by Lt. Col. Raymond Peacock

Most youth pastors are very interested in getting youth into the church. Some are equally interested in getting youth out of the church and into the community doing good works. This chapter is for those who may want to do the latter but are hesitant to do so. This may be because they need answers to the following questions.

Does Youth Have Something to Give?

Some might argue that youth have limited resources and therefore little to give. Both the youth pastor and youth themselves can derive encouragement from the story of Peter and John in the third chapter of Acts. There, a lame man asked them for a contribution. Peter admitted his poverty but didn't dwell on it. He said, "I don't have a nickel to my name, but what I do have, I give you" (Acts 3:6 The Message).

Peter had three things: sympathy, faith, and Jesus Christ. Sympathy will only get you so far, but without Peter's compassion for the crippled man there would have been no miracle. The world needs more, more tenderness, more feeling, more sensitivity and our young people have plenty of this just like Peter, who had sympathy gave it to the crippled man.

Peter had faith as well. The lame man had lain at the gates of the Temple for years. Others carried him there every day so he could beg. But the power to heal the cripple didn't come from an institution like the Temple, it came from an individual who believed something could be done for a lame individual who had been carried by others for years. Youth are frequently full of hope and this hope can be expressed in faith.

Of course Peter had Jesus Christ. Sympathy and belief are not enough. These must be anchored in the one who is love personified—Jesus Christ. Peter definitely had Jesus when he said, "In the name of Jesus Christ of Nazareth, rise up, and walk" (v. 6). "In an instant his feet and ankles became firm. He jumped to his feet and walked" (v. 7). Isn't it great when we give Jesus Christ to those in need? He adds power to our sympathy and faith.

There's another familiar New Testament story that encourages both pastors and young people to know they have something to give to others. This is the story of the feeding of the five thousand. John's gospel records the disciples' words like this: "There's a little boy here who has five barley loaves and two fish. But that's a drop in the bucket for a crowd like this" (6:9). We've often been told that a little in the hands of Jesus is much. The boy's lunch fed five thousand people but he had to surrender his resources to Jesus before they could be used for this miraculous purpose. Jesus transformed the boy's insufficient means into sufficient ends for those hungry people.

What Does a Youth Pastor Need to Know to Get Youth Involved in Good Works?

As a youth pastor, your training may be in the areas of biblical studies, music, evangelism, discipleship, youth dynamics, worship, or leadership. But you still may feel you are stepping into deep water when you venture into serving those with developmental, financial, health, or age related needs. You know you want to help and not hinder. You know you want positive things for those you are helping and for the youth who are serving. You've determined that faith, sympathy, surrender of what little we have, plus Christ's power is enough for service. Still, you have unanswered questions.

Will your youth have the skill to adequately meet the need? Several studies have shown that those who most effectively help a person in need are paraprofessionals or so-called natural helpers, not professionals. The professionals have extremely important roles when it comes to analysis and training, but when it comes to getting close to the people, the natural helpers delivers "high touch" in this "high tech" age. So, know this first: Simply being willing to touch others in a helpful way is a good beginning.

Where can you find a meaningful project that will involve your youth in helping others? There really are at least four answers to this: 1) Your congregation, 2) Your neighborhood, 3) Your community and, 4) Your world.

Your congregation: Who needs help within your own congregation? Older people, sick people, and people experiencing a crisis to name a few. What do these people need? Grocery shopping, home repair, grass mowed, snow shoveled, and more. You can learn of these needs by placing a form in your church's weekly bulletin that asks members to list their needs.

Your neighborhood: I love this story about a church whose membership was declining: The members determined they would go to the neighborhood school and ask the principal if there was anyway they could help the children there. The principal said this was the first time in fifteen years that anyone had come from the neighborhood church and asked to help. Indeed, the school needed readers, tutors, library, and homework helpers. Many of the students were from single parent families whose parents had limited time to help their children. It wasn't long before the church became known as the church who cared about single parents and their children. As a result, the church began to grow as it served the school and established relationships with the children and their parents. Mostly adults who helped during school hours, but some teens found an hour or two a week to help out at the school. Who is in your neighborhood that needs help?

Your community: Most communities have non-profit organizations with volunteer coordinators. The volunteer coordinators are skilled in matching volunteers with appropriate projects. For instance, not long ago, a boy working to become an Eagle Scout was looking for a project. He went to his local Salvation Army and discovered they needed someone to build shelves for their food bank. Even more exciting, his scoutmaster lined up three more Eagle Scout candidates looking for projects. The Salvation Army, the Red Cross, the United Way are three major agencies in every town that usually welcome volunteers. A simple call indicating you have youth willing to volunteer, especially during the holidays, will probably be met with enthusiasm by the volunteer coordinators of these organizations.

Your world: Mission trips are a favorite of youth. I know one mixed team of adults and teens that is preparing to go to New Orleans this summer and help victims of Hurricane Katrina. Their church is responding to the call to help people who still need food, shelter, clothes, and health care nine months after the disaster struck. Service is needed up to two years following a disaster that has destroyed a community's infrastructure.

Many denominations sponsor youth teams to go to other countries for one month to a year. Check to see what your denomination does along these lines. However, if your church is non-denominational or independent, there are organizations who take youth from all churches on their teams. Youth With a Mission (YWAM) is well-known for this. To explore others, search the World Wide Web for Christian Youth Missions Organizations.

Why Is It a Good Idea to Involve Youth in Service Projects?

I once asked a group of youth pastors why youth should serve others. Here are some of their answers:

- ✔ Service projects help youth to focus on others rather than themselves.
- ✔ Service projects give youth experience that shapes their adult choices.
- ✔ Service projects introduce youth to those less fortunate.
- ✔ Service projects teach youth that some find themselves in circumstances not of their own making.
- ✔ Service projects provide and introduction to other cultures and languages.
- ✔ Service projects reinforce that God cares for the least, the lost, and the lowest.
- ✔ Service projects provide opportunity for growth and leadership development.

So get out there. Get involved. This list is not finished. See what your students teach you about why it is good to serve others.

What Kind of Love Is This?

by Amy Jacober

In this lesson, students will:
- ✔ Learn what God demands of love
- ✔ Articulate the difference between what the world's and God's love
- ✔ Consider pragmatic ways to love others
- ✔ Identify specific ways fall short of loving as God desires

Stuff you'll need:
- ❏ Digital cameras with memory sticks, enough for several teams
- ❏ Computer
- ❏ Screen or wall
- ❏ Cut out hearts
- ❏ Memory stick reader
- ❏ Projector
- ❏ Pre-printed scavenger hunt list
- ❏ Markers

Memory Verse
And though I have the gift of prophecy, and understand all mysteries and all knowledge, and though I have all faith. So that I could move mountains, but have not love, I am nothing. And though I bestow all my goods to feed the poor, and though I give my body to be burned, but have not love, it profits me nothing. —1 Corinthians 13:2–3

Scripture
1 Corinthians 13

Lesson in a Sentence
We would live differently if we loved in the way of 1 Corinthians 13.

The Big Picture
God's love is radical. The love He expects of us is equally so. We have been taught too often that Christianity is about a checklist of good and loving things to do. We learn to watch our language when certain people are around, go to church to see and be seen, and give just enough to ease our conscience. God has other plans. He calls us to love in humanly impossible ways. We are to love the unlovable because they are worthy of love. We are to love others like only God can do. Love from God's perspective is not about finding a date or gaining someone's attention. It is about giving attention and dying to self. Love is the most precious gift of all and it costs far more what most of us know.

Focus

Option 1—Digital Scavenger Hunt

This is a great way to create a lot of fun fast. Be certain you have a way to show the pictures when your students return. Using digital cameras, have a memory stick reader to upload them to your computer. Then show the pictures as a slide show projected on a screen. Ask your students for help if you are unsure how to do this.

Split into at least two teams, if possible split into male and female teams. Try to keep team sizes between five and ten. You can write your own rules but begin with something like the following:

Rules:
- Every team member must be in the picture unless otherwise specified.
- There must be a separate picture for each item, no doubling up!
- Keep it clean!
- If the picture needs only one or a few members of your team, each team member must be in a picture before a member may be pictured twice.
- Do as many pictures as you can but be safe and courteous.
- You have thirty minutes to get as many pictures as you can. Do not be late coming back.
- Have fun.

Create a list of items that are specific to your area. You may want to begin with the following things. Ideally, lists should be thirty or so items to take the entire thirty minutes.

Photo List
- ❏ Your entire team making a pyramid
- ❏ Your entire team's bare feet
- ❏ Your entire team doing a wheelbarrow race
- ❏ Your entire team doing an air band
- ❏ Your entire team standing/sitting on a wall or fence
- ❏ Your entire team under a car
- ❏ Your entire team doing a group hug
- ❏ Your entire team doing their best impression of dead cockroaches
- ❏ Your entire team making funny faces
- ❏ Your entire team with the pastor
- ❏ Your entire team upside down
- ❏ Your entire team dong jumping jacks
- ❏ Someone on your team doing a one handed push up
- ❏ Someone on your team doing the splits
- ❏ Someone on your team standing on their head

When students return, have one person upload the pictures for the slide show.

Option 2

Split your group into two, a male and female group. Separate by sides of the room or, if you are able, send one team to another room close by.

Instruct each team to create questions for the other team as if it is their one chance to ask what the opposite sex thinks about relationships. There are a couple of ways to handle the next stage: a) bring the groups back together and trade questions to answer in the large group under the guidance of leaders or b) trade questions and have the guys prepare answers for the girls under the guidance of a male leader and the girls to prepare answers for the guys under the guidance of a female leader.

This can lead to a great discussion. Be certain to not to let this take up all the time for the rest of your lesson.

Discovery

Have your students read 1 Corinthians 13 out loud together in pairs. Give each pair a sheet of paper with, "1 Corinthians 13," written at the top and with a line down the middle. On one side, write, "What love is," on the other side write "What love is not." Ask the students to analyze 1 Corinthians 13 using these two columns.

Life Application

Love is easily one of the most discussed and misunderstood of all topics. The explanation of love in 1 Corinthians 13 is like no other.

Ask your students to call out all of the things the world associates with love. Write these on a dry erase board. Ask what is the difference between the world's perspective of love God's perspective of love that they have found in 1 Corinthians 13?

Is it possible to love in a way that is: patient, kind, not envious, not boastful, not proud, not rude, not self-seeking, not easily angered, not keeping a record of wrongs, not delighting in evil, rejoicing in truth, protective, trusting, hopeful, persevering and never failing?

Ask your students to flip their paper over and list each description of love on one side of the paper. Next, have them discuss and brainstorm a pragmatic way to describe each description of love. For example, love being patient might be seen in patience with a younger brother or an annoying person at school. Love not being rude might be seen in politeness to a teacher at school. There is no single right answer but there certainly are wrong answers. Spend some time discussing what they brainstorm. Which descriptions of love are easiest to think of examples for? Which were the most difficult?

Here's the kicker, any one of these is good, but not good enough. This description of love means all of it. Love requires all of these at all times. A God size task can only be accomplished through the power of God.

How does this impact the way we think about relationships with other people? If we really are seeking to love like this, what would this do to the dating scene in school? To friendships? To all relationships?

Making it Personal

Remind your students that love does not just happen. It is a choice and moves beyond just a feeling. Invite your students to ask God to show them in which area of love they fall short. Play a song and give time to talk to the Lord for a few moments. After asking God, have each student choose one description of love as a challenge to his or her life this week. Pass out a heart cut out to each student and have him or her write the love description on the heart as a reminder.

If you chose the digital scavenger hunt activity, show it at the end of the lesson. Tie it in by mentioning that none of these pictures just happened. They followed specific instructions. 1 Corinthians 13 is our manual of instruction for how to love.

Memory Verse Activity

On the back of the heart, write out the memory verse. This is a long one so you will need to encourage your students to take it seriously. Consider a few ways to remember to look at the heart throughout the week; use it as a bookmark, tape it to the bathroom mirror, tape it on the dashboard of your car, slide it in the cover of a folder, etc.

Service Option

Challenge each student to do a love experiment this week. Loving the way the world loves is easy. Loving the way God requires is hard but worth it. There is not a set way to do this. Each student chooses one tangible way of loving someone else. It can run the gamut from helping a friend in class understand something, tutoring younger kids, paying for someone else's lunch, etc. As best they can, encourage them to tie their love experiment to the description of love they have taken as a challenge for the week.

Songs

"Because Of Your Love" by Paul Baloche on *A Greater Song*

What Kind of Love Is This?

by Amy Jacober

Memory Verse

And though I have the gift of prophesy, and understand all mysteries and all knowledge, and though I have all faith. So that I could move mountains, but have not love, I am nothing. And though I bestow all my goods to feed the poor, and though I give my body to be burned, but have not love, it profits me nothing. —1 Corinthians 13:2–3

Scripture

1 John 4:19–21

Lesson in a Sentence

We would live differently if we loved in the way of 1 Corinthians 13.

Focus

Human Sculpting

Ask for volunteers in pairs. One person is the sculpture, the other is the sculptor. Have the sculptor put the other person in a position. The sculpture must cooperate as long as they are able. The sculpture may end up standing on one foot pointing up to the sky with his right hand and covering his eyes with his left hand. The rest of the group gets three guesses what the sculptor is trying to create. Just like real art, what is intended is not what is seen. The sculpture then tells the group what he thinks he is. The sculptor does the same. There is no right answer. The point is that one person did something (the sculptor) and the other responds (the sculpture). Play this game through a few times.

TEACHER'S NOTE:

It is always better to stop an game while your students are still enjoying it than playing it too much.

Discovery

Ask your students how they respond when someone has done them wrong? Do they ignore it? Get revenge?

How do they respond when someone has done them right? Do they treat hem well? Be kind?

Read 1 John 4:19–21.
What does this mean to you? What does this say about love?

Application

Of all books in the Bible, this one talks again and again of love. What it is, how we are to respond and where we get it. This coupled with what we learned in 1 Corinthians 13 takes the idea of love to a whole new level. Most of us think that if we meet the right person, we can love.

Ask your students:

- According to this passage are we able to love on our own?
- Who makes it possible to love?
- If God is love and we love because He first loved us, do we get a choice in who we love?
- Is there a difference between loving and liking?

Invite your students to ask questions and challenge this passage. What happens when we have a brother who is jerk? Who lies about us? Who hurts us? Do parents really love when they give consequences for our actions? What does love look like in the real world?

Close by thanking God for His love and asking Him to help each person to be more loving.

A Love Feast

by Amy Jacober

In this lesson, students will:
- ✔ Be aware that God lavishly loves them
- ✔ Comprehend that while God loves them and invites them into a relationship, he will not force matters
- ✔ Consider both a literal and metaphorical meaning of inviting the blind, crippled, poor and lame to the table
- ✔ Understand that it is possible to take God's love for granted

Stuff you'll need:
- ❏ A banquet with all the trimmings and decorations
- ❏ Invitations; 2 per student
- ❏ Pens

Memory Verse

But God demonstrates His own love toward us, in that while we were still sinners, Christ died for us. —Romans 5:8

Scripture

Luke 14:12–24

Lesson in a Sentence

God offers extravagant love.

The Big Picture

God's love knows no bounds! He offers love to all but that does not mean that all people actually acknowledge or receive this love. Despite his offer, many people find all kinds of reasons to not come to Him. At this time of year, love seems to be all the conversation. Realistically, many students want to know that someone cares, listens, and knows they exist, wants to spend time with them, and believes that they are important. They miss the love offered by Christ or simply choose to not take it, looking for something else. Not only do we need to help our students recognize love but to authentically give love. It is not just for the popular or well off. It is for those who do not fit in, for those who struggle and are different. Receiving and giving love go hand in hand.

Focus

Option 1

Open with a lavish meal. Use china plates and tables set with tablecloths and candles—the whole nine yards! You needn't spend a fortune. Use what you have around church and enlist a few parents to help. If possible, ask a few volunteers to come as severs. If you do not want to offer a full dinner, make it a very fancy dessert. Whatever it is, make it look like a lot of effort went into making the evening a success.

Option 2

Invite a disabled person to share their story. What is it like to get around in a wheelchair? How do others look at you if you walk with a cane or are missing a limb? What difficulties are faced if you are blind? Many people do not know anyone with a disability and church buildings are often not hospitable to them. It is not that people are opposed to someone with a disability as much as they are just not considered. They are an exception; not a part of the community.

In the parable, it is those who were least likely who attended the banquet. The wealthy and successful missed Jesus. When we read that Jesus loves all people, it really means all people.

Some students feel they are unlovable. For a person with a disability, the acceptance and love is a life-long battle. This can be a powerful time of testimony not only for your students to connect with someone and hear their story but also to realize that even though they are not perfect, Jesus can and does love them.

Discovery

Hand out an invitation and a pen to each person.

The invitation may be a simple sheet of paper with the following printed on it:

You are cordially invited
To the banquet of a lifetime
This is no ordinary meal
It is food for life
At this feast you will know love like never before
Your host is the creator of the universe
Your Lord, God, and Savior
RSVP

As you read Luke 14:15–24, ask them to jot down any questions they have on the back of the invitation. Read through the passage a second time and ask them to listen for the character with whom they identify. Is this

The one reclining at the table?
Family?
A rich neighbor?

Poor?

Crippled?

Lame?

Blind?

One with a new piece of land?

One with new oxen?

One with a new wife?

The servant?

Ask your students to share the character with whom they identify and why.

Next, ask them to share the questions they jotted down at the initial reading. Let this lead your discussion of the passage.

Life Application

Ask your students to re-read the invitation as printed.

We all find times to refuse this invitation.

In small groups, brainstorm all of the excuses we give for not attending the banquet. Write these on the front of your invitation.

Making it Personal

Ask your students to look over all of the excuses their group named. Which one is the excuse they use? Are they too busy? Are they too young and having fun and hope to come to the banquet later in life? Have they been burned by people and are looking to Christians instead of Christ for their faith? The list is endless. Ask them to circle the one that most speaks to their life.

After a few moments, offer to trade invitations with your students, the one with all of the excuses written on it for a brand new, fresh clean one.

Ask each student to take this home and consider each day how they would respond to an invitation to be in the presence of God. To follow Jesus is more than a one-time banquet. It is an ongoing relationship.

Service Option

Find a local soup kitchen and volunteer to help serve. After you have been there, spend some time with your students unpacking the experience. Were the people treated like guests? Was it a service offered with dignity or were the people treated as second-class citizens? How did your students feel being there? Consider the food we waste every year. What can you do to serve others on a regular basis? Volunteer monthly? Consider ways to fight hunger around the world?

Check into the *30 Hour Famine* sponsored by World Vision as a way to show love and give to the poor, the lame, the blind, and the crippled.

Song

"Face of Love" by Sanctus Real on *The Face of Love*

A Love Feast

by Amy Jacober

Memory Verse

But God demonstrates His own love toward us, in that while we were still sinners, Christ died for us. —Romans 5:8

Scripture

John 13:35; John 15:12; 1 Thessalonians 3:12; Romans 12:9; 1 Peter 1:22; John 13:1; John 15:19; John 15:13; 1 John 3:16; Deuteronomy 6:5; 1 Corinthians 13:13; 2 Thessalonians 3:5; Galatians 5:22; Psalm 31:23; Jeremiah 31:3; Colossians 3:14; Ephesians 3:17; Ephesians 3:18; Ephesians 3:19; 1 John 4:8; 1 John 4:18; 1 John 4:19

Lesson in a Sentence

God offers extravagant love.

Focus

Throw a big Valentine's party. Be as extravagant as you are able. If you lack decorating skills, enlist others to get this set up. Set the tone, have music playing, balloons, table-cloths, snacks (don't forget to make some of the snacks healthy) and games. Write a valentine for each student.

This evening will be quite difficult for some students. They don't feel love at home or at school. They long for loving relationships. Let this be the night they experience being loved and find opportunities to offer love. Scripture can be learned by experience as well as study.

Discovery

Write a verse about love on different strips of paper. Have enough for one for each student. Use the suggestions above and use a concordance to find more if needed. Place a strip of paper in a balloon, blow it up, and tie it off. Tie a string to the balloon. Give one balloon to every student and ask him or her to tie it to his or her shoe. The object of the game is to pop someone else's balloon while keeping yours safe. Once you do pop a balloon, collect the strip of paper. The person at the end with the greatest number of strips wins.

Have each person with a verse or verses to read them aloud. Shower your students with scripture about love, from God, from others, for others, etc.

Life Application

Today is Valentine's Day. You have heard many ways that you are loved and are to love others.

Have a table set up to make valentines for those in your church who may be in need of encouragement. Bring colored paper, scissors, glue, glitter, and markers. Many go day after day in loneliness and struggle. After making the valentines, see if you can arrange a time to take some of your students to hand deliver these.

Remind your students of all of the verses that say we are to love one another. A few hours of visiting with those who are in need is a small way to give the love God has given to us.

Memory Verse Activity

The greatest love we can receive is that given by God for our salvation. God loved us so much that while we were still in sin, while we were still far from Him, while we did not honor Him or earn His love at all, Jesus gave His life that we may live.

Pass out a paper heart to each student. Ask them to write the memory verse on the heart. After they are finished, have them exchange the heart with someone else. Keep this heart in a place where you can be regularly reminded of the love of Christ.

The Greatest

by David Upchurch

In this lesson, students will
- ✔ Understand love from a biblical perspective and discover practical ways to show that love to their friends.

Stuff you'll need:
- ❏ Chairs in a circle
- ❏ Movie clips

Memory Verse

Love the Lord your God with all your heart and with all your soul and with all your strength. —Deuteronomy 6:5

Scripture

Matthew 22:34–40

Lesson in a Sentence

A true follower of Christ loves God with all that he is and loves his neighbor as much as he loves himself.

The Big Picture

Love for God is the heartbeat of our mission and that love compels us to love our neighbor in concrete ways.

Focus

View a movie clip or organize a discussion on the topic of the greatest. To get students thinking about this, organize into groups based on a certain subject like basketball: "If you think LeBron James is the greatest basketball player, join this group; Michael Jordan here, Kobe Bryant this group, Pete Maravich here." Then suggest other categories like musical style—Rap, Pop, Country and Western, Opera; Greatest band—Beatles, U2, Dave Mathews Band, Brooks and Dunn; Greatest school subject—English, Math, History, Physics; Greatest food—Granola, Pizza, Ice Cream, Asparagus; Greatest city— New York, Los Angeles, Dallas, Ardmore; etc.

Movie Clips

Shrek and *Shrek 2* tell of the effect of true love; *Hitch* shows how love takes risks; *Fever Pitch* tells how love is bigger than an individual. These summaries were taken from *www.movieministry.com.* Register at the website for access to the complete illustrations, but this is a good start if you've seen the movies.

Background

By defining the positions of the Pharisees and Sadducees we can see how we are similar to them.

The Pharisees began as scribes used by political leaders to enforce the law in the Maccabean revolt (165–63 BC). Observance of the law was the most important thing to them. Factions within the Pharisees disagreed over the fine points of the law and they forgot God's intention. They argued over a multitude of interpretations of the laws dealing with ritual—the temple and worship—and morality—business and everyday life. This confused the people and made worship difficult. The things of God had become ritualistic and void of life.

The Sadducees immersed themselves in culture. Generally conservative in theology and of the priestly class, they vied for religious power and status that they might gain from the political power, Rome. They were usually of the aristocratic class and in touch with Greek culture and customs. As a result, they had money and material things. Tradition and doctrine slowed their rise to power so they bought the office of the high priest from Rome.

What contemporary organizations in life or at your school are like the Pharisees and Sadducees? What do you see in your life that is like the Pharisees or Sadducees?

In Matthew 22:34–40, Jesus is questioned about one of the hot topics of the day. The conversation betrays the sin of the Pharisees: self-righteousness. They want to know what is the ultimate law because keeping the law is more important than the motive of the heart. Human effort is preeminent.

How often do we hear people say, "I don't need any help, I can do it." Or, "My hard work got me here. I've earned it." Religionists teach, "Try harder. Do more." Dependence on God is not important to them.

Do you recognize it when you fall into this trap? Jesus' answer to the Pharisees defines the law of love—the primary law. This ends the debate concerning the law.

How do we live the law of love?

Discovery

The "Friend" Game

Make a circle of chairs using one fewer chair than there are people. Instruct group members to sit down with one person in the middle designated as "it." That person begins, asking someone in the circle, "Do you love your friend?" If the person answers, "No," everyone tries to switch chairs before "it" sits in one of the chairs. No one may sit in his or her original chair. If the answer is, "Yes," "it" says, "Everyone who is wearing blue" (or has blue eyes or writes with their left hand or any similar phrase). Everyone who fits that description moves chairs while "it" tries to sit, too. Play this for until it gets too crazy or is not involving everyone.

Life Application

Love must be defined—Matthew 22:37.

In this verse, the expert in the law poses a great question for a law-keeping person. But we are under grace so the law of love takes precedence. Jesus quotes Deuteronomy 6:5, which was the heart of God's covenant with the Israelites. This is the first sentence in a Jewish worship service to this day and the first verse a Jewish child memorizes. However, knowledge of this verse, this law, is not life changing. To do it requires self-effort.

For love to grow it must be nurtured.

What do you need to nurture that kind of love?

What difference does it make that Jesus showed the very kind of love he is talking about?

The order of the heart, soul and mind implies that the attitude of the heart needs to be correct. Do you agree? This kind of love will result in obedience to God, which in turn fuels our spiritual growth and thirst. How much quicker do we obey when we know someone loves us? Think about family relationships vs. government.

Activity

Bring in a yearbook. Notice the activities listed and the pages of signatures and what they say. You may point out how well you've kept up with those friends and what they wrote. The lesson is: What will you be remembered for?

In verse 39, Jesus quotes from Leviticus 19:18 which deals with relationships between fellow Jews. Jesus is going outside the boundaries. Think about Jesus' dealing with people throughout the Gospels. He was loving and accepting. He pointed out sin without condemning. The Jewish leaders were debating when they should have been obeying. How broad are your social relationships? How well do we experience true community?

The phrase *The second is like it* implies equality with the first commandment. You can't emphasize piety for God over social concern. Divine love by necessity works itself out in interpersonal love. 1 John 3:14–18; 4:8; 10–12, 20–22 make it clear that loving others is the way to love God. Think about our love for ourselves. It's instinctive. Wouldn't it be great if our love for others were that way, too?

Looking back at verse 34, the Pharisees had hoped to silence Jesus. The Greek word silence can also mean "to muzzle." They have their trap turned on them as they were the ones muzzled.

All of the Law and the Prophets hang on these two things (v. 40). This includes that the whole of scripture at that point in time. This is law and life in its totality for a follower of God.

Connections
The Good Samaritan—Luke 10:25–37
1 Corinthians 13
2 Corinthians 5:14–15

Personal Application
In what ways can you show love for God by loving those you wouldn't normally love? Introduce yourself to a neighbor or someone new. Remember several things about them and begin praying for them. Who are five other people you can start praying for and loving immediately?

The Greatest

by David Upchurch

Memory Verse

You shall love the LORD your God with all your heart, with all your soul, and with all your strength. —Deuteronomy 6:5

Scripture

Psalm 139

Lesson in a Sentence

The forgiveness of God causes us to love and follow Him more.

The Big Picture

The love of God is the greatest force in the earth. Through faith one steps out in new life thirsty for more of Him every day.

In this lesson, students will:

See themselves like God sees them and rejoice in forgiveness and new life.

Discovery

Read Psalm 139:1–12, 23–24. Notice that David starts the psalm in the past tense "searched" and finishes in the present "search." All of the hiding and trying to get away leads David back to the one who never left. Then he realizes the eternal truth: The best place to be is with God. David wants to keep the closest possible relationship with God so he is continually conscious of God working in his life even if it seems dull and boring. It's as if the ordinary becomes extraordinary because of God's presence and communion. To keep such a relationship with God is to keep short accounts between you and God. This means you are quick to confess when you've wronged God.

Think about David's life, despite being a great warrior and king he had a man murdered and committed adultery. These are big time sins. However, David was heart broken when he realized his sin and confessed it (see Psalm 51). David pursued God and God said David was a man after His heart. David didn't lose sight of the fact that he was responsible before God even if he was king. Wrapping up the chapter David reminds us that God leads us forever.

Activities

Remind students of how God forgives through writing in the sand. Set a station off to the side that contains a box full of sand. Ask students to write a specific sin in the sand and then pray confessing that sin. Before they leave they wipe away the sin.

Songs

Use one of these songs or one of your choice for a meditation with the students. It helps to have the lyrics printed out or on a screen so that they can reflect after they have heard the song and also they can journal a response to God's grace and love.

"Sorry"—Shawn McDonald
"Don't Want to Grieve You"—Vineyard Music
"Who Am I"—Watermark
"Come Ye Sinners"—Robbie Seay Band
"Rescue"—Desperation Band
"Crooked Deep Down"—Derek Webb
"Set Free"—Billy and Cindy Foote

Connections—Other Scriptures

Psalm 51—David's confession
Job 28:28—Job's philosophy to fear God and shun evil
Psalm 8—David wonders about man
Romans 2:4—God's kindness leads to repentance
Romans 8:1—No condemnation in Christ
Galatians 5:6—Faith expresses itself through love

Love Your Neighbor

by Amy Jacober

In this lesson, students will
- ✔ Struggle with tangible ways to love others
- ✔ Consider who is a neighbor
- ✔ Learn direct commandments from scriptures for living with and among neighbors

Stuff you'll need:
- ❑ Two basketballs and a court
- ❑ 3 x 5 cards
- ❑ Pens or pencils

Memory Verse
You shall not take vengeance, nor bear any grudge against the sons of your people, but you shall love your neighbor as yourself; I am the Lord. —Leviticus 19:18 (NASB)

Scripture
Proverbs 3:27–30

Lesson in a Sentence
We are to love others even when it is difficult.

The Big Picture
We all know people for whom we love to do things; people whom we take care of. Usually we consider these people our friends. But scripture calls us to treat our neighbor as we would want to be treated. This is still easy when we get to identify our neighbor. We look for people who look, sound, and think like us. Except our neighbor is also that person we don't like; who is lazy; who will never be able to help us in any way. Loving our neighbor means learning not only to love but also to recognize and acknowledge our neighbors locally and globally.

Focus

Knock Out

If you have a basketball court nearby this is a great game! You will need two basketballs. Have your team line up at the free throw line. The first person in line tries to make a shot. As soon as the first person has released their ball, the second may try to make a shot as well. The second person knocks out the first by making a basket before the first. If the first person makes the basket, she gives the ball to the second person in line and the third person now tries to knock out the second. Play continues with each successive person trying to knock out the person in front of him or her until there is only one player remaining.

This game does not require a lot of athletic ability. Don't be afraid to try it! A warning, if you make it down to the final two or three people, you will be running quite a bit but worth it!

For a more tame option, you can make the same point by playing nearly any board or yard game. Whatever you choose, be certain the point is to best the other players and put yourself on top.

Discovery

Read Proverbs 3:27-30 out loud for the group. Split the class into at least three groups. Each group creates a skit interpreting these verses and shares its skit with the others.

After reading and interpreting the passage, ask the students:
- Who do we consider our neighbor?
- Do we think about only local neighbor or global neighbors?
- Why should we care about others?
- Do Christians have any greater obligation to care for our neighbors than anyone else?
- How can we pour out good to those around us?

Life Application

Plot to carry out random acts of kindness. How can you, as a group, devise to help others? Are there neighbors in your church who need help with anything? Do they need help with yard work or babysitting? Is your church in a neighborhood that needs to be cleaned up? Brainstorm all of the ways and write up a list that you may help others.

Personal Application

Choose one of the items placed on the list. Have each student write down on two, 3x5 cards one act of kindness they will try to accomplish this week. Have them take one card home with them and post the other card in the classroom. All of the others can check with each other to see if the good deed was done. Even with the best of intentions, many of us forget to follow through.

If you use a web page or e-mail with your students, send a reminder in mid-week.

Song

"Love Is a Miracle" by Delirious? on *The Mission Bell*

Love Your Neighbor

by Amy Jacober

Memory Verse:
You shall not take vengeance, nor bear any grudge against the sons of your people, but you shall love your neighbor as yourself; I am the Lord. —Leviticus 19:18 (NASB)

Scripture
Mark 12:28–31, Galatians 5:13–15

Lesson in a Sentence
We are to love others even when it is difficult.

Focus

Option 1
Do a little research to learn about your community before the meeting. Check with your local chamber of commerce to find current statistics on population, socio-economic make-up, number of businesses etc.

Take a walk with your students and look at the shops, homes, empty lots, schools and other things in your neighborhood. Talk about how your students view the neighborhood. Do they know any of the business owners? Do they know the people in the homes? What kind of reputation does this part of your town have? Ask your students to observe what they experience on this walk: the sights, sounds, smells, and overall feel.

When you return to your church, ask the students what they saw. How long had it been since they took a walk and really paid attention to the neighborhood? As your students share what they experienced, offer a fuller picture with the information you've gathered. How does the appearance of the neighborhood support or contradict the reality of the statistics?

Option 2
Show a clip from the movie "Mean Girls." There are many scenes from which you can choose: scenes in the lunchroom, hallway, shopping, or looking at the book. This movie is chock full of examples of girls who are mean to each other.

After showing the clip, ask what parts could they relate to and what parts did they think were far-fetched. What do mean girls and guys do at your students' schools? Remind them that they should not name names or turn this into a gossip session.

Discovery

Ask your students to tell you what they think is the greatest commandment that God ever gave? Encourage them to wrestle with this. If they know the passage that says to love God and love their neighbor, push them to talk about what this means in today's language.

Read Mark 12:28–31 and Galatians 5:13–15. We understand that we are to love God even if we don't always do this well. But, this is a lesson for another day. This lesson is about loving our neighbor. We prefer to pick and choose whom we consider our neighbor. Most often, we consider those we like, those we see as worth our time to be our neighbor. Those who are different or those we consider enemies are not our neighbors. Jesus blew this idea out of the water.

Every person, mean or not mean, bully or not, rich, poor, able bodied or not, male or female. comes as a fellow human and therefore is to be viewed as a neighbor.

Life Application

Ask your students:
- Whom do they find hard to love?
- How can they learn to love even an annoying person or a bully?
- Why would God ever call on us to love people like this?
- Why doesn't God teach them a lesson to get them to change?
- What does how treat difficult people say about what we believe about?

Scripture says to love others as we love ourselves. In this way we acknowledge the interdependence of all people. This is not about charity, it is about seeing other people as God sees them, not as we see them in our flesh.

Close with a talk about the struggle to loving others with an attitude that glorifies God and not the self.

Standing Tall

by Sharon Koh

In this lesson, students will:
Identify situations when they may compromise standing as believers in Christ. These may include cheating at school, viewing inappropriate scenes in movies, lying, bullying, and showing racial prejudice. When students identify these situations, allow them time to consider ways to handle them.

Memory Verse

I am the LORD your God, who brought you out of Egypt, out of the land of slavery. You shall have no other gods before me. You shall not make for yourself an idol in the form of anything in heaven above or on earth beneath or in the waters below. You shall not bow down to them or worship them; for I, the LORD your God am a jealous God.
—Deuteronomy 5:6–8a

Scripture

Esther 3:1—4:17

Lesson in a Sentence

Idols present themselves to us in many different forms. Therefore, it is important to make good choices about when and where take a stand for God.

The Big Picture

When God instructs us not to have any other gods before Him, He does not limit the definition of the word *idol* to physical objects. Idols can also be people, ideologies, or actions.

There are times when we face difficult choices. At these times, it takes courage to stand up for what we believe and not bow down to something that will compromise God's place in our lives.

The following are case studies that a teacher/youth pastor may adapt or add to as appropriate for the issues their students are dealing with:

Jimmy, who trained for the football season all summer, has been struggling with his grades at school. If he does not make a 2.5 GPA, he will not be allowed to play football. His friend, Charlie, knows of someone who will do Jimmy's homework for him for a small fee. What would you do if you were in Jimmy's position?

Grace, the president of her youth fellowship, is attending an R-rated movie with friends. An explicitly sexual scene appears in the movie. What would you do if you were Grace?

Katie has been invited to a sleepover with her JV basketball team. When she gets there, she finds that everyone is drinking beer and wine coolers. What would you do if you were in Katie's situation?

Timothy's parents trust him because he is responsible and cares for his younger siblings. They go out of town for the weekend and leave his younger brother and sister in his care for three days. On the first day, as he drives them to the ice cream shop, Timothy hits a trash can in the parking lot, denting his parents' car. What would you do if you were in Tim's situation?

Focus

Break students into small groups (preferably with a mature Christian adult or leader in each group) and give each group a case study. Allow them ten to fifteen minutes to discuss the situation and decide how they would respond if they were in a similar situation.

Discovery

Read Esther 4:10–17. Both Mordecai and Esther have opportunities to stand up for what they believe. What are these two opportunities?

Read Esther 3:2, 3 again. Why does Mordecai refuse to kneel down and pay honor to Haman?

Mordecai and Esther are Jewish people. Read this week's memory verse in Deuteronomy 5:6–8a. How do Mordecai and Esther uphold this commandment?

Read Esther 4:11. Why is Esther fearful about speaking to the king even though she is the queen?

Why does she decide to petition for her people anyway? (See verses 13 and 14.)

Life Application

Even if we are not faced with the threat of death as the consequence for our daily decisions, often circumstances require that we take a stand for God and the things of God. Allow students time to think about such situations in their own lives. What is their most common dilemma?

Personal Application

Some people wonder how to identify critical situations in their lives. Not all difficult circumstances are spiritual crises. Signs of such a crisis are the questions, "What are they going to think of me?" and "What if they don't like me anymore?" Allow students time to reflect on this and to think of situations in their own lives when such questions arise in their own minds.

TEACHER'S NOTE

This lesson is meant to be applicable to the students' real life. Therefore, it may be necessary to create a safe environment where students can honestly reflect on their experiences without fearing what others in the class may think about them. The teacher should carefully place students in groups and set up rules of confidentiality and respect.

Songs

"Jesus, You Alone" by Tim Hughes

Standing Tall

by Sharon Koh

Memory Verse

"I am the LORD your God, who brought you out of Egypt, out of the land of slavery. You shall have no other gods before me. You shall not make for yourself an idol in the form of anything in heaven above or on earth beneath or in the waters below. You shall not bow down to them or worship them; for I, the LORD your God am a jealous God."
—Deuteronomy 5:6–8a

Scripture

Daniel 3

Lesson in a Sentence

Shadrach, Meshach, and Abednego demonstrate exceptional courage in a life-threatening situation by refusing to worship Nebuchadnezzar's image of gold. We can be inspired by their courage to reserve our worship for God alone.

TEACHER'S NOTE

This lesson is essentially the same as the one based on the Esther text. It gives further inspiration from the example of different biblical characters. As you repeat the exercise from the previous lesson, allow students to go deep in their reflection about these difficult situations in life.

The Big Picture

When God instructs us not to have any other gods before Him, He does not limit the definition of the word idol to physical objects. The idols in our lives can be people, ideologies, or actions.

There are times in our lives when we are presented with difficult choices when it takes courage to stand up for what we believe and not allow ourselves to bow down to something that will compromise God's place in our lives.

The Role of a Lifetime

by Whitney Prosperi

In this lesson, students will:
- ✔ Learn about how God used Joseph to spare many lives.
- ✔ Identify some of the realms of influence in which God has placed them.
- ✔ Become aware of the ways God wants to use them to affect their world.

Stuff you'll need:
- ❏ Poster board for each student
- ❏ Markers
- ❏ Scissors
- ❏ Pens
- ❏ Sheet of paper for each student
- ❏ Magazines
- ❏ Tape or glue
- ❏ Words to the hymn "Take My Life And Let It Be"

Memory Verse
Whatever you do, work at it with all your heart, as working for the Lord, not for men, since you know that you will receive an inheritance from the Lord as a reward.
—Colossians 3:23–24

Scripture
Genesis 41:14–57

Lesson in a Sentence:
God wants to use you to make a difference for Him in your world.

The Big Picture
God has designed each one of us for a purpose. He has given us gifts, talents, and interests that we might use them for His kingdom on the earth. Whether or not we'll let Him use us is up to us. We have each been given realms of influence in which we can make a difference.

Joseph's life leading up to Genesis 41 was unpredictable and tragic, yet he still chose to allow God to use him where he was. He saw that God had placed him in Egypt to save the lives of many people. He considered his hardships significant because God used him in them.

We may have questions about certain situations in our lives. Why does God allow sad or hurtful things to occur? But, like Joseph, who never lost his trust in God, we can let God use us in our difficulties. In Joseph's case, the lives of many people were spared through him.

Focus

Give each student a piece of poster board and some markers. Ask them to depict their "role of a lifetime." They can write out a description, create a collage out of photos in the magazine, or draw a picture. Do not over-explain what you mean. Instead, allow them to think creatively. After the students have finished, encourage them to share their creations with one another.

Discovery

Ask the students:
- Who can tell a little about the life of Joseph?
- What are some of the high points of his life?
- What are some of the low points?
- What are the outstanding features of Joseph's personality?
- Describe his general attitude toward life.

As a group, read: Genesis 41:14–57 and discuss these questions:
- Look back at verse 16. What does this tell us about Joseph?
- How did God give Joseph favor with Pharaoh?
- What did God cause Joseph to do that saved many lives?

In verse 14, Joseph was brought from the dungeon into Pharaoh's presence. Think of all he endured: He had been sold into slavery by his jealous brothers, wrongly accused by Potiphar's wife, and thrown into prison. He could have become bitter. But he wasn't. Instead, he believed that God would use his pain and trials for good. Indeed, God used these trials to save lives.

Ask the students:
Have you ever been treated unfairly when God used this for your good or for the benefit of someone else? If so, would you be willing to share a little bit about the situation? (For middle school students you may want to give them some scenarios and examples to get their minds working.)

Joseph found himself in Egypt and decided to let God use him there. Think of where God has you right now. Consider your family, your school, church, and friends. Are you wiling to let God use you in those realms of influence? If so, how will you cooperate with Him in this?

Life Application

Give each student a piece of paper and pen. Ask them to write down their realms of influence. For instance, ask them to list their family name, school name, church or youth group name, and other groups with which they are involved.

Beside each entry, ask the students to list ways in which God could use them in each of these places. For instance, how could He show their families His love through them?

Are there opportunities to serve, speak an encouraging word, or keep their mouths closed at appropriate times? Urge students to think creatively and ask God to show them ways they can make a difference.

Personal Application

Remind students that God may have put them in a particular place to make an eternal difference for Him. Ask them to think about will happen if they don't allow God to use them. What void will be there? What won't happen that should happen?

Songs

Give your students the words to "Take My Life And Let It Be." If they know the tune, you may want to sing it together. If not, suggest they use it at home in prayer.

The Role of a Lifetime

by Whitney Prosperi

Memory Verse

"Whatever you do, work at it with all your heart, as working for the Lord, not for men, since you know that you will receive an inheritance from the Lord as a reward."
—Colossians 3:23–24

Scripture

Genesis 50:20

Lesson in a Sentence

God wants to use you to make a difference for Him in your world.

Focus

When things don't go our way, we often become focused on the negative and don't look to God. Share a story of when you experienced a painful situation that God used for your and others' good. Be open to with your students. You'll be amazed at how they remember your life experiences more than other things you try to teach them.

Discovery

Ask several students to read Genesis 50:20 from different translations.
Ask the following questions:
- How did God turn evil into good in Joseph's life?
- In Joseph's opinion, why was he placed in his high position?
- In what position has God placed you so you can be a part of someone's salvation?
- How will you take the opportunity God has given you?

Life Application

Joseph worked hard even though he was often in difficult situations. Think through the different jobs God has given you. You are a student, family member, and you may have a job in the community. How can you honor God in each of these areas of your life? Remember, as you study, work at your job, or help around the house you have the chance to work as unto the Lord. What are some practical ways you can do this?

Ask God to help you see your life like Joseph did who knew that God had a special purpose for him and so honored Him in every choice and action. God has a special reason for creating you. How can you live each day with the attitude that you are making a difference because of the work of God in your life? Write out a Bible verse to remind you of this fact and place it on your mirror or in one of your schoolbooks. Ask a friend to hold you accountable for the choices you make. Choose to live purposefully.

Submission to God

by Carina Proano

In this lesson, students will:
- ✔ Learn to authentically trust in the invisible but ever-present God
- ✔ Recognize personal weaknesses
- ✔ See their need to hope in God
- ✔ Get a glimpse of God's sovereignty
- ✔ Learn to respect others' opinions
- ✔ Realize the importance of guidance and shared wisdom
- ✔ Become able to invite others to keep them accountable

Stuff you'll need:
- ❏ Enough blindfolds for half the students
- ❏ Two handouts: questionnaire and song lyrics
- ❏ Pens or Pencils
- ❏ Bibles
- ❏ Discussion starter sheets for leaders
- ❏ CD Player
- ❏ Ginny Owens' songs "I Am" and "This Road"
- ❏ Additional adult volunteers and/or student leaders

Memory Verses

Trust in the LORD with all your heart, and lean not on your own understanding; in all your ways acknowledge Him, and He shall direct your paths. —Proverbs 3:5–6

Scriptures

Acts 9:1–16; Exodus 3:1–18; Genesis 50:15–21

Lesson in Sentence

We walk by faith and submit to God even though we do not understand everything that is happening in our lives.

The Big Picture

Hard times are a reality in this world. Chaos and pain come into our students' lives without their consent or control. At such times, submission to God's will is perhaps the most difficult of spiritual disciplines. It is counter to natural desires because we do not want to answer to anyone. But, the discipline of submission teaches that we are under the authority of Christ. With this realization, circumstances that are out of our control become an opportunity to cling to God.

Focus

All the students team up with a partner. Everyone sits in two rows opposite his or her partner, takes off their shoes, and throws them in a pile on the floor between the two rows. One person in each team is blindfolded. Each blindfolded person must find his or her partner's shoes in the pile. The partner can advise "That is not my shoe" until the correct pair is found. Then the blindfolded players must tie the shoes on their partner's feet. The first team to finish, wins.

When the game is finished, ask both the blindfolded players and the sighted players if they were frustrated or thought the game was difficult. Were there any moments when they wanted to give up? Were there any times when they wanted to tear the blindfold off? Then bridge the gap between the game and the big picture:

When we can't see what is going on, we feel out of control. When we can't control events in our lives, we feel as though there is something wrong with us. But there are times when it is all right to feel out of control. In God's design, we cannot control our lives so we must submit our will to His will. Such submission and dependence on God become our worship to him.

Discovery

Divide students into groups of three to five members led by either an adult or student leader. Assign one of the three scripture passages to each group. Each passage will be used more than once depending on the number of groups. Make sure every group has a Bible and the leader has a discussion starter sheet. The groups read their assigned passages and the leaders use the questions as a guide to discussion.

Life Application

Once each group is finished their discussion, leaders distribute the student questionnaire. Allow at least ten minutes for the students to fill out this questionnaire alone. Then, gather the students back into their groups. Tell them to discuss their answers if they feel comfortable doing so.

Some questions that could promote discussions:
- Describe a situation or event that was out of your control.
- How did the situation end?
- What does surrender mean to you?
- Has God ever failed you?

When these discussions are done, pass out the lyrics to both songs. Ask the students to find a comfortable place in the room where they can concentrate on the words of the two songs that you will play.

Play "I am." After the song is finished, use the following questions as a discussion starter:
- Has anyone ever felt incapable of being used by God?

- Does the idea of being used by God overwhelm you?
- How can we see the bigger picture?
- How do you fit into the bigger picture?
- What happens when we put our trust in God?

Before playing the next song, "This Road," explain that trust in God doesn't guarantee an easy life. The submission to God's will, may include trials, pain, struggle, loneliness, frustration, and any of the hardships that Jesus promised his followers.

Play "This Road."

Personal Application

After the second song finishes, allow the students five minutes to practice the spiritual discipline of silence. Through this silence, invite the students to come up with one situation in which they need to surrender to God. This situation may be in the past or something with which they are currently struggling. Wrap up this lesson on submission to God by telling the students that despite their discomfort, the change God brings to their lives will benefit them and the kingdom of God when their daily actions become a living worship unto Him.

Finally, be sure that you, your adult volunteers, and youth staff are available to privately talk with students about any issues that arise a result of this lesson.

Submission to God

by Carina Proano

Memory Verses

Trust in the Lord with all your heart, and lean not on your own understanding; in all your ways acknowledge Him, and He shall direct your paths.—Proverbs 3:5–6

Scriptures

Acts 9:1–16; Exodus 3:1–18; Genesis 50:15–21

Lesson in a Sentence

Submission is freedom from the need to have it your own way.

Focus

Welcome your students to "Country and Western Night." They will learn how to line dance. Most students will not have very much experience in line dancing and will need instruction. Ask someone in your congregation who is familiar with line dancing to help you or teach the kids yourself. Expect some kids to pick it up from following your lead and some kids to give up quickly. The transition between the dance and the lesson on submission will take place after all the students have had a chance to learn the dance.

Tell the students that submission to God is a lot like learning how to dance. In the beginning, no one knows the steps and it is necessary for them to learn from a teacher. It takes listening, watching, learning, and practicing repeatedly.

Discovery

Break the students into groups of three to four people, preferably the same groups that were formed during the main lesson on submission. Make sure every group has a Bible. Assign to each group one of the three above verses. The groups are to come up with a skit that could resemble the story in their verse. This can either be a modern-day interpretation of the story or a re-enactment. Give the groups ten minutes to come up with their skit. Finally, the groups perform their skits for everyone.

Life Application

The students continue to discuss how they can include submission in their lives. Guide them by asking them to consider the practical benefits of practicing submission. Introduce the idea that they each would have an accountability partner for the rest of the school year. Such accountability partners assist each other to practice submission to God. Do not assign accountability partners but allow the students to choose someone they trust and respect. These partners should meet on a regular basis and set boundaries for their relationship. They should discuss what they will do to keep each other accountable, how often they would like to talk about submission to God, and different modes of keeping each other mindful of submission.

Submission Survey

1. How do you typically respond when trouble hits your life?

1————2————3————4————5————6————7————8————9————10
Don't Worry;   Minor Freakout!   It's the end
Be Happy   of the world!

2. Who do you turn to most when you are faced with hard stuff?

God	Teacher
Parents	Pastor/counselor
Siblings	None . . . I keep to myself
Friends	Other _____

3. Which of the people on the list in question 3 do you trust the most?

4. Is it easy for you to trust someone other than yourself?

1————2————3————4————5————6————7————8————9————10
Yes, I'm   I'm a little guarded   I can't trust
an open book   anyone

5. How do you respond when someone points out something wrong in your life?

1————2————3————4————5————6————7————8————9————10

Completely   Respect their opinion   Allow their words
defensive   to affect your behavior

6. Do you feel as though you are accountable to anyone for your behavior?

7. If yes, whom are you accountable to?

Worship

by Amy Jacober

In this lesson, students will:
- ✔ Recognize of the mandate for worship in scripture
- ✔ Learn different ways to worship
- ✔ Identify who or what they worship

Stuff you'll need:
- ❑ Several pre-printed sheets with scriptures and directions
- ❑ A small table
- ❑ A chair
- ❑ A vase with a lily in it
- ❑ Paper
- ❑ Crayons
- ❑ Markers
- ❑ Tape
- ❑ Beanbags or floor pillows
- ❑ MP3 player w/worship songs
- ❑ 3 x 5 cards
- ❑ Tea lights or votive candles
- ❑ Matches or a lighter
- ❑ Pictures of Christ

Memory Verse
Give to the Lord the glory due His name; Bring an offering, and come before Him. Oh, worship the Lord in the beauty of His holiness! —Chronicles 16:29

Scripture
1 Chronicles 16:11; Psalm 46:10; Psalm 96:1-6; Psalm 150; Matthew 6:25–34; Ephesians 6:18; James 4:8

Lesson in a Sentence
Worship is the acknowledgment and response to that which is worthy.

The Big Picture
We all worship. Even those who do not follow Jesus worship something. The old saying is that one needs only to look at a person's schedule and checkbook to see what they worship. While schedules have gone the way of PDA's and checkbooks are nearly passé, the principle remains. Our students lack control over both these. They are scheduled by school requirements. As for what is in their pockets, wouldn't it be interesting to see what they spend money on in an average month? That is a completely different lesson but still a good indicator here.

Worship is often a highly volatile topic. People have strong beliefs about what should and should not be a part of worship. This is often the focus more than who is being worshipped. Scripture offers a variety of ways worship with no admonition that it is an exhaustive list. In fact, worship is a way of life, not a once a week activity. Teenagers are by nature radical and passionate. What to do with all of this passion is the question. A lifestyle of worshipping God moves their relationship with Christ from a list of do's and don'ts to an all encompassing, radical focus. The fact is, they will worship something.

This lesson, unlike all of the others is unique in that the Focus and Discovery sections are combined. This gives you the freedom to be flexible time- wise and to debrief the experience in the way that is best for your group.

Focus/Discovery

Have your room prepared ahead of time for this activity. Choose a worship CD to set the tone in the room. You may also consider lighting by placing candles throughout the room.

As your students enter, tell them that they are entering holy ground. Ask them to slip off their shoes and set them to the side. Let them know that in the midst of a busy week, God is ready to meet them and you are offering time and space to do so. Hand each student a paper that says the following:

> Draw near to God and He will draw near to you. Cleanse your hands you sinners; and purify your hearts you double minded. —James 4:8

> Welcome! Life is busy and often overwhelming. We do not often make time for God. This evening, you have the time. There are several stations around the room for you to visit. For the first half of our time together you can do what you choose to do. You may sit at one station for the entire time or go to several, there is no right or wrong way to do this. Breathe deep the presence of Christ and know that the one who loved you with His very life desires to meet with you now.

The stations:
Lilies of the field
On a small table, place a vase with a lily in it. Set a single chair in front of the table. Have printed a paper that says: Look at this lily and meditate on Matthew 6:25-34.

More than words
Set out paper, markers, crayons, and a few rolls of tape. Have printed a paper that says: Sometimes words just can't be found to express your relationships with God. In whatever way you feel, draw, color, and create a message to the Lord or describe you are hearing from the Lord.

Be Still
Create a space to relax. If you have beanbag chairs, set them out. If not, use pillows and create a comfy space on the floor. Have printed a paper that says: Read Psalm 46:10 and meditate or rest in His presence.

Sing a new song
Set out headphones and an MP3 player with a variety of worship songs and hymns

loaded on it. Print Psalm 96:1-6 on a sheet of paper. Have printed a paper that says: Read this Psalm while listening to music.

A Psalm of Praise
Have printed a paper that says: Read Psalm 150. This is a Psalm of praise. Take a few moments and write out your own psalm of praise in your own words.

Who Is God?
Set out 3 x 5 cards and markers. On a sheet print the following; To praise and worship God we need to know who He is. Take a marker and write a word to describe God. Set this out for others who come behind you to see.

For Others
Set out votive candles or tea lights in containers. On paper print Ephesians 6:18 and the following: "We are encouraged to pray for others. Think of someone who needs someone's prayer right now. Light a candle and offer a prayer for that person. The candle is to remind you that you are doing something seemingly small but very powerful."

Seek His Face
Find at least five pictures of Christ. Check art books and the Internet. The more of these you have the better. On a sheet of paper print 1 Chronicles 16:11 and the following: what does it mean to you to seek the face of Christ?

TEACHER'S NOTE:
Worship is an English word meaning "worthy" or "that which is worthy." It connotes time, attention, focus, and adoration. When we hold something dear to our hearts, when we wrap our lives around whatever captures our attention, we are worshipping. Many of us talk about loving God, following Jesus and being Christian. What we don't do so well is live as though He is worthy; walk the walk as much as we talk the talk.

Life Application
Spend time discussing what you just experienced together. Ask for initial thoughts. If your group is not talkative, begin with the following questions to guide the conversation.

- What did you learn about worship from this experience?
- What has God communicated to you in this time?
- What was your favorite station? Why?
- What was your least favorite station? Why?
- What do you think was missing?
- How can we take some of these things into our daily lives?
- What other ways can we worship God in our daily lives?

Making it Personal

Worship can be one of the most difficult concepts to grasp, especially when we don't "feel" God's presence. Nowhere in scripture does it say that we will always "feel" God but it does say we are to praise Him. We are to worship Him.

Ask your students to pick a way to worship the Lord this week and share this with a neighbor, praying for one another to do this throughout the week.

Song

"Let the Worshipers Arise" by Pocket Full of Rocks on *Song to the King*

Worship

by Amy Jacober

Memory Verse

Give to the Lord the glory due His name; Bring an offering, and come before Him. Oh, worship the Lord in the beauty of His holiness! —1 Chronicles 16:29

Scripture

Then he said to me, "These words are faithful and true." And the Lord God of the holy prophets sent His angel to show His servants the things which must shortly take place. "Behold, I am coming quickly! Blessed is he who keeps the words of the prophecy of this book." Now I, John, saw and heard these things. And when I heard and saw, I fell down to worship before the feet of the angel who showed me these things. Then he said to me, "See that you do not do that. For I am your fellow servant, and of your brethren the prophets, and of those who keep the words of this book. Worship God." —Revelation 22:6–9

Romans 15:16—proclaiming God
Hebrews 13:15—Praising God
Philippians 2:17—dedicating lives
Philippians 2:25—sharing fellowship
2 Corinthians 9:12—charitable giving
James 1:27—acting justly
Matthew 25:45—caring for the needy
Psalm 19:1—all creation declares God's glory
Psalm 95:6–7—Come worship and bow down

Lesson in a Sentence

Worship is the acknowledgment and response to that which is worthy.

Focus

Worship Skit by Jacqueline Eleanor Foreman

Opening Scene—Jane in sanctuary dancing, singing, and jumping around praising the Lord.

Kelley (Enters the sanctuary in disapproval): Jane, what do you think you are doing?

Jane (Stops what she is doing to answer Kelly): Praising the Lord of course!

Kelley: You call that praising the Lord? It looks like you are jumping around like some one at (insert the name of the current boy band here) concert. That is not how you praise the Lord.

Jane: If this is not how I am to praise the Lord, how exactly would you praise the Lord?

Kelley: Well first you must realize that praising the Lord is something that is quiet and personal. It is for you and God alone. Next, you need to be by yourself where no one can see you. Last, there is only one way to give God the praise he needs and that does not involve singing or dancing but just sitting in prayer.

Jane: Well I know from reading scripture that the Bible tells us that there is more than one way to praise and honor our Lord. And while sitting quietly in your room in prayer is one way, there are many more ways. Dancing, singing, keeping a journal, playing an instrument, enjoying God's presence in nature, serving the Lord, and any form of art are all many different and great ways of worshipping God. There are many other ways as well. The Lord did not limit us in the way to worship him.

Kelley: Wow! I never heard or even thought of worshiping God like that. Sorry for what I said. Let's go get some tea and crumpets.

End

Ask what the students thought of how worship was presented in the skit. Have they ever been somewhere or known someone who thought worship was to be done in one very specific way? What do they think about the two extremes of worship; loud and active or silent and sedate?

Check out what the Bible actually says about worship. By no means is this an exhaustive list. If you know of a few other verses you think are important, add them.

Discovery

Tape a large piece of paper on the wall in a central location with markers nearby. Break into small groups. Pass out a strip of paper with the passages below printed on them. Give at least one to each group. Ask them to read the passage and in a word or two tell what can be learned from it about worshipping God. After a few minutes, have each group share what they learned. As they do this, have them write the word or phrase on the butcher paper to better understand what it is they learned.

Psalm 19:1—All creation declares God's glory
Psalm 95:6–7—Come worship and bow down
Matthew 25:45—Caring for the needy
Romans 15:16—Proclaiming God

2 Corinthians 9:12—Charitable giving
Philippians 2:17—Dedicating lives
Philippians 2:25—Sharing fellowship
Hebrews 13:15—Praising God
James 1:27—Acting justly
Revelation 22:6–9—God alone deserves our worship

Life Application

Share in small groups what is difficult, easy, confusing and refreshing about worship.

- What makes you want to worship?
- What keeps us from worshipping?
- What purpose do you think worship serves?

Look at all that is written on the butcher paper. Are there any points with which you disagree? Are there any with which you agree? What is missing?

Making it Personal

Worship is a choice. There is no one way to do it nor is there any one time it is to be done. It is a part of every aspect of life.

- How do you personally struggle to keep the right attitude toward God?
- What expression of worship is new for you?
- What expression of worship is a struggle for you?
- Choose one pragmatic way to worship God this week.

Practicing a Religion vs. Enjoying a Relationship

by Joyce DelRosario

After weeks of living with a frantic schedule, I found myself in a predicament while driving to meet with one of my volunteers. As I drove I found myself physically feeling more and more sick. I had busied myself into exhaustion, so I cancelled my next two meetings and went home to rest and reflect on how I got to this point.

My mind turned to the person I often identify with in scripture, Martha. In Luke 10:38-42 Jesus is at the home of Mary and Martha. Martha was doing what she knew best, serving Jesus Christ. She was busy in the kitchen preparing a meal for him. I'm not the greatest cook, but I do find great joy in preparing and sharing a meal with the people I love. There is something about being able to offer a part of myself that blesses others physically, spiritually, and emotionally.

Martha may have felt the same. She was a great minister who opened her home to Jesus. This was good and right. When Jesus arrived she went into action, her thoughts were on what had to be done. I suspect she had a mental to-do list: Serve drinks, check; shove dirty laundry under bed, check; prepare food for the guests; check. Preparations, protocol, and service to her guest—these occupied Martha's mind.

My days are filled with such a list. The list has grown so large that I have enlisted the aid of a PDA, computer calendar, day planner, and Post-It notes. Serving is a busy proposition for me! I meet with my volunteers every week as a group and individually, I plan Bible studies, I meet with other youth pastors in the area, I preach on occasion, I sit on planning teams and committees, I read books on how to live and serve well then discuss them in group settings with my brothers and sisters in Christ, I travel to one conference or camp to another, I listen to the Christian radio station while driving from one meeting to the next. From the time I wake up to the time I go to bed I am efficiently practicing my religion. I am Martha.

All of this is done with the best intentions. When I gave my life to the Lord, I meant it and set out on a mission to prove my love and devotion to Jesus. But, I sometimes look around and ask, "Where is everyone else?" Why am I the only one sweeping the church basement after our meeting? I look at friends and family who all seem to have time to be at home. They seem to have time to sleep. Where are they while I'm slaving over the kitchen stove? To me, they look like Mary, Martha's younger sister. Younger siblings are great, but when things need to be done, the older siblings can get frustrated. To Martha, Mary was the lazy one. Doesn't she care that there is an important guest to feed? Doesn't she care that there are things that need to be done? We have youth group tonight! We have a mission trip to plan! We have Sunday School and Bible studies! What is Mary doing? How can she just sit there and listen to Jesus instead of serving him?

The older sibling is fed up with doing all the work; pulling the whole load. So, Martha complains to Jesus. She has what I call the "That's Messed Up" syndrome: "That's messed up! Lord, don't you care that my sister has left me to do the work by myself? Tell her to help me!"

"Martha, Martha. You are worried and upset about many things, but only one thing is needed. Mary has chosen what is better."

In Jesus' eyes, Mary chose the better way. I think Martha was right in serving, but she had forgotten the point of it. She did everything she was supposed to do. She was acting responsibly. She was serving Jesus; trying to please him. She was trying so hard that Jesus noticed her worry and distress. Martha was so wrapped up in her to-do list that she forgot the reason for her busyness.

Meanwhile, Mary sat quietly at the foot of Jesus. She knew that there were things to be done, but the sight of the Savior, the sight of the Son of God, a glimpse of the one who could heal physical pain and mend broken souls, caused the world around her to fade away. She could only see His face. She could only sit in awe of Him. Mary did not move. She was at rest in the presence of God. Mary knew what the Psalmist meant when he wrote, "Be still and know that I am God."

In other words, Mary chose the better way.

Jesus did not say that Martha was wrong in what she was doing, but points out that Mary chose the better way. She chose "the one thing that is needed". Mary tended to her relationship with Jesus Christ.

Martha practiced religion; Mary had a relationship.

I define religion as the amalgam of superficial practices that identify people with the same beliefs. Christianity, Buddhism, and Islam are identifiable by their various practices. The youth worker's personal religion includes such practices as planning retreats, implementing fundraisers, and getting parent permission slips together. All of these must be done. They make possible our times with young people. When Martha worked in the kitchen, it had to be—everyone had to eat. Although these practical things are important, we youth workers, servants of Jesus Christ, must remember the better way— our relationship with the Lord.

It bugs me when people ask if I'm religious. This conjures images of candle lighting, chanting, and ponderous processions. I want to answer, "No! I'm in a love relationship with Christ." But, the real reason I don't like that question is that it hits too close to home. If I were to answer truthfully, I would admit I spend more time with religious busyness than I do tending to my relationship with Christ.

Martha did what was right, good, and necessary, but Mary chose the better way. My prayer for myself and for all of my brothers and sisters in Christ is that each day when we awaken, we will truly awake and choose the better way. We may be in a religion, but a marvelous relationship with Christ is within us. Let us go forth and minister compelled not by a to-do list but by the love of Christ.

For the love of Christ compels us, because we judge thus: that if One died for all, then all died. —2 Corinthians 5:14

Help Along the Way

by Amy Jacober

In this lesson, students will:
- ✔ Learn of the tradition of Palm Sunday
- ✔ Be able to retell the story of the Jesus' triumphal entry into Jerusalem
- ✔ Discuss what it means to praise God

Stuff you'll need:
- ❑ "The Crowd or the Cross" video. This may be purchased at *www.worship-housemedia.com.* It is found in "Igniter Video, Volume 1." There are five videos in this series.
- ❑ Video or DVD player
- ❑ A television
- ❑ Paper
- ❑ Pencils
- ❑ Dry-erase board & markers

Memory Verse
Blessed is the one who comes in the name of the Lord; We have blessed you from the house of the Lord. —Psalm 118:26

Scripture
Matthew 21:1–12, Isaiah 62:11–12, Zechariah 9:9

Lesson in a Sentence
Even on the way to His death, Jesus helped others.

The Big Picture
We live in a busy world and in busy times. We all have important deadlines to meet. Teenagers are no exception. They have soccer practice and music rehearsal, youth group, and school deadlines. In the midst of this busyness, most of us barely have time to take care of ourselves let alone to look around and see the needs of others. Yet, on the way to the cross, Jesus modeled concern for others.

The needs of others deserve our attention. We must find a way to slow our busy lives, re-prioritize, and help the needy and the lost.

Focus

Show the video "The Crowd or the Cross." This is a three-minute presentation that prompts us to consider what we will choose: the crowd or the cross? It brings up a host of questions that are ideal springboards to the consideration of what it means to follow Jesus.

When Jesus approached Jerusalem, He was greeted like a celebrity. The red carpet was rolled out, the crowds were cheering, and praises were all around. As we already know, this reception was short lived. But temporarily, the crowd was seeking Jesus and praising Him. Talk with your students about what the crowd (the present world) is following and praising and whom Christians follow and praise.

Discovery

In groups of three or four, have your students read Matthew 21:1–11. You may need to remind them that this portion describes what happened as Jesus entered Jerusalem on the first day of the week He was to be crucified. As they read, pass out a piece of paper and pencils to each group. Encourage them to reread the passage several times and write down as many questions about it as they can. There is no question too silly or small and no question too deep or big. This is a time to brainstorm and get into the passage.

Have the groups trade questions. Each group then chooses two or three questions to answer or discuss. This exercise is meant to encourage them to read scripture, learn the stories, and begin to wrestle with scriptural ideas. Younger students will tend to be more literal and older students more conceptual. This is normal and both are valuable.

Sample questions may be:
- Who was with Jesus at this time?
- Why did Jesus need a donkey and her colt?
- What does Hosanna mean?
- How do we respond when we hear that the Lord has need of something we have?

Connections

Isaiah 62:11-12 and Zechariah 9:9 both speak of the prophecy mentioned in Matthew 21:5. Why was it important that this prophecy be fulfilled? Would we still understand Jesus to be the Messiah had this not been mentioned? How does prophecy help us better understand scripture and what it means to follow Jesus?

Life Application

You've just looked at the story of Jesus' entry into Jerusalem. This is one of the most beloved and best-known stories in the Christian tradition. It tells of praising Jesus, of changing your patterns and recognizing Him. Spend a few moments brainstorming ways that we recognize Jesus in our daily lives. Write these on one half of a dry-erase board.

Now spend a few moments brainstorming the ways and reasons we praise God. In the passage, they threw garments and tree branches on the ground so Christ would not have to walk on dirt. We won't have an opportunity to praise God in this way but there are unique ways we praise him today. Write these on the other half of the dry erase board.

Some of your students may need encouragement to realize for how much we have to praise Him for. This exercise does not diminish the fact that some have hard lives. It does put things in perspective, however. For example, even the very air we breathe is a gift from God. Our present lives are not perfect and never will be. But we are not alone. The Lord is with us even in the most difficult of circumstances.

Make it Personal

Read Matthew 21:10 out loud for the whole group. In this verse, the whole city was stirred to ask, "Who is this"?

Discuss with the students in this way: Imagine if you had been in Jerusalem then and heard that question, how might you have responded? How would you respond today? If you meet someone this afternoon who has never heard of Jesus, knows nothing of Palm Sunday, what would you say? You may have the students role-play this scenario with their neighbor or write out their ideas.

Songs

"Lead Me On" by Matt Papa on *Matt Papa*

Help Along the Way

by Amy Jacober

Memory Verse

Blessed is the one who comes in the name of the Lord; We have blessed you from the house of the Lord. —Psalm 118:26

Scripture

Matthew 21:12–17

Lesson in a Sentence

Even on the way to His death, Jesus helped others.

Focus

Option 1

Play a game of freeze tag. After playing, ask what life is like when it is interrupted. Some of us are easily distracted and welcome any disruption. Others are focused and either hate disruptions or don't recognize them when they come. Realistically, we all get so focused on our own life that, short of being grabbed and told to freeze, we breeze on and take care of our lives without notice of others.

Option 2

Replay "The Crowd and the Cross," the video that you used in the previous meeting. The middle of Holy Week is a good time to reflect on what it means to follow Jesus, even to the cross.

In the above lesson, students are asked to consider how they might answer the question asked in Matthew 21:10—"Who is this?" Who is Jesus to them? Do they understand the significance of the life, death, and resurrection of Jesus?

Following Jesus is not for the faint of heart. It does not guarantee an easy life or that problems will disappear. The world's way seems so much easier than this. So, many ignore the cross. If we acknowledge that following Jesus is hard but is worth it, our students won't see Christianity as hypocritical. If we take a hard look at what it means to practically follow Jesus, we can better grasp the difference between following the crowd and following Jesus Christ to the cross.

Discovery

Ask the group to read Matthew 21:12–17. As the students read, have them make a list of every person mentioned in this passage and everything that Jesus does.

After the lists are made, assign one word to each action. For example: *Chastizing* describes Jesus' overturning the moneychangers' tables. *Healing* or *helping* describes His healing of the blind and lame.

Discuss these things in this way: Have you ever noticed that hearts and flowers did not surround Jesus' life? Nor was He simply an angry judge. He carefully attended to each circumstance and individual. When in the final week of his earthly ministry, He still managed to take care of individuals. Interestingly enough, He addressed their needs more than their wants. No one wants to be chastised like the moneychangers were, but they needed such discipline. Scripture tells us that God disciplines those whom He loves. Discipline can come in the form of encouragement for those who are distressed or in rebuke for those in error. Each act is equally loving.

Ask for stories of times your students' needs were met when someone addressed them as an individual. For example: A neighbor noticed a boy was home alone after school with nothing to do. That neighbor showed an interest in the boy, welcomed him into his garage every afternoon, and taught him auto repair.

Application

This passage tells of Jesus' capacity to love others in the middle of his own trials. We are not he, so this may seem impossible for us to imitate. Yet, even in our worst moments, the Lord is with us. Our own burdens are more bearable when we help others in their difficulties.

Discussion Points

How can we find encouragement to help others by studying Jesus' example? What are some pragmatic ways to address the needs of others instead of only one's own struggles?

Close with a reminder of "The Crowd or the Cross." Ask your students to remember that Jesus was on his His way to the cross during this week 2000 years ago and to daily consider who they will follow—the crowd or the Lord.

How Jesus Gives Peace of Mind

by Whitney Prosperi

In this lesson, students will:
- ✔ Learn about the disciples and their encounter with Jesus post-resurrection
- ✔ Internalize the truth that Jesus is with them and will give them peace
- ✔ Understand how to live in the awareness of His peace and presence

Stuff you'll need:
- ❑ Costumes for skits, though these are not absolutely necessary.

Memory Verse

Peace I leave with you; my peace I give you. I do not give to you as the world gives. Do not let your hearts be troubled and do not be afraid. —John 14:27

Scripture

Luke 24:26–49

Lesson in a Sentence

Jesus is with us even when we don't recognize His presence and will give us peace as we set our minds on Him.

The Big Picture

There are times when we feel that we're alone. We may experience turmoil, tragedy, fear, illness, or worry. Whatever the situation, we must remember we're never without hope. Jesus promises His presence to us and will give us peace.

Just as the disciples were worried and fearful after Jesus Christ's crucifixion, sometimes we experience anxiety about the past. We may also feel fear of what lies ahead. When we feel anxious we simply need to turn to Him and allow Him to give us His peace. The more time we spend in the Word, the more we'll be conscious of the Lord's presence near and around us.

Focus

Divide into three small groups. Give them each Group a portion of the selection from Luke 24. For example, verses 26–32, 33–43, and 44–49.

Each group will work out a way to dramatize its portion before the group. Give the groups some time to practice before they perform. Encourage the other groups to pay attention and clap for each group's skit.

Discovery

Ask the students these questions:
- Have you ever felt all alone with God very far away? If so, describe the situation and your emotions.

- Were you alone? Explain your answer.

Read Luke 24:26–32 as a group. Ask the students these questions:
- Did the disciples recognize Jesus? Explain your answer.

- What has taken place in the chapters before this one? Why do you think this affected their ability to realize they were talking with Jesus?

- Have you ever been in a situation in which God was with you but you were so focused on the circumstances that you didn't notice?

- What did Jesus do to help the disciples recognize Him?

Sometimes overwhelming circumstances of our lives prevent us from seeing the obvious—that God loves us, is with us, cares for us. We need God to open our eyes to see that He is with us.

Recall a time when you were overcome by feelings of aloneness. Then share how God reminded you of His presence. Maybe He used a friend's words, a song, or a Bible verse. Describe this to your students and don't be afraid to be open to them.

Have your students take turns reading verses 33–49. Ask them:
- How do you think the eleven disciples felt when Jesus suddenly appeared to them?
- Imagine if you were one of them. How would you have reacted?
- What were Jesus' first words to the disciples when he appeared?

Just think about that for a minute. He could have said anything in the world to them and He spoke peace over their lives. Maybe you need the peace of God in your life today. You might be facing unpredictable circumstances and you don't know how things are going to turn out. You maybe feel fear. Jesus speaks these same words to you.

Ask a student to reread verse 45.

Explain how God is the one who gives understanding when we read His Word. When we pray as we are reading or studying the Bible He will help us know how to apply that passage directly to our lives.

The more time we spend in His Word the more we'll sense His presence and hear Him speaking to us.

Life Application

There are three practical ways to be reminded of God's presence.

Memorize His Word

- Talk to Him constantly throughout the day
- Praise Him
- Ask students to think about what they have learned by practicing one of the above. Give students the opportunity to tell about how these disciplines have helped him or her realize the constant presence of God. If no one wants to share about this, tell about your own experience.

Personal Application

Ask your students to choose one of the three options shared above and encourage them to try this in their daily lives this week. If they chose to remember God's presence through praise, encourage them to find new ways to express worship and praise to God. If it is through memorizing scripture, ask them to find one or two verses to memorize. If they chose to focus on talking to God throughout the day ask them to write out reminders to themselves and place them where they will see them to jog their memory about this commitment.

You may even want to allow the students a time to share about what they learned through this exercise at your next gathering.

TEACHERS' NOTE

Be sensitive to the fact that not every student in your group may be a Christian. If you sense that you need to share how to initially invite Jesus into one's life for the first time, go ahead and do that at whatever point you feel appropriate.

How Jesus Gives Peace of Mind

by Whitney Prosperi

Memory Verse

Peace I leave with you; my peace I give you. I do not give to you as the world gives. Do not let your hearts be troubled and do not be afraid. —John 14:27

Scripture

Philippians 4:6–7

Lesson in a Sentence

Jesus is with us even when we don't recognize it and will give us peace as set our minds on Him.

Focus

Ask students to focus their minds on nothing for one whole minute; that is, sit in complete silence. Next, ask them to share what kinds of things raced through their minds in that minute. Explain that our brains are designed to focus on something. When we focus them on God and His Word we'll find that we have peace that passes understanding.

Discovery

In pairs, read through Philippians 4:6–7 and answer the following questions:
- What is it okay to be anxious about?
- What are we supposed to pray about?
- According to this passage, how are we supposed to pray?
- What promise does God give us when we follow His advice about prayer?
- How is God's peace described in this passage?
- In what way can you apply this promise to your own life?

Application

How can you remind yourself of God's presence working in your life? One way is to set your mind on God and His Word.

Ask someone to read Romans 8:6. Now ask these questions: Is there something that you constantly worry about? Are you tempted to become discouraged when you think about a certain thing? If so, ask God to help you pray as soon as you think about that thing.

TEACHER'S NOTE
Be sensitive to the fact that some of your students may be struggling with some very difficult things. If you sense this, you may want to make yourself available to talk with students one-on-one after the session. As always, you want your students to know that you are there for them.

The Plain Truth

by Joyce DelRosario

In this lesson, students will:
- ✔ Learn about our identity created by God before the Fall.
- ✔ Understand the definition and cost of sin.

Stuff you'll need:
- ❑ Two clear vases
- ❑ Popcorn
- ❑ Apple cider
- ❑ Baseball card
- ❑ Pencil
- ❑ Magazine pictures of models
- ❑ Any items representing value
- ❑ Sand
- ❑ Two vases, one filled with water
- ❑ Oregano or pills
- ❑ Barbie doll
- ❑ Dollar bill
- ❑ Sliced apple

Memory Verse

The thief comes only to steal and kill and destroy; I have come that they may have life, and have it to the full. —John 10:10

Scripture

Genesis 1:26–31; 3:6–12

Lesson in a Sentence

Though we were made in the image of God to be in relationship with Him, sin has separated us from God.

The Big Picture

Made in the image of God, Adam and Eve were to have a relationship with God. But here's the problem: When God made Adam and Eve, He told them, "I love you so much because I made you. You have a choice of whether or not to love me back. If you love me, then you'll live in the boundaries that will keep you safe and give you life. Or you can choose to do things your way and risk being separated from Me." Adam and Eve chose to do things their way even though they knew it's not what God wanted. So, we have been born into a messed up world; a world separated from God.

The Bible says that the wages of sin is death (Romans 6:23). There is a price to pay for sin. Without that relationship with God, we are destined to death.

Focus

Ask the students describe the vase with the water in it. Is it pure, clean, clear? Then have a student pour the water back and forth between the two vases. This represents the relationship we were intended to have with God. We were made in God's image and as a result were able to relate with Him, signified by the pouring back and forth of water.

Have the students pick up items on the table they feel are sinful and discuss why they chose what they did. What did they chose to leave on the table? Why did they do this?

Discovery

Fill the empty vase with popcorn and ask the students if the vase is full. No? Why not? Then fill the vase with sand. Is it full? No? Why not?

Empty the sand out of the vase. Then have the students choose items from the table with which to fill the vase. Once the vase if full of the chosen items ask the students if the relationship between the vases is the same as when only water filled the vase. Note that you can pour water into the vase with the other things, but it gets muddled. Also, it is not possible to pour the vase of items into the vase with water without offending the water vase. We can ask God to be a part of our life, but it's not the same as when we allow Him to fill us entirely.

No matter how much we fill the vases with stuff it can never be full. There will always be empty places, voids that have not been filled. John 10:10 says Jesus came to give us "life to the fullest." The only thing that can truly fill our lives is God. But because of sin, we can spend our life trying to fill it with all sorts of things.

Memory Verse Activity

Have students bring a vase to decorate. Write the memory verse on the vase with paint pens or permanent markers. Throughout the week, have them fill the vase with things that occupy their days. By the end of the week, they will have a visual depiction of what they fill their life with. The verse on the vase will serve as a reminder that only God can truly fill us.

Quotable Quotes

The worst sin toward our fellow creatures is not to hate them, but to be indifferent to them: that's the essence of inhumanity. —George Bernard Shaw

The Plain Truth

by Joyce DelRosario

Memory Verse

For sin shall not be your master, because you are not under law, but under grace.
—Romans 6:14

Scripture

Romans 6: 11–14.

Lesson in a Sentence

We were born into sin, but, when we give it to the Master, it cannot master us.

Focus

Gather newspapers and magazines. Have the students find evidences of sin in them. The students can glue the clippings onto a drinking glass like a collage. After the glue dries, have the students take their glass outside. Set up a large metal garbage can there. Decorate the garbage can with the following verses if you'd like. Make sure the area is clear and safe. Have safety goggles and rubber gloves on hand.

Hand each student a sheet of paper with one of the following verses printed on it:
- Genesis 4:7
- Matthew 6:14
- Romans 5:16
- Romans 5:20
- Romans 5:21
- Romans 6:6
- Romans 6:10
- Romans 6:14
- Romans 6:18

Add more verses or repeat them to account for every student.

Have each student take his or her glass of sin and read the verse out loud. Then they smash the glass into the garbage can. Make sure they are wearing the safety goggles and gloves. This loud and destructive act is meant to be a victorious act against sin. Please make sure to take every precaution to ensure the students' safety!

Discovery

Describe the pictures on your drinking glass. Describe how you felt when you read the verse and broke the glass. Did you have any difficulty breaking the glass?

Talk about the evidence of sin found in the magazines and newspapers. Now read the scriptures over again. What does the Bible have to say about the things you found in the clippings?

Application

CONFESSION

An excellent way to keep sin from mastering us is to allow people keep us accountable for our thoughts and actions. The Bible tells us that two are better than one and that iron sharpens iron. Confession is way for us to sharpen one another and to help bring to light the sin that so easily entangles us. It also gives us a way to build authentic community.

Dietrich Bonhoeffer wrote:

In confession there takes place a breakthrough to community. Sin wants to be alone with people. It takes them away from the community. The more lonely people become, the more destructive the power of sin over them. The more deeply they become entangled in it, the more unholy is their loneliness. Sin wants to remain unknown. It shuns the light. In the darkness of what is left unsaid sin poisons the whole being of a person . . . In confession the light of the gospel breaks into the darkness and closed isolation of the heart.

Take the time to create a safe place in your youth group for confession. This may not happen right away; build slowly toward a place of trust and discipline. This exercise can break down walls and bring authenticity to the individual student and to the group as a whole.

Begin by breaking up into smaller groups. Separate the boys from girls in groups of no more than four people each. These groups must be able to meet consistently with one another in order to establish trust and familiarity. Pairs are also fine for this exercise.

Begin each confessional time in this way:
- Use a full two minutes to talk about the past week. Talk about family relationships, school, friendships, etc.
- What was the highlight of your week?
- What was a downer for you this week?
- Share a something you have struggled with this week
- Then have the group pray over that person.

TEACHER'S NOTE

Ending the time of confession in Communion will build your community. Read Dietrich Bohhoeffer's *Life Together* for further insight into this exercise. The chapter titled "Confession and Communion" will help you establish the proper tone and theology for walking through this with your group.

Earth Day

by Joyce DelRosario

In this lesson, students will:

✔ Learn of God's call for us to take care of the earth
✔ Identify ways we can take care of the earth
✔ Implement projects in our homes and churches to help take care of the earth.

Stuff you'll need:

❑ Items typically thrown into the garbage (pop cans, paper towel tubes, egg cartons, newspapers, etc.)

Memory Verse

Then God saw everything that He had made, and indeed it was very good. So, the evening and the morning were the sixth day. —Genesis 1:31

Scripture

Genesis chapters 1 and 2

Lesson in a Sentence

The earth and everything in it is ours care for.

The Big Picture

How concerned should Christians be about the environment? Is it something we should leave to the Sierra Club and Greenpeace? At the creation of the world humans were given one task: Take care of what God created.

Let's pretend that someone asks you to take care of his or her house for a year. During that year, you eat all the food in the kitchen and leave it empty. You don't bother to clean the house because you won't be there forever. In addition, you make no repairs so that much of the house becomes useless. When the owner of the house comes back what do think he will say?

God has given us a home to live in for a little while. We are responsible to take care of this home that we call earth. We should not use up all the resources to the point where they can no longer be replenished. We must to keep things clean so that life can continue. We must to take care of the earth so that its wonder can continue far past our stay here.

Focus

Choose option 1 or 2. Be certain to watch your time and not get carried away with this part of the lesson!

Option 1

Discuss the possible origin of each item. Then answer the following questions:
- What materials were used to make this item?
- Are these natural resources?
- Is there a possibility of running out of this resource?
- Invent ways to reuse these items for a different purpose. Create an infomercial to demonstrate these ways. Find as many ways to reuse all the items.

Option 2

Take the group to an area in your town where there is garbage on the roads. Call your local "Adopt a Street" or "Adopt a Highway" group and volunteer to clean up a road. After you clean the road, discuss the items that were found on there. Are these items that could harm the environment? How did cleaning the streets help the earth? What would happen if no one cleaned the road?

Discovery

In Genesis 1 and 2 God creates a magnificent world. Then God puts Adam in charge of naming the animals and caring for the earth. Have the students lie down and close their eyes. Read the above passage very slowly and ask them to picture being present during the creation. Ask what images they see. Ask them to describe the animals and plants they see.

Have the students open their eyes and talk about how it may have felt to be Adam and Eve. How would they feel if God just asked them to take care of everything around them? What would be their concerns? What would they be excited about? What's the first thing they would do? What does this mean for us today? How can we take care of God's creation in today's society?

Life Application

Talk about what it means to be a steward. How are we stewards of the earth?

Give the students each a small potted plant or small fish to take care of for the week. When they return to the next class ask them how they are doing in caring for these things. Discuss what it means to take care of something.

Have the students write the memory verse on his or her flowerpot or fish bowl. Every time they feed their fish or water their plant ask them to say the verse out loud and meditate on what the verse means for the existence of the plant or fish.

Connections

Look up the word *steward* in the concordance. What did stewards do? What were their duties? Who did they serve? What does that mean for us as stewards of the earth?

Take the Earth Day footprint quiz at *www.earthday.net/footprint/index.asp*. Notice your impact on the earth. Discuss how our stewardship impacts the earth.

To find out ten ways to combat climate change look up *www.earthday.net*. For more information, go to *www.getgreen.com*.

Earth Day

by Joyce DelRosario

Memory Verse

God spoke: Let us make human beings in our image, make them reflecting our nature so they can be responsible for the fish in the sea, the birds in the air, the cattle, and yes, Earth itself, and every animal that moves on the face of Earth. God created human beings, he created them godlike, Reflecting God's nature. He created them male and female. God blessed them: "Prosper! Reproduce! Fill the earth! Take charge! Be responsible for fish in the sea and birds in the air, for every living thing that moves on the face of the Earth." —Genesis 1: 26–28 (The Message)

Scripture

Genesis 1

Lesson in a Sentence

Let's take charge of the earth.

Focus

To take charge means being proactive to find ways to respond to the God's call to be good stewards of the earth. Find ways your youth group can take charge of the earth by reducing waste, reusing materials, and recycling waste.

Discovery

Look up *www.earthday.net* and find "Religious Earth Day In A Box." Implement an Earth Day celebration in your church, school, or community.

Stones of Adversity

by Whitney Prosperi

In this lesson, students will:
- ✔ Learn about the sinful decisions made by God's people
- ✔ Understand the reality of God's discipline
- ✔ Recognize when they need to repent from disobedient choices

Stuff you'll need:
- ❏ Large sheet of paper
- ❏ Construction paper
- ❏ Markers
- ❏ Scissors

Memory Verse

And without faith, it is impossible to please God, because anyone who comes to him must believe that he exists and that he rewards those who earnestly seek him.
—Hebrews 11:6

Scripture

Deuteronomy 4:27–31

Lesson in a Sentence

If, after we have experienced God's discipline in our lives, we turn back to Him in repentance, we will find Him.

The Big Picture

God has told us in His Word how to live in obedience to Him. In Deuteronomy He also told the people how He wanted them to live. But they rebelled, choosing their own way. So just as God promised, they had to suffer the consequences for their actions. God also disciplines us when we choose to go against what He tells us in His Word. Just as a parent lets a child learn through negative consequences, God lets us do the same. Sometimes it seems that the lessons learned "the hard way" are the easiest to remember.

If you have experienced a time of discipline for sin, remember that God will forgive you. When we admit our sin and repent from it, we'll find that God is waiting to restore and heal us. He promises us that when we seek Him with all of our hearts and souls we will find Him. He is not hiding from us. In fact, He wants to be found.

Focus

Announce that you are going to play a game called "Truth or Consequences." Ask students to break up into groups of three to four people. Give them butcher paper and markers and ask them to make two columns on their paper. At the top of one write the word "Truth" and at the top of the other write "Consequences". Now have them list truths from life and God's Word in the "Truth" column and, in the "Consequences" column, the possible consequences for going against those truths. After they compile their lists, have the groups share them with the class.

Discovery

As a group, read Deuteronomy 4:27–31 and discuss the following topics:
- Describe the Lord's discipline of His people.
- Why were they being disciplined?
- Did God give them a warning before He disciplined them?
- What good news does God share with them according to verse 29?
- What caused the people to repent and return to the Lord?

Now share with your students a story about a time when you experienced God's discipline in your life. Relay as much or as little information as is appropriate. What happened? What were the consequences? How did God get your attention so that you turned back to Him? How did He restore and heal you? What lessons did you learn?

Discuss

- Why do you think we learn lessons the hard way so much faster than any other way?
- Describe a time when your parents disciplined you and you later realized that they were doing it for your good.
- Were you later glad they disciplined you? If so, what lesson did you learn?

God disciplines us so that we will return to Him. He knows that if we are left to our own ways and our own sinful choices, that we will self-destruct. When we experience consequences for our actions, God is, in fact, acting mercifully. He disciplines us because He loves us.

When we learn from past mistakes we won't stray from God's ways so easily the next time. It's one thing to hear a warning from God. It's another to heed it and obey. God's people had been warned repeatedly but they still chose to go their own way. It is often the same with us. We know the right thing to do, but choose to willfully go in the other direction.

Discuss

• Has there been a time when you chose to disobey God even though you knew you were going to suffer consequences? What happened? (Encourage your group to be discreet and to protect the privacy of anyone else that may have been involved in the situation.)

• How did you experience God's discipline and forgiveness?

God is waiting for us to return to Him and to seek Him. He doesn't want us to stay in the pit of our sinful choices, rather to be restored and forgiven.

Life Application

Maybe you have experienced a time when it seemed God was far away. It might have been in the past or maybe it is right now. Possibly, you feel like God is distant because of your sinful choices. If so, it's important to remember that God has not moved away from you; you have moved away from Him and He is calling you to come back. He promises that we will find Him when we look for Him. Does that describe you? Are you looking for Him or are you focused on other things?

Making it Personal

In what ways can you seek God? Is there something you can do to put knowing Him above the other priorities in your life? Maybe there is a sinful habit to cut out of your life. If so, confess it to God and then ask a trusted friend or youth leader to pray about it with you and to hold you accountable.

Maybe good things are getting in the way of your relationship with God. Are you too busy? Is there something in your schedule that you need to cut? This might not necessarily be bad; rather something you need to take a break from. Maybe you will take a time out from TV or a favorite activity or sport. When you do this, you'll find you have more time to seek God. And when you seek Him, He promises you will find Him.

Stones of Adversity

by Whitney Prosperi

Memory Verse

And without faith, it is impossible to please God, because anyone who comes to him must believe that he exists and that he rewards those who earnestly seek him.
—Hebrews 11:6 (NIV)

Scripture

Deuteronomy 30:1–3

Lesson in a Sentence

If, after we have experienced God's discipline in our lives, we turn back to Him in repentance, we will find Him.

Focus

God is waiting for us to return to Him. If you have experienced a time of rebellion or sinfulness in your life, are you willing to repent and come back to God? Answer that question silently in your mind. I'll give you a minute to think about it. (Leave a moment or two of silence so that students can think about their choice.)

Discovery

Call on different students to read Deuteronomy 30:1–3 aloud. Discuss with each student:
   • What does God promise in this passage?
   • What does that tell us about His character?

Now read Romans 2:4 as a group. Discuss:
   • What is God's attitude toward people who sin?
   • What leads us to repentance?

Read 1 John 1:9. Discuss:
   • Can we say there is no sin in us?
   • If we confess our sins to God, what is his promise in return?
   • How does this make you feel?

Isn't it wonderful that the kindness of God causes us to return to Him? He is a compassionate Father, waiting to forgive us. He won't take away the consequences for our sin but He will restore us to a right relationship with Him.

Life Application

Have you found yourself in a season of sinful choices? If so, God's mercy and kindness is calling you back to Himself. You may feel like you have wandered too far, but God is pursuing you. God promises that He will take you back. His mercies are unending. Will you repent from your disobedience? To repent simply means to turn around and go in the other direction. Are there things that you need to turn from so you can fully turn to God? If so, go to Him honestly and humbly and confess your sin. Ask Him to forgive you. He promises He will do this.

To Tell the Truth

by Amy Jacober

In this lesson, students will:
- ✔ State the difference between truth and a lie
- ✔ Understand that telling the truth can sometimes be difficult
- ✔ Recognize that telling the truth is what God desires

Stuff you'll need:
- ❑ *The Best and Worst of American Idol* video or DVD
- ❑ Fact sheets, typed and copied

Memory Verse
The truthful lip shall be established forever, but a lying tongue is but for a moment.
—Proverbs 12:19

Scripture
2 Samuel 12:1–7 (8–15)

Lesson in a Sentence
Lying may work for a season but truth will last.

The Big Picture
We do not live in a world that values truth. In fact, we veil many opinions with truth. It seems the only things that are said with conviction are opinions. Truth, letting your yes be yes and your no be no, is negotiable. Many students find they do not behave as they would like and find it hard to be consistent in every situation. They resign to the whim of the moment. Most students say cheating is wrong. But, in a class with a teacher who does not explain things well, cheating becomes an option. Stealing is considered bad. But borrowing money indefinitely from a friend is not considered stealing. Little indiscretions lead to bigger ones. Plus, this behavior is acceptable in the adult world. This models a life of deceit and cover-ups.

This lesson seems like a no-brainer, but to live its message is against the trends in our culture.

Focus

Option 1

Don't Believe the Hype

The world tells us lies as if they are true. Sadly, some people get caught up in this. *The Best and Worst of American Idol* shows people who believe their own hype. Choose a clip where several people tell the camera how great they are yet their audition says otherwise.

What makes people think they have talents that they really don't possess? What about the "American Idol" judges? What purpose do they serve? Does one tell the truth more than the others?

Option 2

Truth Telling

Type up and photocopy the following "facts." Some of these are clear-cut, some fall into the realm of opinion. This is intentional. Ask your students to determine which ones are true and which are false. You may want to work with one or two of your students to add a few local or personal facts to the list.

- The tower of Pisa was designed to lean. (F)
- Jerusalem is north of Bethlehem. (T)
- Sonic is the best fast food in the country. (I say true!)
- The Great Wall of China was built to be able to have ten soldiers or five horses to be able to travel abreast. (T)
- The Anne Frank House is in Amsterdam. (T)
- Star Wars is considered one of the best films in history. (You decide)
- The first still photograph was taken in 1826. (T)
- Hamburgers were invented in Hamburg, Germany. (F)
- The Mona Lisa may be found in the National Gallery of Art. (F)
- Placing north at the top of a map is the best way to draw a map. (You decide)

Feel free to add ideas about your students as well. Try things like this:

_____ in our youth group can eat fifteen pieces of pizza.
_____ has never chewed gum.
_____ can say all the books of the Bible in order.
_____ kisses his cat goodnight every night.

Have your students work in pairs to answer these questions. On some, they may get frustrated as there is no true or false answer. That won't keep them from giving one, though! Often we create our own truth to serve our purposes. This has been going on in the world for a very long time. Check out the following story in scripture to see the struggle that can come when deciding between truth or a lie.

Discovery

Tell the story of 2 Samuel 11. While this passage has many lessons for us to learn, tell the facts and focus on the struggle David has with truth. David slept with Bathsheba and then arranged for Uriah, her husband, to come back from war to be with his wife. When Uriah turns out to be above reproach, David then sends him to the battle to be killed. David was so caught up in his own lie that he started to believe it himself.

In groups of 3, read 2 Samuel 12:1–7. Ask each group to write this as a modern day story.
  • What is the story in this passage?
  • Ask each group to share their modern story.

TEACHER'S NOTE

Nathan was a prophet. While it was his role to speak God's truth, it was not an easy role.

If you have a group that likes to go deep and you are comfortable handling this, move on to verses 8–15. This gets tough. You will want to spend time thinking through this passage and how it fits in the larger context of scripture before entering into discussion with your students.

Life Application

You've just heard several modern renditions of this same passage. Give each group the following list of questions:
  • What was it that David did that was so horrible?
  • How hard do you think it was for Nathan to speak truth to David?
  • Why did Nathan tell a story rather than just telling David he had done wrong?
  • How do people handle being told when they have done wrong? What if the person speaking to them is speaking truth?
  • What makes telling the truth easy?
  • What makes telling the truth hard?

Sometimes, telling the truth can make life more difficult. David tried this and look where it got him! Share stories of times when you told the truth knowing it might get you in trouble. What happened in the end?

Making it Personal

Are you more like Nathan or David? Do you tend to tell the truth no matter what or do you tend to cover up one lie with another?

Consider the ways you honor the Lord. Spend a few moments in prayer inviting students to consider their own lives. Ask the Lord to reveal where truth is needed in their lives. Do they need to come clean on a dating relationship? In school? With parents?

Songs

"Ooh Aah (remix)" by Grits on *7*
"Fullness found" by Todd Agnew on *Reflection of Something*

To Tell the Truth

by Amy Jacober

Memory Verse
The truthful lip shall be established forever, but a lying tongue is but for a moment.
—Proverbs 12:19

Scripture
John 14:1–6; 2 Samuel 7:27–29

Lesson in a Sentence
Lying may work for a season but truth will last.

Focus

Have each student write a lie on a facial tissue with a crayon so the tissue doesn't tear. On the count of three, tell each student to tilt their head back, place the tissue on their mouth and then blow. The object of the game, to be the last person to keep their tissue in the air using nothing more than blowing with their mouth. No hands!

Ever notice how much work it takes to keep a lie going? Just like trying to keep the tissue in the air, it is possible but it takes a lot of energy and focus.

Discovery

Have half of your students read 2 Samuel 7:27–29 and the other half read John 14:1–6.

One passage is about the truth of promises from God, the other is about Jesus being truth. Both seem simple yet are difficult concepts to grasp.

Ask each half to explain their passage to the others in the form of a newscast. Have them consider the narrative of the passage, what questions would they want to ask about it and what details did they feel needed to be explained. Choose one or two people from each group to present this to the entire group through either a news anchor or a news anchor and interview.

Life Application

How do you understand truth? This word is used in both of these passages in very different ways. In them, passages we learn that God's word is true and that God Himself is truth.
- Why is this so hard to get?
- Why is it so unpopular to declare any one things as true?
- Do you think it is possible to have one truth?

Jesus declares that He is the way, the truth, and the life.
- Do you believe this? Why or why not?
- What does this mean to you?
- How does this impact your daily life?
- Do you really live like someone who knows the truth or someone still seeking?
- What does it take to commit to something?

We live in a world that accepts many views as true. Tolerance has become the buzzword for this idea. In the pursuit of tolerance, many have lost their bearings. This is dangerous. There is nothing wrong in seeking to understand others but there is something wrong in being influenced by every idea.

Discuss truth and tolerance with your students.
- How do they view these concepts?
- How do they view the fact that sticking to what you believe is true may mean not accepting someone else's view?
- How do we work through those difficult issues in a way that honors God?

Motherly Love

by Amy Jacober

In this lesson, students will:

✔ Learn that mothers are mentioned and respected in scripture.
✔ Recognize what has been passed to them from their mothers.
✔ Know that mothers have a purpose.
✔ Consider how best to say, "Thank you" to their mothers.

Stuff you'll need:

❑ A collection of habits and/or traditions for each student (see Focus).
❑ *Stepmom* video or DVD
❑ 2 x 4 papers
❑ Markers

Memory Verse

Honor your father and your mother, as the Lord your God has commanded you, that your days may be long, and that it may be well with you in the land which the Lord your God is giving you. —Deuteronomy 5:16

Scripture

2 Timothy 1:1–7

Lesson in a Sentence

Mothers can be an encouragement to their children through faith.

The Big Picture

To school; to practice; to church! A mother may feel more like chauffeur than an encourager. Yet, in the midst of her busyness, a mother encourages her children in a thousand little ways. She runs the gamut from loving nurturer to strict disciplinarian, all with the goal of helping her children grow. Christian mothers nurture their children's faith from the day they're born. They teach, counsel, and confide; nurture and protect. Their lives are offerings poured out before the Lord as a spiritual act.

Focus

Option 1

Gather information from the mothers of your students about their family's habits and traditions. This might be a video compilation showing mothers, grandmothers, and aunts sharing something the student does that stems from a family pattern. This can be anything—eating or sleeping habits, speech patterns, abilities or gifts, physical characteristics, etc. A grandparent and a parent did these things that now the student does.

A low-tech option is to read a written description of each habit or tradition and ask your students to identify the person to whom it belongs.

Ask each student:
- Do you realize this is a part of who you are?
- Do you know that this is passed down in your family?
- Can you think of any other quirks that have been passed down in your family?

If you have a deeply engrained quirk or habit, share this story. The more your students hear from you, more likely they are to share. This needn't be a time to reveal darkest secrets but is a good time of sharing.

Option 2

Show a clip from *Stepmom*. Preview the film to choose the clip that best suits the needs of your students. This movie tells how hard it is to a mother and what happens when roles shift. Adults struggle; there is no manual of how to best navigate changing waters.

Discovery

Have two of your leaders read 2 Timothy 1–12. The first reads verse 1 and the second reading verses 2–12 as if he or she were the apostle Paul.

This letter is from Paul to Timothy. Paul functions like a father encouraging his son Timothy. Not only is Paul telling Timothy to be encouraged and not shaken in his faith but to recognize from where he came. He specifically mentions Timothy's grandmother Lois and mother Eunice who was a believing Jew; her husband was a Greek (Acts 16:1).

Discuss

Why would Paul bother to mention someone who had influenced and taught Timothy?

Why is it significant that Paul mentions Timothy's grandmother and mother?

Paul calls Timothy "my dear son" but nowhere does scripture say that Paul was Timothy's physical father. Why does he use this phrase?

What does it mean?

Verse 5 speaks of Timothy's, Lois' and Eunice's genuine faith. What does genuine faith have to do with verses 8–12?

Life Application

Students must hear the stories of those who have gone before. Just like Lois and Eunice passed on lessons to Timothy, we must pass on our stories. Invite a woman or several women to share stories of seeking the Lord and passing on faith in reference to 2 Timothy 1:1–12. Ask about a time when suffering or struggle came because of honoring the Lord. You may also want to ask about the worries or concerns that come to a parent when children become adolescents and make their own decisions. It is best to invite women whose children are grown and out of your youth group.

Make it Personal

We all pass things on to others. You've heard of Paul, Lois, and Eunice, all of whom chose to pass on their faith. You've heard some women of this church tell of the ups and downs of holding to faith as they passed it on to their children. What about you? Will you pass on your faith to someone younger?

Some of your students come from homes with godly mothers. Others come from homes where mom is not seeking Jesus at all. Still others' mothers are absent—actually or emotionally. Remind your students that this passage from 2 Timothy covers not only Timothy's biological family—Lois and Eunice—but his spiritual family as well—Paul. We may forget that God provides family for us beyond biology. In God's family, both men and women have much to offer a young person by way of teaching, discipline, and nurturing.

Invite your students to take a few moments to consider how their lives display their relationship with God. Are they ashamed of the gospel or known as one who follows Jesus? Chances are they fall somewhere in between. What does this say about their faith? What changes need to occur in order to be like Lois and Eunice, people of genuine faith?

After a few moments of reflection, transition into a time for students to consider their own mother, grandmother, aunt, or other person who pours faith into their lives. What specifically has he or she offered them?

Pass out markers and pieces of paper roughly 2-in. x 4-in.—a size similar to that of a grocery coupon. On one side of the paper, tell your students to write a thank you for what their mother or other significant person has given to them. On the other side, they will devise a coupon to be redeemed within the year. This can be good for a free car wash, dinner, house cleaning, child care or anything else that may be meaningful.

Close by praying for your students' mothers and their relationships.

Motherly Love

by Amy Jacober

Memory Verse

Honor your father and your mother, as the Lord your God has commanded you, that your days may be long, and that it may be well with you in the land which the Lord your God is giving you. —Deuteronomy 5:16

Scripture

Exodus 2:1–10

Lesson in a Sentence

Mothers can be an encouragement to their children through faith.

Focus

Who's your mother? Every May the magazines at grocery checkout counters run stories about celebrities and their mothers. Take one or two of these stories to read to your students. Often the people they admire are strongly supported by their mother as a personal cheerleader, disciplinarian, and grounding force. Often these stories are about a mother-child relationship that is not biological. Today, someone other than a biological mother raises many teenagers.

Discuss

- Do you think of celebrities as having mothers?
- What do you think is different about their relationships as compared to your relationship with your mother?
- What do you think is the same?
- Why do mothers embarrass teenagers?
- What do you appreciate about your mom?

Activity

Often magazines run pictures of celebrities and their mothers. Collect a few of these magazines, some blank paper, and tape or glue. Cut out five to ten of these pictures. Tape one half of the picture—the celebrity—on one paper and the other half—the mother—on a different sheet. Play celebrity-mom match. This helps the students to understand that famous people actually have a family life; their moms are (usually) normal people.

Discovery

We all have an idea of what a good mother is. She is there for you; she protects and provides. What do your students think of a mother who got pregnant at a young age and gave up her child to adoption? Is she a good mother? Is it possible that the most loving thing will be the least desirable?

Have someone who is an engaging reader read Exodus 2:1–10. This story tells of Moses' mother's decision to give him up at the beginning of his extraordinary life.

Life Application

Discuss:

- Do you think Moses' mother did the right thing?
- What would you have done?
- How do you see God at work in this passage?

God values mothers and children. Against all odds, God honored Moses' mother for her quick thinking. He even allowed her to serve as a nurse to Moses for Pharaoh's daughter.

Discuss:

- Have you ever seen God create a miracle out of a bad situation?
- What was the experience like?
- What would you do if God asked you to do what seemed to go against all wisdom?

Have your students make a list of the most difficult decisions they think their mothers have had to make. Write these out for all to see but be discreet in what you reveal. Perhaps they gave up their dreams; they risked being hated by their children to keep them safe; their career plans changed. Ask: Are these decisions that you think you could make easily?

Share one or two stories of your growing up years; stories about your anger or embarrassment at your mother. Be certain to choose one illustrating that your mom was right even though you didn't understand it at the time.

Youth Ministry Sourcebook

Resting to Remember

by Sharon Koh

In this lesson, students will:

Gain an understanding of the biblical mandate to rest from their work. It teaches them a habit to instill in their lives now, while the pressure making something of one's future is insistent and immediate. It is important to emphasize that the idea is not just to rest but also to rest and remember God and the things of God.

Stuff you'll need:

❏ Pleasant music, preferably with no lyrics. For example, pleasant music mixed with sounds of nature and other calming tones
❏ A restful, quiet location
❏ A blanket or pad for each student

Memory Verse

By the seventh day God had finished the work he had been doing; so on the seventh day he rested from all his work. Then God blessed the seventh day and made it holy, because on it he rested from all the work of creating that he had done. —Genesis 2:2, 3 (NIV)

Scripture

Hebrews 4:9,10

Lesson in a Sentence

The Sabbath rest a gift during which we remember God.

The Big Picture

At a time when productivity is value and busyness is virtue, it is easy to think that restfulness is laziness. The Sabbath rest is a gift; a time to remember when the work in creation was complete and completely good. Adam's sin upset this restful state in ways that we are still trying to understand. But the Bible promises a time will come when there will be eternal Sabbath rest. God rested on the seventh day of creation because His work was done. We rest to remember when God's work of creation was done and to anticipate a time when all God's work will be complete.

Focus

Dim the lights in the room and ask students to make themselves comfortable on their blankets. If the space allows, have students lie on the floor. Read the memory verse Genesis 2:2, 3.

Tell the students, "Today we want to take time to remember when God's work of creation was done and look forward to the time when all God's work will be done."

Play the music and allow 15–20 minutes for reflection. When the time has passed, explain: "This is what the Sabbath is all about—remembrance and expectation. God is in charge of all our work, so we leave this in His capable hands."

Discovery

As a group, read Hebrews 4:9, 10 and discuss:
- Why is the Sabbath rest offered to the people of God?
- According to this passage, what does participating in this rest entail? That is, can you expect to experience when you enjoy the Sabbath rest?
- Why do we participate in the Sabbath rest?

Life Application

Have your students reflect on their practical lives. Ask them if they typically build a time of rest into their schedules (not including sleep). Is this something that they only do when everything is done and they are exhausted? Remind them that God's work was complete on the seventh day of creation and we rest to remember that time. Remind them that we also rest in anticipation of the time when all the work of God's purpose will be done. All work and all creation belong to God.

Personal Application

Ask students to reflect about how this lesson affects them. Does it put rest in a different light? Encourage them to build Sabbath rest into their regular schedules as a healthy habit. If there is time, ask them to be specific about the time of their Sabbath rest and set up some way to hold them accountable to these intentions. It may help your students to hear about your own enjoyment of the Sabbath rest.

Connections

Exodus 5:12–15 is one of the primary instructive texts on the Sabbath day. Allow students to ponder this scripture and the seriousness of this commandment.

Resting to Remember

by Sharon Koh

Memory Verse

By the seventh day God had finished the work he had been doing; so on the seventh day he rested from all his work. Then God blessed the seventh day and made it holy, because on it he rested from all the work of creating that he had done. —Genesis 2:2, 3 (NIV)

Scripture

Luke 6:1–11; Luke 13:10–17

Lesson in a Sentence

Jesus is Lord of the Sabbath.

The Big Picture

The Jews received the laws governing the Sabbath day but got carried away with the regulations surrounding their observation. Today, followers of Christ should uphold the Sabbath. It is important that we remember God who completed the creation and is completing His plan for the ages. However, so we do not make the same mistakes as the Jews, the life of Jesus teaches us important things about the Sabbath.

In this lesson, students will:

• Learn how Jesus viewed the Sabbath and view this in the context of the larger lesson on the significance of Sabbath rest.

Discovery

As a group, read Luke 6:1–11 and Luke 13:10–17. Ask the students what these texts tell us about Jesus' attitude towards the Sabbath. Point out the tension between respecting the Sabbath for the reasons stated in the main lesson above (remembrance and anticipation). Also, help students to appreciate why it was easy for the Jews to get carried away in the observation of this commandment. Help them to understand what it means that Jesus is Lord of the Sabbath.

If there is time, go through Matthew, Mark, or Luke and find all that is recorded here about Jesus healing, teaching, and visiting on the Sabbath. It is striking how many of Jesus' healings and visitations take place on the Sabbath. Note the Lord's teaching in response to the reactions at these events.

Spirit-Filled Living

by Kyle Cravens

In this lesson, students will:

- ✔ Identify the Holy Spirit and His role in their lives
- ✔ Recognize that life without the Spirit will be filled with sin
- ✔ Recognize the fruit of the Spirit-filled life
- ✔ Be challenged and motivated for Spirit-filled living

Stuff you'll need:

- ❏ Jelly-filled doughnuts
- ❏ Tape
- ❏ Paper
- ❏ Molding clay or Play-Doh
- ❏ Pens or markers
- ❏ Blank note cards and pens
- ❏ Poster boards with questions
- ❏ Wide rubber bands
- ❏ Large sheet of paper
- ❏ Note cards with questions
- ❏ Fruit (real, plastic or cut-out shapes)

Memory Verse

I say then: Walk in the Spirit, and you shall not fulfill the lust of the flesh.
—Galatians 5:16

Scripture

Acts 2:1–4, Galatians 5:16–26, Ephesians 5:15–20

Lesson in a Sentence

The Holy Spirit empowers us to live a life that glorifies Christ.

The Big Picture

We are born into sin. The only way to overcome this is to accept Jesus as Savior. When we take this step, we receive forgiveness and the Holy Spirit takes up residence in our life. We become controlled by the Spirit and our lives take on qualities that glorify Christ. This is no guarantee that life will be easy, but through the Spirit, we find hope and the ability to persevere during difficult times.

Focus

Provide a snack of jelly-filled doughnuts for students as they enter the class. Begin the session by saying, "Today, we will learn about living a life filled with the Holy Spirit." Choose Option 1 or 2. Be certain to watch your time and stay on track during this part of the lesson.

Option 1
For Older Learners
Before class, write each of the following questions on a poster board and post around the room:
- Who is the Holy Spirit?
- What is the role of the Holy Spirit?
- How do we receive Him?
- What does a life without the Spirit look like?
- What is the evidence of a life with the Spirit?

Number these poster boards one through five. Divide the class into five groups by assigning each student a number one through five. Instruct students to find the poster board with their number and answer the question. After one minute, instruct the groups to rotate to the poster to the right. Do this until all groups have had a chance to answer all five questions.

Option 2
For Junior High Learners
Adapt the activity above to junior high learners by taking the five questions and making them into stations as follows. Assign each group to a station.

Station 1: Draw a picture of who the Holy Spirit is to you.

Station 2: Mold clay or Play-Doh into symbols that represent the role of the Holy Spirit.

Station 3: Create a comic strip on butcher paper depicting how we receive the Holy Spirit into our lives.

Station 4: Write a short story of how a life without the Spirit looks.

Station 5: Write a song using the theme music from a classic television show but changing the words to capture what a life filled with the Spirit will be like.

Refer to these stations when the lesson below mentions the poster-board questions. Allow groups to share at those times.

Discovery

Instruct students to be seated with their group. Pull down posters numbered one, two, and three and share the student's responses to the questions. If none of the answers are correct, be prepared to share correct answers to the questions.

Before the session, write the following questions on note cards:

• What was the Jewish celebration of Pentecost?
• What significant event in the life of Christ occurred in chapter 1 (Acts 1:9)?
• How did the Holy Spirit appear?
• What did the Spirit do?

Distribute these to each group and direct them to read and discuss Acts 2:1-4 using the questions. Instruct each group to be prepared to share discussion with the large group.

Read aloud the scripture and allow groups time to share. Lead a discussion about the Holy Spirit:
• Came on the earth at Pentecost after Jesus ascended into heaven
• Comes to live within us when we accept Christ
• Gives us power to glorify Christ in our lives.

Ask students to consider the fact that when we accept Christ, the Spirit resides within us. Ask:
• How should this fact motivate how we live?

Provide each group with a poster board and marker. Instruct them to read Galatians 5:16–21 and make a list of the acts of the flesh. Allow time for students to share what they listed. Note these on the board. Pull down poster number four and compare this to the list students just made. Ask students to respond to the warning found in the latter part of verse 21.

Hand each group a piece of plastic fruit, real fruit, or a fruit shape. Instruct each group to describe their fruit—its shape, color, taste, texture, benefits, etc. Allow time for groups to share.

Read aloud Galatians 5:22–26. Pull down poster number five and compare what students listed to the scripture you just read. Assign one of the scriptural fruits of the Spirit to each group. Instruct them to discuss their fruit and create a skit that demonstrates evidence of this fruit in a person's life. Allow time for each group to share.

Ask a volunteer to read aloud Ephesians 5:15–20. Discuss this scripture using the following questions:
• Why is the warning in verse 15 so important?
• What does "make the most of every opportunity" mean?
• How can we do this?
• How can we understand what the Lord's will is?
• Does verse 20 mean that we are to be thankful in the good as well as the bad?

Life Application

Instruct students to stand and completely exhale. Then, when you signal, direct them to take a deep breath and hold it as long as they can. When need to take a breath, they must sit down. Keep this going until one student is left standing. Award this student with a small prize.

Say: "Just as our bodies have a need for oxygen, so we need the Holy Spirit to live a life that glorifies Christ.

Take a doughnut and ask: "What happens when you bite into a jelly-filled doughnut?

(The filling oozes out.) Demonstrate this and ask: "Is the Holy Spirit oozing out of your life? Do others see Him in you?"

Option

Divide class into two groups and instruct them to come up with a cheer about what they have learned. Allow each group to share their cheer. Lead each group in this cheer: "We've got Spirit, yes we do, we've got Spirit, how bout you?" (pointing to the other group). Do this exchange several times. End this time with everyone cheering, "We've got Spirit, yes we do, we've got Spirit, the Holy Spirit!"

Making it Personal

Provide a note card to each student. Ask students to respond to the following questions on their card:

What changes do you need to make to reflect a Spirit-filled life? Write a step by step plan to do this.

Which fruit of the Spirit do you need to show more of? Write a practical way to make this fruit more evident in your life.

Provide each student with a wide rubber band. Instruct them to write on it, "Be filled with the Spirit." They can wear it on their wrist like a bracelet as a reminder during the upcoming week.

Pray that the Holy Spirit will fill each student that they will glorify Christ in their life.

Quotable Quotes

If the Holy Spirit can take over the subconscious with our consent and cooperation, then we have almighty power working at the basis of our lives; then we can do anything we ought to do, go anywhere we ought to go, and be anything we ought to be. —E. Stanley Jones.

Spirit-Filled Living

by Kyle Cravens

Memory Verse

But you are not in the flesh but in the Spirit, if indeed the Spirit of God dwells in you. Now if anyone does not have the Spirit of Christ, he is not His. —Romans 8:9

Scripture

Titus 3:5–6, Romans 8:1–17

Lesson in a Sentence

When we accept Jesus Christ as Savior, we no longer live in bondage to our flesh but are controlled by the Holy Spirit.

Focus

Before class, draw the outline of a person on two posters. Label one poster "Fleshly Life" and the other "Spirit-filled Life." Write characteristics of the flesh and qualities of a life filled with the Spirit on individual slips of paper and place these, one each, in balloons. Fill the balloons with varying degrees of air—some full, some like they have been blown up for a couple days, and some that are practically deflated.

Provide each student with a balloon. Ask your students which balloon they would want to give to someone as a gift and why. Most will want to give the full balloons. Instruct students to pop their balloons and read the slip of paper in it. Direct them to tape the characteristic written on their slip to either the poster with the outline of the fleshly life or the one with the outline of Spirit-filled life. Say: "We need to be in such a relationship with Christ that the Holy Spirit is welling up inside us like a full balloon. We should desire to be fully controlled by the Spirit. No one wants to live life like a deflated balloon."

Discovery

Ask a volunteer to read Titus 3:5–6 aloud and another volunteer to share the meaning of these verses in their own words. Demonstrate the meaning of these verses in this way:

Fill a clear glass about three-fourths full with a dark liquid such as cola. Place this in a clear plastic box. Take a pitcher of water and pour the water into the glass. Keep pouring until all of the dark liquid has flowed out of the glass into the box and the glass is filled with clear water. Explain that the dark liquid is flesh and when the Holy Spirit is poured into us, we become reborn and renewed.

Invite students to take turns reading aloud Romans 8:1-17. Emphasize being set free in verse 2.

Instruct students to close their eyes. Ask for volunteers to share what comes to mind when they hear the word *bondage*. Ask: "What have we been set free from? Make reference to the two posters. Ask students, "At the end of your life, how do you want to be remembered—as fleshly or Spirit-filled?" Point out that verse 16 refers to us as children of God while verse 17 refers to us as heirs of God. Ask students how these statements make them feel. Ask if any student has a family photo handy. If so, allow time to share some of these photos. Ask: "Why do we have family photos taken?" Say: "When we accept Christ as Savior, we become part of the family of God."

Ask an adult to take a photo of you and the group. Post this photo on a church bulletin board and label it "Part of the Family of God".

Life Application

Remind students of the lesson on Sunday. Ask those students who were in attendance then to share at least one thing that stood out to them.

Distribute note cards and pens to each student. Ask students to consider things that control their lives, write these on their card, and pray over them asking the Holy Spirit to take control. As an act of giving up these things, instruct your students to place their card in a box labeled "Controlled by the Spirit." Say: "God made the ultimate sacrifice by sending his Son to die on the cross for sin. Now, by faith, we can live a Spirit-filled life."

Instruct students to find a partner and discuss specific ways to live a life filled with the Spirit and then pray for each other and also for friends who do not have Christ in their lives.

Connections

Many scriptures refer to the Holy Spirit. Challenge students to search for these during their daily quiet times and to bring what they find to class next week. Give them a start, telling them to search the book of Acts.

Kids with Disabilities Are Just Kids (With Disabilites)

by Ruben Alvarez

I remember feeling like I had lost my best friend, because that is what had happened. As the tears ran down my face, I asked John, my youth pastor, "Do dogs go to heaven when they die?" I don't remember exactly what his answer was—something about animals not having a soul to be redeemed but that there would be animals in heaven. Whether or not this is theologically correct, at thirteen years old, I chose believe that I would see my dog in heaven one day. You see, I had not been a Christian for long and I depended on John to help me sort through my Christian faith.

Now I am forty years old and John is still one of my best friends and my mentors. But, of all that he has seen me through over the years, the death of my dog stands out. He came to my house, sat outside with me, put his arm around me, and was there for me as I grieved over my dog. Since he was my youth pastor, some may say he was just doing his job. I say he was going the extra mile. To him I was not a disabled child. I was a kid in his youth group who needed his comfort and happened to have a disability.

If truth were told, for John my disability was always secondary. It never really became an issue until I was eighteen and we went on a trip to Austin, Texas with the youth group. I think it was the first time John ever had to sit down with me and grapple with the fact that, for a weeklong trip, I might require more assistance than he was used to giving me. If my memory serves me well, I think he began by saying, "Well, since we are going to be gone for a week, I was just wondering if there is anything you think I need to know so that I can help you."

I know it wasn't easy for him to bring up because my personal care issues were not really something he'd ever had to worry about. Imagine his relief when he found out that I only needed help putting on my socks and shoes, buttoning small buttons, and shaving. As I have aged and my mobility has become more limited, I require a little more assistance than I did in the past. As always, when I am with John I am comfortable asking for help and he never hesitates to give it. But I have never felt like I'm his service project. I have always felt like I was another part of the group; first as a youth, then as a colleague, but always as a friend.

I've been involved with youth ministry for nearly twenty years, both with able-bodied and disabled kids, though most of those years I served kids with disabilities. Most people think that ministry to the disabled is some sort of specialty that you have to be called to. My contention is it is no more special than youth ministry itself. My pastor never started out with the intention of creating a specialized ministry to disabled youth. His goal was to minister to me and my needs; speak into my life the things that God wanted me to hear; teach me what it meant to be a follower of Christ; give me the tools that I needed to become a man of God. This foundation enabled me to follow my passion to educate the church about people with disabilities. You see, with the foundation that John gave me I was able to figure out for myself what it meant to be a person with a disability who follows Christ. I figured out how be a model of hope to people with disabilities. John did not set out to teach me these things, he simply taught me who Jesus Christ is and how He loves me and how much he and his wife Karen loved me in

Christ. The Lord was able to teach me all the other stuff I needed to know for my life and calling.

We Christians have all received Christ into our hearts as our personal Lord and Savior. So, we have all been given the Great Commission to preach the gospel to the world (Matt. 28:16–20). Some of us are privileged to preach that gospel message to young people. And as every good youth pastor knows, within the youth culture there are many subcultures. No matter what aspect of the culture a young person identifies with, we must remember that we simply minister the gospel to kids. Yes, it is important to identify what kids interests are, but only as a means to understand how best to serve them. So, serving kids with disabilities is not a different calling or a specialized ministry. If you are called to youth ministry then you are called to kids of all kinds.

Ironically, the disabled culture mirrors the rest of our society because people with disabilities tend to gather with each other, much like soldiers that have seen battle. This could be because they deal with life and death issues everyday. But the most remarkable thing is that young people with disabilities come in all colors and yet still manage to find common ground instead of differences. For that reason, I believe that disabled youth and their able-bodied peers need to merge so that they can learn from one another. But this will only happen if the youth pastor models this attitude.

As servants of Christ, we've not only been given the Great Commission, but a biblical mandate be on the lookout for those that are hidden away and forgotten by society. We must extend the gospel invitation to these as well. This understanding is based on the parable of the great banquet in Luke 14:16–21.

I am affiliated with Young Life's Capernaum Project. Here we say, "To minister to the disabled, you be comfortable with being uncomfortable." It is my wish that every youth pastor expose him- or herself to the disabled community. This will not be easy at first. It may even be downright uncomfortable. You can either be intentional about starting a disabled ministry or take the way of my youth pastor, John, and be unintentional about inspiring a kid with a disability. The way to bet involved with a young person who happens to have a disability, simply love the kid first. Meeting the needs of his or her disability will come out of this.

God may be calling you to a ministry to the disabled or simply drawing you the one disabled person. But if he has called you to kids, he has called you to all kids. Remember, kids with disabilities are just kids (with disabilities).

Quiet Time?

by Ben Donley

In this lesson, students will:
- ✔ Understand the necessity of sitting quietly with God
- ✔ Realize that God has something to say to them personally
- ✔ Be challenged to choose a time and a place to hear God
- ✔ Learn to pray like Elijah did and believe that God will answer

Stuff you'll need:
- ❑ CD boom box
- ❑ Any CD that you crank super-loud
- ❑ Markers and pens
- ❑ Sheets of paper with lists of step-by-step directions on them*

Memory Verse

Be still and know that I am God; I will be exalted among the nations, I will be exalted in the earth. —Psalm 46:10 (NIV)

Scripture

1 Kings 19:11–18

Lesson in a Sentence

God is speaking, and we practice silence and solitude to be sure we hear Him.

The Big Picture

The world is noisy and distracting. There are many voices steering us to do this and that. Our schedules are so jammed that we hardly stop to be alone. This combination of rush and noise prevents our finding any solitude in which we may hear God speak about what is true, what is best, and what is yet to come.

If you are tired of guessing about what to do next; of stumbling through life confused, you need to hear from God. He sees everything as it is and thus can give you a perfect perspective. But to hear, you must pull out of the action and wait attentively.

TEACHER'S NOTE

As the leader, you will decide what step-by-step directions will be on the student's papers. You can direct them to draw or write different objects or words in various locations and in various colors on their papers. For example: "Draw a red circle at the top right corner of the page." During the game, these directions will be hard to hear because of the loud music, so you do not have to be too creative, or complicated. Use different directions for each pair of students.

Focus

Distraction Game

Form your students into pairs. One person is the director and is responsible to communicate the directions from the sheet you give them to their teammate. This teammate listens to their director's instructions and then does it accurately on the blank paper. When you say, "Go," every director opens their instructions and verbally communicates to their teammate what is written there. The first team to draw their picture accurately gets a cool prize.

Say: "On your mark, get set…" but stop to say you forgot some very important instructions. This is where the challenge comes in. Tell all of the directors to stand shoulder to shoulder. Move them all twenty-five or thirty feet away from their respective teammates who are also standing shoulder to shoulder with their backs to the directors. Then place the boom box in the middle of the groups, turn it on at a high volume and say, "Go".

As the directors yell directions to their teammates, walk up and down the lines distracting everyone with annoying and irrelevant comments. Give them a few minutes to struggle with this. This game reveals communication problems that result from distance, noise, distraction, etc.

Option

Randomly choose a couple of teams and move them closer together. They will do better than everyone. This will prove a point later.

At an appropriate time, stop the game and check the results. Proclaim the winners and give them a prize.

Discovery

Ask for comments about the game:
- What made the game difficult or frustrating?
- What would have made the game easier?
- What would have happened if the teams had been closer together?
- What if there had been no distraction or music?
- What if the teams could have seen each other?

Read 1 Kings 19:11–18 as a group. Ask the students, "Who knows anything about Elijah?" Introduce Elijah the prophet. Explain the relationship between Elijah and the political leaders of his day. Tell why Elijah was running away; that his life had been threatened by political leaders and he was afraid that he would soon be killed.

Break the students into small groups to discuss the following questions about Elijah:
- When God asked Elijah why he was at the mountain, how did Elijah explain his situation?
- How did God speak to Elijah?

- How did God get his attention?
- What made it easy for Elijah to hear from God?
- What did God say to Elijah?
- How was God's perspective different that Elijah's perspective?

Life Application

Bring the group back together. Tell them that Elijah needed direction and was able to get it from God because he was alone and quiet; removed from the distraction of his everyday situation. The communication from God changed Elijah's perspective about his life and gave him the proper direction. Elijah needed to hear this from God. When he went away to be alone and quiet, he heard God.

Tell the students, "The Bible tells us that God is a communicating God who speaks to His people about all sorts of things in all kinds of ways."

Discuss these questions with the group:
- How do you think that God is speaking to people today?
- How are the communication problems from the game similar to the communication problems we experience in prayer with God?

Making it Personal

Prayer is much more interesting when God gets His message through to you. Tell a personal story about how God directed you during a time of silence and solitude; how that experience changed your life. You may wish to show a clip from the television show "Joan of Arcadia." The main character in this show regularly receives messages from God.

Ask the students:
- What do you think would change if you received regular direction from God?
- What makes it difficult for you hear from God?
- What can you learn from the game and from Elijah that might help you communicate better with God?
- What can you learn from the game might help you communicate better with God?
- What can you learn from Elijah that might help you communicate better with God?

Encourage your students to get alone and quiet with God for ten to thirty minutes a day this week. Tell them to separate themselves from noise, distraction, technology, and human contact and to listen for God. Ask them to experiment and write a daily report about the struggles of solitude and silence and what they hope God will communicate to them.

Quiet Time?

by Ben Donley

Memory Verse

Be still and know that I am God; I will be exalted among the nations, I will be exalted in the earth. —Psalm 46:10 (NIV)

Scripture

James 5:17–18

Lesson in a Sentence

Persistent prayer accomplishes amazing things.

Focus

Relevant Visuals—Show your group a clip from the movie "Bruce Almighty." There are several from which to choose. Make sure to choose one that demonstrates Bruce's ability to change situations supernaturally as when he changes the weather. This will go along with the rest of your lesson.

Tell the students, "In this movie, God takes a vacation and Bruce is given the ability to do everything that God can do. All of God's powers are his."

Ask them, "What does Bruce do with this power?"

God may not go on vacation and leave the earth in the hands of a human being, He does give His followers the ability to change situations through prayer.

Discovery

Elijah's prayers changed the weather, caused fire to fall from heaven, and raised a boy from the dead. Read James 5:17–18 (NIV) and ask the following questions.

- Why do you think that these verses point out that Elijah was like us?
- How is Elijah like you"
- How is he different?
- What is significant about Elijah's prayers?
- Do these prayers work?
- What do Elijah's prayers tell you about his faith in God?
- What does earnestness in prayer mean?
- What does righteousness have to do with praying?
- What does righteousness look like in the real world?

Life Application

According to James, the followers of Jesus should pray powerfully enough to have an impact on this world. Tell your students a story about something God did in your life because of earnest, righteous prayer. If you do not have a personal story, research and tell your students of someone famous—a celebrity of sports figure—who had such an experience.

Break the students into small groups and have them share their answers to the following questions:

What do you think are your barriers to powerful prayer? Is it faith, earnestness, righteousness, or something else?

What are some situations in your life or in this world that you would like to affect with powerful prayer?

Close the evening with a personal confession of your own struggle with these questions and pray accordingly.

Day-to-Day Missions

by Alicia Claxton

In this lesson, students will:
- ✔ Redefine missions as a calling God has given every believer
- ✔ Consider ways they can testify to God's faithfulness in their lives
- ✔ Make a point to share God's love with those around them

Stuff you'll need:
- ❑ Dominos (see Focus: Option For Small Group)
- ❑ Large bowl of water
- ❑ Pennies (see Focus: Option For Any Sized Group)
- ❑ Sheets of paper with scripture quotes (see Personal Application)
- ❑ Blank sheets of paper and markers (see Memory Verse Activity)

Memory Verse

How beautiful on the mountains are the feet of those who bring good news.
—Isaiah 52:7a

Scripture

Isaiah 52:7; Matthew 28:16–20; Acts 1:8

Lesson in a Sentence

"Missions" is a lifelong passion and act of obedience for every follower of Christ.

The Big Picture

Too often, we assign the task of missions to those who feel called to fulltime ministry or others who seem to be more comfortable with evangelism. However, the calling to share the Gospel and to give testimony of God's faithfulness is for every believer. We may not all travel to far away places, but each of us is given the opportunity to share the life-changing message of Jesus Christ. "Missions" is the work of God's grace through those who are willing to bring good news to the world around them no matter where they are.

Focus

Choose either option below. Be certain to watch the time. Don't get carried away with this part of the lesson.

Option for a small group:

The Domino Effect—Have students place dominoes on edge on a table or floor in any pattern they choose—make sure they are all within touching distance of one another. Once all the dominos are set up, tip the one over and watch how that one affects the rest.

Make the transition to the lesson by saying, "Today we are going to talk about the impact we can have in the world. Like the domino effect, we can make an impact on this world when we touch one life with the gospel. That's what it means to be a missionary."

Option for any sized group:

Give each student a few pennies. Place a large bowl of water on the floor or table and have students flip their pennies into the bowl from across the room. Once everyone has had a chance, have them gather around the bowl of water. Take one penny, drop it into the bowl, and let them see the "ripple effect." No drop is unmoved when something even as small as a penny hits the water.

Make the transition to the lesson by saying, "Think about what happens when you skip a rock across water. A ripple effect extends far beyond the spot where the rock hit. Similarly, we can make an impact on this world when we touch one life with the gospel. That's what it means to be a missionary."

Discovery

Open with a word of prayer.

Have a student read Isaiah 52:7 and discuss with the group:
- What are we encouraged to do according to this verse?
- What is the figurative meaning of our feet in this verse?

Have a student read Matthew 28:16-20 and discuss:
- What does Jesus tell His disciples to do in these verses?
- What promise does Jesus give them in verse 20? Is that promise for us as well?

Have a student read Acts 1:8 and discuss with the group:
- What does it mean to be a witness for Jesus?
- To whom are we told to witness?
- Where can we find the power to impact our own world?

Tell of your experience in the day-to-day gospel or of others in your church that share the message of the gospel in their daily lives.

Life Application

Ask students to think about the most memorable mission/outreach project they have been a part of (mission trips, community outreach projects). Give them an opportunity to share what they learned or experienced as a result of participating.

Making it Personal

Print the quotes from the "Quotable Quotes" section of this lesson on separate sheets of paper and tape these on the wall around the room. Encourage students to read each quote. Once everyone has done this, ask them to consider what "missions" means to them. Are they willing to bring the good news of salvation to people in their lives?

Memory Verse Activity

Before students arrive, write the memory verse in large letters on butcher paper or poster board and hang it at the front of the room. As you begin, ask everyone to take off their shoes. Give each student a large sheet of paper (legal size or bigger) and a marker. Instruct students to put the marker between their toes and write the memory verse on their paper – remind them that they can look at the verse up front as they write. This activity will require students to look at and write down the words in a way that will help them remember it in the future. For fun, give a prize to the one who writes the verse in the most legible "foot writing".

Connections

There are many verses in the Bible that deal with people on mission to share the Gospel of Jesus Christ. Encourage students to study the missionary journeys of Paul.

Songs

"Hands & Feet" by Audio Adrenaline (video available at *www.audioa.com*)

Quotable Quotes

The Great Commission is not an option to be considered; it is a command to be obeyed. —Hudson Taylor, missionary to China
The spirit of Christ is the spirit of missions. The nearer we get to Him, the more intensely missionary we become. —Henry Martyn, missionary to India and Persia
He is no fool who gives up what he cannot keep to gain that which he cannot lose. —Jim Elliot, missionary who lost his life trying to reach the Auca Indians of Ecuador
This generation of Christians is responsible for this generation of souls on the earth! —Keith Green
If you found a cure for cancer, wouldn't it be inconceivable to hide it from the rest of mankind? How much more inconceivable to keep silent the cure from the eternal wages of death. —Dave Davidson

Day-to-Day Missions

by Alicia Claxton

Memory Verse

How beautiful on the mountains are the feet of those who bring good news.
—Isaiah 52:7a

Scripture

Matthew 5:13–16; Romans 10:8–16

Lesson in a Sentence

"Missions" is a lifelong passion and act of obedience for every follower of Christ.

Stuff you'll need:

- ❏ A bowl of unbuttered, unsalted popcorn and a bowl of buttery, salted popcorn (see Focus)
- ❏ A jar of unsalted peanut butter and a jar of regular peanut butter (see Focus)
- ❏ A few unsalted crackers and a few regular crackers (see Focus)
- ❏ Two or three Blindfolds (see Focus)
- ❏ Footprints made out of construction paper (see Making It Personal)
- ❏ Map of your city or state (see Making it Personal)

Focus

Have an old-fashioned taste test with your group. Ask for a few volunteers for this contest. *Make sure these volunteers do not have food allergies.* While your students are blindfolding the contestants, pull out the bowl of unsalted popcorn and the bowl of buttery, salted popcorn. Allow each contestant to taste and vote on the one they liked best. You can change volunteers·or keep the same students for the next contest. This time place a spoon of unsalted peanut butter and a spoon of regular peanut butter in front of each contestant and ask them to decide which one they like better. You can stop there or do one last contest. Place a few unsalted crackers and a few regular crackers and see which one they liked best.

Make the transition to the lesson by asking the following questions:
- • What was missing in some of the food you tasted?
- • Why do we use salt on our food?
- • Think of your favorite salty snack (chips, popcorn, peanuts, etc). What would it taste like without the salt? Do you think you would like it if it wasn't salty?

Discovery

Open with a word of prayer. Have a student read Matthew 5:13–16. (Note: Depending on the size of your group, you can divide students into smaller groups to answer the following questions or work through them together as a large group).

- What does verse 13 mean when it says, "You are the salt of the earth"?
- How are we like salt?
- Verse 14 talks about light. How important is light to our everyday lives?
- Have you ever been in a place that was totally dark? What did you do?
- How did you feel when you finally found a source of light?
- Do you think people who are lost without Jesus Christ might feel similar to someone who is walking around in the dark? Why or why not?
- How can we be light to this world (verse 14)?
- What is the goal or ultimate purpose of letting our light shine before others?

Life Application

To be salt and light does not simply mean we behave differently than the worldly people around us. It is a calling to live and share the life-giving message of Jesus Christ. Though we sometimes complicate that message, scripture clearly states how to be saved.

Read Romans 10:8–11 with your students and help them understand how to communicate the gospel to others. Also, spend a few minutes talking about the reality that some will reject the gospel. Remind them that we cannot "save" anyone, only the power of the Holy Spirit can convict and restore the lost. We are the messengers, Christ is the Savior!

Personal Application

Place an oversized map of your city or state on the floor. Give each student a paper footprint and a pen. Instruct them to read Romans 10:12–15 and to think about their own attitude toward those who have not yet believed in Christ. Challenge the students to write on their footprint the names of people from their school, work, neighborhood, or family that they hope will believe in Christ. Finally, ask them to lay their footprint on or near the map and spend a few minutes praying that they might take the gospel message those people whose names are on their footprint. After they've had some time pray silently, close the session by praying for your students.

From Generation to Generation

by Amy Jacober

In this lesson, students will:
- ✔ Appreciate that others take time to teach them
- ✔ Learn that we all have much to learn
- ✔ Recognize the importance of study to become rooted in the faith
- ✔ Discuss what it means to follow Jesus

Stuff you'll need:
- ❏ Lego sets
- ❏ Seedling plants
- ❏ Note cards or card making supplies if you choose to make Father's Day cards

Memory Verse

Now there was a man of the Pharisees, named Nicodemus, a ruler of the Jews; this man came to Him by night, and said to Him, "Rabbi, we know that you have come from God as a teacher; for no one can do these signs that You do unless God is with him."
—John 3:1–2 (NASB)

Scripture

Colossians 2:6–7, Ephesians 4:11–13

Lesson in a Sentence

Instruction in the faith is a gift from God.

The Big Picture

We all need instruction in life and faith, much of which is conveyed by our experiences. However, today is Father's Day, reminding us that our fathers are our first instructors. When we take their instruction and become rooted in the faith, we can better weather life's storms.

Few students ask for more homework or longer term papers but, eventually, they love having learned. As we follow Jesus, we must learn what this means in our everyday life. Instruction from others helps but we must also realize that God is our greatest teacher.

Focus

Option 1

Split into at least two teams with a small Lego set for each team. Using these sets, the students will build a small car, boat, or other small item. Aim for two to four students per team. Give the instructions, the picture, and the Legos to half the teams. The other teams can have no instructions, picture, or other help.

Notice if anyone is annoyed or frustrated at this exercise. Assembling a Lego car is not life changing, but the point is clear: It is easier to accomplish something if you are given instructions.

Lead a discussion by asking your students if they have ever had a teacher who was not clear in his or her instructions and were marked down because of this. Be certain to point out the difference between a teacher who does not teach well and one whose students don't pay attention.

Option 2

Bring in several seedling plants, the kind that come six to a pack. Tell your students to separate the plants without breaking any roots. This, of course, is impossible.

Ask the students why this is so hard.

Discovery

Divide into two groups and consider the following scriptures:

Group 1—Read Colossians 2:6–7 and have the group discuss the following questions.
- What does it mean to be rooted, established, and built up?
- What do the above terms mean in this passage?
- In what ways have you been instructed in the faith?
- What does it mean to you to be a follower of Jesus?

Group 2—Read Ephesians 4:11-16 and have the group discuss the following questions.
- Why do we have different roles in the church? In life?
- Do you think we value these roles equally? Why or why not?
- What does the phrase *children being tossed about by waves* mean?
- How do we learn what it means to follow Jesus?
- How will others who come behind us learn this?

Read Ephesians 4:15 for both groups and discuss with them the following questions:
- What does it mean to grow into Jesus in all aspects?
- Is this possible?
- Are there parts of our lives that are off limits to such growth?
- Should there be parts of our lives that are off limits?
- What in your life would have to change in order for you to grow in all aspects?

Life Application

Today is Father's Day. Take advantage of this both to celebrate and offer an example of a father's role in one's life. You have just discussed scripture about being rooted in faith. This faith has to be passed on.

Invite an experienced father to visit your group and share his story. Ask a father whose child is already grown so as not embarrass any of your current students. This can be a great experience for all of your students. They will see what a man can be. Those without fathers can hear of what God desires of a father. Those with fathers will be reinforced in what they know to be true. Also, your students may begin to realize their own parents are doing the best they can.

Ask the father to share what the responsibility of passing on faith has meant in his life and how he went about doing this. Encourage him to be honest, acknowledging his own fears and shortcomings.

Invite your students to pray for this kind of character and attitude as they grow up. It is also important that they pray to not settle for anything less.

Allow time for the students to ask questions of your guest. Get the ball rolling by asking it there was a time when he was nervous about teaching his children the faith.

Making it Personal

Ask your students to think of one area in their life where they need to grow. Invite them to talk about this and seek out at least one person to help them on this journey.

If you have time, offer a few moments for students to write a note or make a card for their father, thanking him for his role in their lives.

Songs

"Come and Listen" by Dave Crowder Band on *A Collision*

From Generation to Generation

by Amy Jacober

Memory Verses

Now there was a man of the Pharisees, named Nicodemus, a ruler of the Jews; this man came to Him by night, and said to Him, "Rabbi, we know that you have come from God as a teacher; for no one can do these signs that You do unless God is with him." —John 3:1–2 (NASB)

Scripture

Matthew 5:1–12

Lesson in a sentence

Instruction in the faith is a gift from God.

Focus

Play the old game of telephone but combine it with charades. Ask four people to leave the room. One of the students remaining in the room decides on a scenario of any kind. Ask your students to share each scenario with you so they will be appropriate and not too hard to pass on. For example: a gorilla washing a car.

Have one person return to the room and whisper the scenario to him or her. Have a second student return. The first student acts out the scenario for the second student using no words. This continues for the third and fourth students. After the fourth student has seen the scenario, have him or her share it verbally with the rest of the group.

Play this game several times but don't get too carried away. It is always best to end a game while they still want to play.

At the end, point out that this game is a form of translation—taking something passed on to you and interpreting it to the best of your ability.

Discovery

Here, your students will consider the Beatitudes and translate them into the language of their lives.

Place eight poster boards in various places around the room. On each, write one of the Beatitudes. Give markers to your students so they can write their own translations of each passage on the boards.

Read through Matthew 5:1–12 as a group. This is an easy passage to read while sitting in a circle, allowing each student read one verse until all twelve verses have been read.

Ask your students to take three to four minutes at each poster board to reread the verse and consider what it means in their lives. Invite your students to write their own translations into today's language on the poster boards. These may be concrete ways of living or theoretical interpretations.

These can be considered in any order. It is best to not have too many students at any one poster so they more easily concentrate and write on the poster. Play music quietly in the background and encourage a time of authentic meditation. Ring a bell or announce the time to move to another poster. This will prevent some students from racing through the exercise and disturbing those who take it more seriously.

Application

Look over what was written on the posters and discuss as a group.

The Beatitudes are a part of the Sermon on the Mount. This is His direct teaching to His disciples. If we take scripture seriously, we must listen to this teaching. Just like any other time of instruction, sometimes it engages us, sometimes we tune out, and sometimes we find it is too hard. Talk through the Beatitudes with your students. What did they write on the posters that sounds like a good idea but is just not realistic? Why does it seem unrealistic?

Have each person choose one Beatitude and the translations provided and pray about living a radically transformed life according to its truth. Invite each student to seek ways to live out the Beatitude they chose in tangible and consistent ways this week.

Poverty—A Worldwide Epidemic

by Amy Jacober

In this lesson, students will:
- ✔ See a clear pattern of care for the poor throughout scripture
- ✔ Consider the consequences of not caring for the poor
- ✔ Begin to see the poor through the eyes of Christ
- ✔ Understand that they have a calling from God to care for the poor

Stuff you'll need:
- ❑ Colored cards
- ❑ Web site information on poverty
- ❑ Colored paper
- ❑ Markers

Memory Verse
Those who oppress the poor insult their Maker, but those who are kind to the needy honor Him. —Proverbs 14:31 (NRSV)

Scripture
Exodus 23:11; Deuteronomy 15:7; Psalm 41:1; Proverbs 21:13; Proverbs 21:17; Proverbs 23:21; Proverbs 28:19; Jeremiah 17:11; Jeremiah 22:16; Amos 8:11; Matthew 18:23-35; Matthew 19:21; Matthew 25:31–40; Galatians 2:10; 1 Timothy 6:7; Amos 4

Lesson in a Sentence
From God's perspective, care for the poor is not an option.

The Big Picture
Poverty is real and it is not going away. It comes in many forms. No one is immune to its effects. While most of us will never live on the streets, poverty still impacts our lives. God is clear that those who are poor are not only worthy in His eyes, are to be cared for without question. Consistently throughout the Old and New Testaments, God calls for His people to care for the needy.

This can be done in many ways looking at issues of education, housing, nutrition, and employment. There is often a struggle among Christians about involvement in secular community issues. The Bible has no struggle with this. We are already involved by our sheer existence, what kind of involvement is our only choice.

Focus

Option 1—True or False

Hand out a blue card and red card to each student. The colors don't really matter as long as you have two colors. Call out the following information. The students are to hold up the blue card if it is true and the red if it is false. You may want to gather a few facts from your community for an even greater impact. Contact your local Chamber of Commerce or mayor's office for this information.

- There are more than 6 billion people in the world.
- One in three claims to be a Christian
- One in four is under fourteen years old
- One in six does not have access to health care
- One in seven does not get enough to eat
- More than one billion people do not have access to safe drinking water.
- Every five seconds a child dies of hunger.
- Americans spend more than $61 billion on soft drinks every year, fifteen times the budget of USAID, the US government humanitarian aide agency.
- About one of every three girls worldwide does not receive an education beyond fourth grade.
- The infant death rate for the poor is 1.6 that of the infant death rate for the non-poor.
- Inadequate prenatal care is nearly three times higher for the poor than non-poor.
- Twice as many poor children in grades 3-12 have repeated a grade as non-poor children.
- AIDS is considered a pandemic at this time.*

Christians have a responsibility to do something about these issues. Spend a few moments processing this information with your students. Were they aware of how difficult many lives are? What does this make them think or feel?

*Sources: *Faith in Action Study Bible,* Zondervan/World Vision, Grand Rapids: 2005. Couture, Pamela. *Seeing Children, Seeing God;* A practical theology of children and poverty. Nashville: Abingdon Press, 2000.

Option 2

David Smith wrote a great book about the world's people called *If The World Were A Village.* A professor from Philadelphia University named Lloyd C. Russow has written a web site about these issues— *http://faculty.philau.edu/russowl/villageof1000.html.*

Create your own quiz for your students based on this information. Highlight the large numbers living in low-income nations, those lacking clean water and access to sanitation, literacy, and the small numbers of those with access to computers, telephone lines, and automobiles.

Discovery

Create a scripture mosaic. Be certain you have a clear wall somewhere in the room. If you did not choose Option 1, you will now need to hand out paper to your students. Give one of the scriptures below to a student or a team of students depending on the size of your group. Ask each to read the passage and draw a picture representing what the passage is saying. When they are through, have each tape their picture to the wall and explain what their passage said. In the end, you will have a wall full of mandates from the Lord for all to see. Each of these mandates requires that we care for the poor. Before your meeting time, have a banner prepared to tape up over your newly created mosaic saying "What does the Lord require of you?" When they are through, tape this above the mosaic.

Exodus 23:11	Jeremiah 22:16
Deuteronomy 15:7	Amos 8:11
Psalm 41:1	Matthew 18:23–35
Proverbs 21:13	Matthew 19:21
Proverbs 21:17	Matthew 25:31–40
Proverbs 23:21	Galatians 2:10
Proverbs 28:19	1 Timothy 6:7
Jeremiah 17:11	

Now here's the hard part that we don't usually discuss. Read Amos chapter 4; this is a tough chapter and the students will need your help in understanding it.

The first few verses seem funny until you realize what they are saying. The entire passage is referring to Israel not doing as God has commanded. The cows of Bashan were the well-fed cattle in Canaan. They are a symbol for the wealthy, self indulgent, oppressive women of Israel—the haves as opposed to the have-nots.

Verse 2 goes on to warn the people that this will not last. In verse 3, sarcasm sets in. Amos says to go ahead and sin even more in false worship. They go to shrines and look like upstanding citizens but is all for show.

Amos goes on to remind them of all that God has provided and the extreme measures to which God has gone to get their attention to no avail. He ends by warning them that if they continue in this way of oppressing the poor, they should prepare to meet their God.

Life Application

Spend some time looking at the scripture mosaic.

The ethos of your group will largely determine the remainder of your discussion time. If your group has spent little or no time considering issues of poverty, you will need to spend some time opening the eyes of your students to the reality of the struggles in the world. If your group is already bent toward considering issues of poverty, use this time to further reflect on what scripture calls Christians to do.

After reading these passages discuss these questions:

- What do you think is the duty of Christians toward the poor?
- How should we view poverty?
- What pragmatic, realistic ways can our youth group address poverty?
- Why is this not talked about among most Christians?
- Why is acknowledging poverty and our responsibility toward the poor a taboo among us?
- How does God say He will deal with the Israelites who oppress the poor?
- Do you think this still holds true today?
- If no, why not? If yes, what might this look like in our day?

Making it Personal

Poverty is not an individual issue though individuals can make a big difference in fighting poverty. Consider some of the ways your group suggested to fight poverty. Which of these ways are things individuals can do? Choose one way to begin to fight poverty and commit to find ways to help. Possible options:

- Tutoring
- Recycling and donating the money to a local shelter
- Research homelessness in your community and volunteer at a shelter
- Conduct a food drive and give the food to a local food bank
- Check on a gleaning program in your community and donate the produce to the local food bank
- Sponsor a child
- Pray for the poor of the world
- Learn the causes of poverty rather than assuming it is caused by laziness or stupidity

Close in prayer for those struggling in the seemingly endless cycle of poverty.

Service Option

There are many organizations offering relief and help for the poor. World Vision is one of these organizations offering two specific programs that are easily accessible for youth groups. In particular, the 30 Hour Famine combats world hunger and One Life Revolution combats the AIDS pandemic. Check them out for pragmatic ways to involve your students in fighting poverty. *www.worldvision.org*

Another well-known and respected organization is Samaritan's Purse. They offer many ways to give back to the community and the needy in the world through Operation Christmas Child and sponsorships. You can check them out at *www.samaritanspurse.org*

A smaller but excellent group that helps indigenous workers establish churches is Empowering Lives. They focus on skills for life training and holistic ministry while capitalizing on the natural resources and strengths in a given area. You can find them at *www.empoweringlives.org.*

Song

"Micah 6:8" by Charlie Hall on *Flying into Daybreak*

Poverty—A Worldwide Epidemic

by Amy Jacober

Memory Verse

Those who oppress the poor insult their Maker, but those who are kind to the needy honor Him. —Proverbs 14:31 (NRSV)

Scripture

Ruth 1:1—2:13

Lesson in a Sentence

From God's perspective, caring for the poor is not optional.

Focus

World Vision offers much information regarding issues of poverty and a Christian response. Spend some time on their site gathering the most current information. You may even want to consider downloading and sharing one of their videos. The images are striking and can convey more than any description. You can also download their global hunger and poverty facts sheet under the 30 Hour Famine section. All of this may be found at *www.worldvision.org.*

Discovery

Have someone read Ruth 1:1—2:13 out loud for the group storybook style. If you have a strong student reader, this is ideal. If not, choose a leader who can read clearly and with animation.

After reading ask the following questions:
- Who are the main characters?
- Did Naomi and Ruth need help?
- How did they end up in poverty?
- What help did they find?
- How are they treated as those in need?

Life Application

Ruth reminds us of an important lesson: many of those in poverty are there through no fault of their own. For her, the death of her husband left her with no way to care for herself or her mother-in-law. Yet, with dignity and grace, she worked hard and was shown mercy. How many reasons can you think of that might cause poverty? List these on a dry erase board. Discuss what you as a group might be able to do about one or more of these.

Talking about helping those who are poor and struggling is a good thing. An often-overlooked topic concerns the attitude with which we offer help. Boaz treated Ruth with respect. He did not look down on her nor treat her as less than human. Nor did he ignore her or pretend not to see her. What can we learn from Boaz about how to treat those in need?

Pray that the Lord to open your eyes this week to see those in need around you. Once seen, ask God to guide you in your next step in treating the poor as Christ would.

Freedom

by Chuck Hunt

In this lesson, students will:
- ✔ Gain a better understanding of the gospel.
- ✔ Have an opportunity to call out to God.
- ✔ Experience a new freedom to worship.

Stuff you'll need:
- ❑ Blindfolds (one for each student)
- ❑ Large sheet of paper
- ❑ Bibles
- ❑ Sharpie pens
- ❑ Nachos

Memory Verse

Stand fast therefore in the liberty by which Christ has made us free, and do not be entangled again with a yoke of bondage. —Galatians 5:1

Scripture

Luke 18:35–43

Lesson in a Sentence

Jesus came to set us free to worship him.

The Big Picture

Spiritual blindness is common to all of us. We are blind to the things that keep us from celebrating Christ. It keeps us from seeing all that God has done for us. It blocks our experience of the fruits of the Spirit.

In the parable of Luke 18:35–43, the blind man calls out to Jesus for mercy and Jesus responds by healing the man of his blindness and enters into a relationship with him. Verse 43 shows that the healing allows this man to worship God in the midst of his community. If we, like this blind man, call out and allow God to heal us, we will find new freedom in our relationship with Christ that will enable us to follow Him with reckless abandon.

Focus

Have each student find a partner. Hand out two blindfolds to each pair allowing each to blindfold the other. Leaders should help so there is no cheating. Tell the students that they are to locate their leaders without taking the blindfold off. Do not allow the students to find any leaders. After frustration sets in, allow them to take off their blindfolds and find their leaders, who are out in the open.

Discovery

Get four to five students beforehand create a living storyboard of the Luke 18:35–43. In the nineteenth century, this was called a tableau. It is like a comic strip in which each panel, or scene, progresses the story. With lights out, the students take their places for Scene 1. Turn on the lights—Scene 1. Turn out the lights, rearrange for Scene 2. Turn on the lights—Scene 2 etc.

Break the other students up into groups and ask them to figure out what Bible story is being acted out in the living storyboard. The first team to find it is the winner, will read the verse for the group, and get a plate of nachos as a prize for their group.

Discuss:
- What did it feel like to search for your leaders and not find them?
- Was it frustrating to search but not find?
- Did you give up?

It is likely that you will have three groups among your students:
- The students that don't care and won't try.
- The students that will huddle together and not search.
- The students that search, bump, and scream their way to frustration.

Draw a parallel between their experience and the blind man in the story. Ask what would have happened if he had been comfortable with being blind and had not called out to the Lord.

Share with the group of a time when you had to call out to God because of your blindness and give an example of what happened when God healed you from blindness. Use this to share with the group that Jesus wants to free them to enter into a relationship with Him. All they need to do is call out to him with reckless abandon.

Life Application

Many of our students are pressured by worldly standards of what they should be and how they should act. The issues that keep students in blindness are numerous: popularity, shame, expectations of family, friends, and society, wealth, poverty, addiction, etc. Most students don't even realize that they are blind. Here is one way to make them aware of it:

Place a list of blinding factors similar to the one above on a screen or flipchart.

Explain that these are the reasons why people are blind to freedom in Christ. Go through the list and comment on each issue. Allow the students to silently claim the reason for their blindness.

Make it Personal

Option 1—High School

Hand out paper and pens and with soft music in the background give students an opportunity to call out to God and answer the question, "What do you want me to do for you?" If the moment allows, give students the opportunity to speak privately to a leader about the ways they are blind. Prepare the leaders with ways to help students call out for freedom. Celebrate with the students the freedom they now have in Christ by jumping, yelling, and singing.

Option 2—Junior High

Give out Sharpie or paint pens and have your students write on a blindfold one thing that keeps them away from God. Instruct them to tie a knot where the words are so that it is private. Encourage them to share it with a leader or keep it in their backpack as a reminder to call out to God for freedom and to celebrate the fact that God sets them free. Celebrate the freedom they now have in Christ by jumping, yelling, and singing with the students.

Option 3—Go Big

Have the students and leaders put on blindfolds. Allow them to move around the room while loud music is playing (for anonymity's sake). Encourage students to call out to God in prayer and celebration. At the end of the music have everyone take off their blindfolds together and celebrate with dancing and huge trays of nachos.

Songs

"Undignified" by David Crowder

Quotable Quotes

For to be free is not merely to cast off one's chains, but to live in a way that respects and enhances the freedom of others. —Nelson Mandela

Freedom
by Chuck Hunt

Memory Verse
Stand fast therefore in the liberty by which Christ has made us free, and do not be entangled again with a yoke of bondage. —Galatians 5:1

Scripture
A new commandment I give to you, that you love one another; as I have loved you, that you also love one another. By this all will know that you are My disciples, if you have love for one another. John 13:34–35

Lesson in a Sentence
We have been made free so that we can love one another.

Focus

Option 1
Show a clip from Braveheart. Use the section of the movie that contains this line by William Wallace: "There's a difference between us. You think the people of this land exist to provide you with position. I think your position exists to provide those people with freedom. And I go to make sure that they have it." Tell the story of how William Wallace was betrayed because of greed for power.

Option 2
Hodge Ball

This game is a cross between dodge ball and hog-ball. You'll need a few playground balls. Divide your group into two equal teams. The game begins with each team on half of the court with at least two balls. The Rules are:
- The object is to send all of your opponents to prison.
- You send opponents to prison by hitting them with the ball.
- Opponents who catch the ball, however, stay free and don't go to prison.
- If you throw a ball that has been caught, you go to prison.
- If you are hit while holding (hogging) a ball you remain free.
- Players in prison regain their freedom by hitting an opponent with the ball.

Discovery

You must be free to be able to love someone. Jesus gives us the freedom and commandment to love.

Place your students in small groups of no more than eight. Have them read over the memory verse and scripture and then discuss:

- What does the word *freedom* mean to you?
- If you were completely free, what would you do?
- If money and time were not a factor, what would you do if you knew you could not fail?
- If everyone were completely free to do what was in their best interest, what would be the result?

This week people will celebrate the Fourth of July—the anniversary of the birth of freedom in this country—with picnics, music, and fireworks. We must recognize and celebrate our freedom in Christ with the same enjoyment, passion, and excitement.

Worship with Anybody, Anywhere

by Keith McDorman

In this lesson, students will:
- ✔ Be challenged to see that God desires all humanity to worship Him
- ✔ Recognize that, having grown up in the church, one can simply go through the motions of worship
- ✔ Understand the terrors of racism

Stuff you'll need:
- ❑ *Family Guy* DVD, Season 3, Episode 19—"Stuck Together, Torn Apart"

Memory Verse
I have sworn by Myself; The word has gone out of My mouth in righteousness, And shall not return, That to Me every knee shall bow, Every tongue shall take an oath. —Isaiah 45:23

Scripture
John 4:16–30

Lesson in a Sentence
True Worship is not found in a certain location or in a certain ethnicity, rather it is found in character.

The Big Picture
Worship is not a matter of where you are, but who you are. The defining quality of worship character, not culture, heritage, ethnicity, or citizenship. Jesus taught that the Samaritans could worship God even though this was offensive to the Pharisees. This abolished the thought that growing up Jewish was needed to worship God.

Focus

Begin with an exciting game of Tomato (see *http://www.indianchild.com/outdoor_games.htm*). To play this game, everyone sits in a circle. The person who is "it" stands in the center of the circle. Each player asks the person who is it an appropriate question. The answer to every question must be, "Tomato." For example: "What color is your hair?" "Tomato." "What do you brush your teeth with?" "Tomato." The first person to make *It* laugh goes into the middle and becomes *it.*

Once this game is finished have the students watch the clip in the episode of Family Guy. The scene is inside of the Quahog police force's van. Joe is taking the van for a joy ride with Cleveland and Peter. The van has the ability to arrest whoever comes inside it. Peter steps into the spotlight and is handcuffed. Cleveland walks into the spotlight and the "minority alert" is sounded. He is then beat to the ground, accused of bearing a weapon, which is conveniently placed at his side.

Discovery

The Family Guy clip is funny but true. It makes light of actual events like the Rodney King incident. The clip mocks the system that treats minorities as if they are a threat.

Read John 4:16-30 and ask your students to listen for the ways the woman at the well is seen as a minority and/or a threat. List these for all to see. Ask your group what they learned about worship from this passage. You may need to read verses 19–24 again. Ask your students what they can learn from this passage.

TEACHER'S NOTE:

To the Jews, Samaritans were half-breeds who sold out to the Assyrians when they were conquered before the Babylonian exile. Jews hated the Samaritans because they had broken the law and intermarried with the enemy. They took on other gods and eventually split from Judaism, becoming a separate people with a distinct set of beliefs. In this passage Jesus tells the Samaritan woman that worship is no longer confined to any specific place, but that it is a matter of character. Jesus took the time to not only talk to a woman, which the disciples were surprised to see, but to explain to her the good news that God is available anytime, anywhere.

Life Application

- Why are there divisions on your school campus? (People have a tendency to hang out with others that are like them.)
- What racial groups have more power than others?

Look back at the list of the ways the Samaritan woman can be considered a minority. Ask your students how this kind of labeling and separation takes place in our world today. Add these to the list. How does scripture instruct us to handle these differences? Through true worship in spirit and in truth.

Making it Personal

- Look at your life and see what you hold on to that hurts others.
- Are there any aspects of your life that you can share but don't?
- Do you have a mind to share with others?
- Who do you hang out with? Who do you talk to the most?

If you refuse to interact with those who are different from you, there is a chance that you are missing out on lessons that God is trying to teach you.

Worship with Anybody, Anywhere

by Keith McDorman

Memory Verse

I have sworn by Myself; The word has gone out of My mouth in righteousness, And shall not return, That to Me every knee shall bow, Every tongue shall take an oath. —Isaiah 45:23

Scripture

James 2:1–8

Lesson in a Sentence

Do not show favor to the rich, but love those who are poor and marginalized.

Focus

Begin by sharing with the group about a time you had to deal with intercultural communication. Be as authentic as possible when discussing the difficulties and what you learned through the process. If you have not had such a personal experience, invite someone from your church to share their story about cultural issues in communication.

Discovery

Have a student read James 2:1–8 aloud for the entire group.

Split into groups of two or three students. Ask one group to act out the situation as presented in scripture. Ask each of the other groups to offer a current situation that could be similar. Be sure to remind the groups that such favoritism is often done very secretly by people who aren't blatant racists but respected Christians.

Consider the following questions:
- What makes a person acceptable to come to your church's worship?
- Is it how they dress? Is it how they talk?
- Must they know all the right Christian things to say?
- Is it that they are God's creation and loved by Him?
- What can we learn about loving others?

Life Application

Much discrimination is not a matter of ethnicity but of privilege. James points out the discrimination and favoritism practiced by those in power. James challenges us to love those who can bring no benefit to you.

Brainstorm the ways that you, your group, or your family have power to help those in need. For example, can you stand up for others at school? Can you adopt a street in your neighborhood and make it safe and clean for others?

After you have created a list of options, invite each student to consider using this power.

Culture War

by Will Penner

In this lesson, students will

✔ Realize that the culture is laden with messages that aren't value-neutral.
✔ Identify some of the negative messages with which they are bombarded every day.
✔ Discover ways to counteract negative cultural influences with Christian values and practices.

Stuff you'll need:

❑ Several old copies of popular magazines; at least one for every two or three students. *Seventeen, Teen People, Rolling Stone, Spin, Blender, Vibe, Vogue,* or *Maxim* are good for this purpose.
❑ One piece of poster board for each group of five students.
❑ Scissors
❑ Glue sticks
❑ Markers
❑ Mirror (small hand mirror or large, full-length mirror)

Memory Verse

For though we live in the world, we do not wage war as the world does.
—2 Corinthians 10:3 (NIV)

Scripture

Romans 12:1–21

Lesson in a Sentence

In order to follow Jesus, we must discern the difference between healthy and unhealthy cultural values.

The Big Picture

We may not realize it, but much of how we dress, speak, and think is dictated by modern culture. TV shows, music, and thousands of other voices subtly define who we are. Plus, our parents and our friends heavily influence us.

Though this doesn't create problems in every area of life, it does so in some. There is nothing wrong with allowing culture to shape certain choices. Other cultural influences can put us in direct conflict with our faith.

Discernment of the difference between healthy and unhealthy cultural values is crucial to becoming a mature Christian. It's not always easy to think critically about cultural messages, but we must learn to do this if we hope to follow Christ in our daily lives.

Focus

Ask your students to close their eyes so they can briefly use their imaginations without any distractions. Ask them to remain silent as they imagine in detail the perfect person of the opposite sex. Suggest the following details allowing no more than five seconds between each:

What color hair does this person have?

What color eyes?

What are other facial features?

What about the upper body?

If you're imagining a female, does she have large breasts?

If you're imagining a male, does he have large muscles?

What, if anything, is the person wearing?

Keep scrolling down his or her body, and notice the legs, feet

Imagine every last detail.

When they open their eyes and look around there may be some nervous self-consciousness. Ask the students to remain silent and say to them, "I'd guess that none of you chose another person in this room as you imagined your ideal. In fact, most of you chose someone you don't actually know personally. Many of you chose a movie star or famous musician, TV actor, or other teen idol. You may have chosen someone you know but changed his or her appearance to more closely resemble someone famous."

The media forms our perceptions of what is beautiful or handsome. We perpetuate these perceptions when we assume the media defines these rightly without critically analyzing the purposes behind cultural messages.

Discovery

Divide your students into small groups with no more than five per group. Two or three per group will work fine. You may choose to divide by gender or age or intentionally create diverse groups. Give each group a few magazines, a poster board, a glue stick, a pair of scissors, and some markers.

Ask each person to spend a few minutes looking through the magazines. Students are to search for advertisements that seem to send a message about what it means to be beautiful or handsome. These can be images, words, phrases, or even entire articles. When they find some, they cut them out and paste them to the poster board.

After a few minutes, have the students stop to briefly discuss the purpose of advertising. The only reason a company buys magazine advertising is to sell something. Therefore:

• What is each of the ads you've cut out trying to sell?

• What is the message the ad is sending you in order sell its product?

Have the students write down the answers to both questions somewhere on the poster. For the most part, the messages will be, "You don't look as good as this, but you could if you buy our stuff."

After a few minutes, have the students stop this activity to share what they've written on their posters. Ask them to do the same with other ads that are selling something other than beauty. Again ask:
- What is each of the ads you've cut out trying to sell?
- What is the message the ad is sending you in order sell its product?

Life Application

We are a consumer-driven culture. In other words, companies thrive when you buy their products. But do you thrive as a believer?
- What would happen if you bought everything the ads tell you to buy? Would you be more beautiful? more successful? happier?

Genesis 1:26–27 says human beings are created in the image of God. Do you think God feels you need to buy all of the stuff these ads are selling so you can be complete? Why do we want to buy these products?

Connections

Have a student read Colossians 3:1–17 as you rip the students' posters in half. Take your time ripping each poster as the scripture is read. This emphasizes the truth that we don't set our minds on these things, but on heavenly things.

Have another student read Philippians 3:12–21 while you invite each person to rip a poster. You might give the students some guidance at this point: perhaps one rip per person, rip quietly, etc. This exercise emphasizes that our citizenship is in heaven, not in this world. So, the voices of our culture shouldn't control our desires.

Memory Verse Activity

Have students pick one of the ripped pieces of poster and write the memory verse on the back of it. Invite them to keep it throughout the week and read it every time the culture tries to sell them something by telling them they're inadequate.

Spiritual Practice

Centering prayer is a difficult practice for many young people, primarily because of its simplicity. We enjoy things that are complex, fast-paced, and constantly moving or changing. Centering prayer is the opposite of all that. It involves focusing gently on one word, phrase, or image, while removing every thing else from our minds.

Invite students to spend three or four minutes in centering prayer focused on the word *beloved*. They don't memorize the word, analyze the word, or even understand the word. The word *beloved* is simply a focal point for their minds and spirits.

Their minds will wander but they need not be stressed about this. They needn't be discouraged if they don't feel spiritual. They should simply continue to return their attention to the word beloved.

Invite the students to find a comfortable position. It may be lying on the floor or sitting in a chair, but it must be as non-distracting to them as possible. As they settle in physically, mention that when Jesus was baptized, the Father looked upon him and called him beloved. God calls each one of us beloved as well. We are beloved of God.

After three to four minutes of silence, invite them back to their normal seating arrangements and ask, "When resisting cultural messages, does it help to know that the Creator of the universe calls us beloved?"

Making it Personal

One reason adults encourage young people to pray and read their Bibles daily is that this provides ammunition for the war between cultural definitions of self and God's view of our lives. When we memorize scripture passages, we store up positive messages to counteract the negative cultural environment.

In closing, have each student stand in front of a mirror or pass a hand mirror around the room. As they do this, read Genesis 1:26–27. Remind them that both outwardly and inwardly they are each a precious child of God. Close in prayer together.

Culture War

by Will Penner

Memory Verse

For though we live in the world, we do not wage war as the world does.
—2 Corinthians 10:3 (NIV)

Scripture

John 17:13–19

Lesson in a Sentence

We are not alone as we learn to be in the world but not of the world.

Stuff you'll need:

Four pieces of newsprint with conflict types written on them (see Discovery below)
Several pads of Post-it Notes
Pens or pencils

Focus

Invite students to use the word *beloved* as an acrostic. Depending upon their maturity level, you could ask the students to write a prayer. Or, they could develop sentences or phrases that describe how God feels about us. Younger groups could simply chose an adjective describing God's love that begins with each letter. They could do this individually or in small groups.

Memory Verse Activity

Ask volunteers to say the week's memory verse. Give a small prize to the first volunteer who gets it correct. Go over the memory verse together as a group once or twice.

Discovery

Discuss the language of war that is often used to describe how we are to live as believers in the midst of the world. Are any of your students uncomfortable with this language? If so, why? Is this metaphoric language helpful to anyone? If so, why?

In literature classes, students are called upon to analyze the elements of a good short story—setting, plot, characters, point of view, and theme. Plot is further defined by a story's introduction, rising action or conflict, climax, falling action, and resolution or denouement.

Conflict is essential to a good story not just because it makes the plot interesting but also because it accurately reflects the human experience. There are four basic types of conflicts. Put each of these on separate pieces of newsprint and post them on a wall before the lesson begins:

Character vs. Character (physical)—the leading character physically struggles against other people, forces of nature, or animals.

Character vs. Circumstances (classical)—the leading character struggles against fate, or the circumstances of life.

Character vs. Culture (social)—the leading character struggles against ideas, practices, or customs of other people.

Character vs. Self (psychological)—the leading character struggles with his or her self, soul, ideas of right or wrong, physical limitations, choices, etc.

It is useful to name the type of struggle in order to better understand a story. Review some biblical struggles and place them in one of the above categories. You might have individuals or small groups brainstorm some biblical struggles. Then, as a group, decide which category fits each struggle, write the name of the struggle on a Post-it Note, and stick this to the category.

Life Application
We can better understand a story through the above process. So, it can be helpful to similarly understand the struggles in our own lives. Take five to ten minutes with the group to identify personal struggles the students and their peers are currently facing. Write these on sticky-notes and place them in the proper categories.

Songs
"Baby" by Lost and Found. This is a great closing song. Follow this with a short prayer that we may realize how valuable and loved we are and to tell other people that they are beloved, precious children of God.

Community

by Will Penner

In this lesson, students will:
- ✔ See the difference between a group based on interests, geography, etc., and a community rooted in love.
- ✔ Foster a sense that community isn't something we're part of by default, but rather something we choose.
- ✔ Develop an appreciation for their communities and a sense of responsibility for the members of those communities.

Stuff you'll need:
- ❏ Blindfolds—enough for half the students.

Memory Verse

Dear children, let us not love with words or tongue but with actions and in truth.
—1 John 3:18 (NIV)

Scripture

1 John 3:11–24

Lesson in a Sentence

Sacrificial love is the backbone of a Christian community.

The Big Picture

American families are more separated from their extended relatives than ever before. People change careers and relocate more than ever before. Due to technological advances, many people, especially young people, have less face-to-face contact with others than ever before. Therefore, we long for true community more than ever before.

None of us is meant to live life alone. Even while surrounded by the perfect creation, God said of Adam, "It is not good for the man to be alone" (Genesis 2:18). When Jesus began his public ministry, he lived and traveled with a group of people.

Most people do not intentionally choose the people that form their community. We hang out with people because we've come to know them through school, athletics, extracurricular events, youth group, neighborhood, or family relations.

What if we were to actively choose the people with whom we spend our time and worked hard to build up relationships? What if we were willing to give up our lives for those people? How would this change our lives?

Focus

Organize the students in pairs with people they don't know well. One person in each pair is blindfolded. His or her partner guides this person on a trust walk through an area you've previously prepared—the room, the church, or the parking lot. The guide can use verbal commands but may not touch the blindfolded person. Create some obstacles such as crawling under a table, climbing over couch, or even wading across a creek. If necessary, enlist adult helpers to spot people in potentially dangerous areas.

Have the teams switch places. Make the second course harder than the first. A playground with equipment like a rope-swing or slide works well for this exercise. You might mix things up by limiting the guides to speaking in a whisper.

Try to end the walk in your normal meeting place, or debrief together somewhere else. But, be sure to do this while the experience is fresh in the student's minds.

Ask what was the most difficult part of the experience; what was fun; what would have made it easier, etc. Ask if it would have been easier if they'd been paired with their best friend. If you get awkward silence at this question, don't push for an answer. In a way, it's a loaded question.

Model for your students the way this experience can feel. Say, "I'd be nervous about being blindfolded and led around by someone I don't know very well. I'd want to trust that person, but I'm not sure I could—at least not completely. I know I wouldn't trust anyone as much as I'd trust a friend. Truthfully, I'd be more careful about guiding my best friend than I would someone I don't know so well. (Note: This is sometimes reversed, especially in junior high boys who might run their friends into trees just to laugh at them.)

Discovery

Ask the students to name the various groups to which they belong, either by choice or by default. For instance: city, school, church choir, school band, residential area, YMCA, soccer team, family, gender, race, religion, musical preference, clothing style, social status, hobby, support group, internet service provider, cell phone provider, myspace.com or other Internet message board, etc. The students can do this individually, in small groups, or together as a large group. It is helpful to write these on a chalk board for discussion

Lead the group in a discussion about what the membership requirements are for each group. Are they mere groupings? Are any of them true communities. Explore the meaning of community.

Life Application

Ask the students, "What are the biggest differences between intentional Christian community and most of those we've mentioned so far?" You may need to help with answers such as:

- There's a different level of commitment.
- An intentional community helps one grow as a whole person rather than just taking what one can contribute.
- Community is something one chooses rather than something to simply fall into.
- It's harder to be part of an intentional community than something like *myspace.com* because one can enter and leave myspace at will.

Many adults cannot name five close friends to whom they could tell anything, do anything for, and who would do anything for them. Truth be told, most young people can't do this either. Encourage the students to write down the names of five to ten people with whom they'd like to grow in friendship. Have them seriously think about this and pray over the names. Do this as a prayer practice.

Invite those who are serious about becoming intentional about their communities to:

- Commit to pray for these people every day.
- Look for ways to grow in friendship with them.
- Search for ways to serve them through their words and actions.

Music

"Friends" by Michael W. Smith. Only use this if it hasn't been overused in your area. Some students will think it's ridiculously cheesy, though it does have a great message. If you want to test the waters, ask a trusted student to listen to it ahead of time and give you honest feedback.

Making it Personal

Read 1 John 3:11–24. and discuss what it means. None of us can fully live up to the kind of selfless love God describes here though it is easier for us to love some people than others.

Have students break into small groups to write a personal ad that describes someone who is not a boyfriend or girlfriend that might be easily loved sacrificially. Help each group as needed, but don't take more than about ten minutes for this activity.

Have a spokesperson read aloud each group's ad. When you're finished, tell the students that the best way for them to find friends like this is to become such a friend Close with a prayer that asks God's help to become more like the people in these personal ads.

Community

by Will Penner

Memory Verse

Dear children, let us not love with words or tongue but with actions and in truth.
—1 John 3:18 (NIV)

Scripture

1 Timothy 4:12–16

Lesson in a Sentence

Whether we like it or not, we have influence over other people.

Focus

Bring a clear glass full of water and one eyedropper full of dark food coloring.

Tell the students, "Whether you want to or not, your presence is going to make a difference in the community" Let one drop of food coloring fall into the water. "How you act impacts everyone around you. No one in the community is immune from this." Let another drop or two fall. "In fact, the longer you're a part of a community, the more power you have within it." Put the rest of the food coloring into the water.

"Every time you do something selfless, it impacts the community in a positive way. Every time you do something selfish, it impacts it in a negative way. You have more power than you know."

Discovery

Have the students perform the David and Goliath story found in 1 Samuel 17. If you have a large group, break it into smaller groups to perform the story, or select a few who will perform for the whole group. Discuss:

David wasn't present when Goliath challenged Saul's army. Why? Because no one thought he was old enough or powerful enough to even be a small part of a large army, much less the champion of Israel.

What happened when David tried to put on Saul's armor? This means that David did not fit expectations of a great warrior. God had prepared him for that day in a unique way. Instead of armor, what was David's weapon of choice? Does this seem odd? Similarly, we may think the gifts we've been given aren't all that useful. But, instead of trying to measure up to other people's idea of who you should be, embrace how God made you and you will do amazing things.

Life Application
Read 1 Timothy 4:12–16 together and review the memory verse of the week.

What do the lesson about our choice of friends and the lesson about our power over other people have to do with each other?

God wants us to be in friendship and community. We are stronger together with others when we are alone. We need others and others need us. They need us just as we are, not as someone we or they might like us to be—cooler, smarter, better looking, etc. God made each of us for a purpose and we're at our best when we can be fully ourselves in connection with a community of people

Song
"Blest Be the Tie that Binds" is found in many hymnals. This is best sung while standing in a circle holding hands followed by a very short closing prayer.

Church

by Will Penner

In this lesson, students will:

✔ Learn how the earliest community of Christ-followers structured their lives.
✔ Develop an appreciation for the role of the local church in the formation of their faith.
✔ Gain a sense of personal responsibility to their local church.

Stuff you'll need:

❏ A copy of this week's worship bulletin, announcements, new member packet, and/or other paraphernalia that helps describe your church.
❏ One large piece of butcher paper spanning the wall—the longer, the better.
❏ Enough markers or crayons for each student to write at the same time.

Memory Verse

I am the way and the truth and the life. No one comes to the Father except through me.
—John 14:6 (NIV)

Scripture

Acts 2:36–47

Lesson in a Sentence

The church is central to our faith—the most complete expression of God's love on earth today.

The Big Picture

Church is more than a building. It's more than the worship service. It's more than rules and rituals. It's even more than the people.

For centuries, theologians have argued about what constitutes the church. Is it simply a gathering of people of like mind or faith? We're not going answer this age-old question today, but we are going to explore how the church is different from other communities in which we participate.

Focus

Imaginative prayer is simply a process by which you allow your mind to fill in details of an experience allowing prayer to be deeper, richer, and more meaningful.

Invite students to settle into a comfortable posture—lying or sitting on the floor, sitting in a chair—anything that does not distract them. As they settle in, tell them not to worry about doing this exercise right. The truth is not in what they imagine, it's in the lessons gained through a deeper understanding of scriptural text.

After a few moments of silence, read Acts 2:36–47. Allow at least twenty seconds of silence read the text again. Then tell the students, "Imagine that you're one of these early believers." Ask the following questions, pausing for a few seconds between questions, though not so long that they think they're supposed to answer out loud:

- How are you dressed?
- What does the countryside look like?
- What do the buildings look like?
- What are the sounds you hear?
- What does it smell like?
- What are the expressions on the faces of fellow believers when they see you?
- How do you feel about them?

Read the text again and invite the students to open their eyes gently. Allow for a few moments of silent transition before continuing.

Discovery

Discuss the imaginative prayer experience by asking the students to talk about their answers to the above questions. Ask:

- How did it feel to imagine themselves a part of this community?
- How is our church different from this description of the early church?
- How is our church is similar to this description of the early church?

Distribute your church's bulletins, announcements, visitor packs, new member announcements. Ask the students to describe the most prominent features in this literature? Can anyone find something in this literature they never before noticed? What about your church is not featured in this literature? Are there any glaring omissions from the description of the early church? If you have access to the church's website during the lesson, ask similar questions about the church's Internet presence.

Option (especially if this has been too discussion-heavy for your group so far):

In groups of 3 or 4, ask students to design a bulletin or pamphlet that could be used to recruit new people or connect existing believers to important functions in the early church. Feel free to be somewhat imaginative, but don't deviate too far from the purposes of that community as dictated by the Acts 2 passage.

Life Application

Who makes all of those programs and events at your church happen? Which parts of the church activities do you take part in? Why? Are the things you're currently doing helping you grow in faith? Are they serving others?

Do you do anything to serve others in your church? Or do you just "consume" what it has to offer you?

Making it Personal

Ask students to write down some ways they'd like to broaden their experience within your church. Ways to serve, ways to learn, ways to commune with God or others. Tell them to seek the blessing of their parents, youth leader, or pastor beforehand, but to consider going outside the "normal" parameters.

For instance, as a teenager, one of them might choose to lead a Sunday School class for parents of teenagers for the next four weeks, helping them "get" the adolescent mindset or teen culture. They could help lead drama with children. They could sing in the adult choir. Or perhaps serve on a committee outside the youth arena. They could visit someone in the church who is sick or old and can't leave home—and do the visiting with an adult or two instead of just when the youth group does it.

Wild Hair Idea

Check with the pastor (and/or Christian education committee, church board, parents, etc.) about the possibility of a field trip to another church to see how they "do church." Try to make the experience as different as possible. For instance, if you're at a charismatic church, take students to a highly liturgical church (maybe an Episcopalian or Catholic service); if your church sings from a hymnal accompanied by an organ, attend a service where the words are projected on a screen and led by a praise band; if your church doesn't have any women in leadership, attend a service where a female is the senior pastor and/or preaches the sermon.

Be sure to allow plenty of time to debrief the experience afterward. Search for those elements you have in common first, pointing to the unity of the church. Then look at each element that's different, studying whether or not it's simply a cultural difference or a theological one.

(Side note: Students will be exposed to other churches in their lifetimes, so it's better to begin that process while you can help guide some critical reflection about it.)

Church

by Will Penner

Memory Verse

I am the way and the truth and the life. No one comes to the Father except through me.
—John 14:6 (NIV)

Scripture

Matthew 18:18–20

Lesson in a Sentence

Whenever we gather with another believer in the name of Jesus, something supernatural is occurring, whether we acknowledge it or not.

Focus

Read through Matthew 18:18–20, but don't discuss it at all.

Take the group outside, or have the group stand around in a circle to "play a game." But spend about two minutes explaining a bunch of complex rules (you have to pass it to the person on your left, unless it's a girl wearing high heels, in which case you have to reverse the order; oh, and if it's Sunday, you have to say, "Alleluia," every time you look someone in the face; etc.) In fact, spend so long explaining the rules that you never actually "play." Once everyone's good and frustrated, look at your watch, and say, "Oops, out of time; next activity."

Then say, "Follow me." Just take off and have them follow you. As you walk around, you'll encounter some people and situations you'd prepared ahead of time. (Teacher note: Prepare them ahead of time.)

Help someone to her feet and have her say, "I can walk! Thank you!" Come across some seemingly insignificant object, and draw a quick spiritual parallel out of it: "Yum, the water from this water fountain is good. But no matter how much you drink, you'll get thirsty again. But I can quench your spiritual thirst so that you never run dry."

Feel free to use examples straight out of the gospels. But also feel free to be creative, as well—even ad lib a bit. And it's okay if it's a little silly; the point will still come through.

Discovery

When you get back to the youth room, ask something like: Have you ever been part of a "movement" before? If so, what? If not, why not?

Unfortunately, a lot of our church stuff today can look a lot like the rules to the game we never did play. The early church, on the other hand, was a lot more like our little "follow the leader" exercise. And truthfully, that's more like what our faith is really like. It's less about following rules and more about following Jesus.

Connections

"The Way" is a term used for Christianity several times throughout the book of Acts (9:2; 16:17; 18:25–26; 19:9,23; 22:4; 24:14,22).

How does this dynamic term (which implies some kind of motion) conjure up different images than the more static ones we tend to typically use (that are often institutional in nature)?

Life Application

How can your church experience be less rules-oriented and more Christ-oriented? What can you do to help others along the way of Jesus?

Youth Ministry—Resources and Relationships

By Will Penner

Youth ministry can wear us out. No matter how much we love working with young people, there are times when all of us wonder if we'll be able to keep going. The idea of preparing one more Sunday school lesson, one more youth group outing, mission trip, car wash, or bake sale can make the hair stand up on the back of our heads.

When those times come, we need places to turn to for help. The nice thing about doing youth ministry is that there are tons of resources out there to help us do what we do. On the flip side, culling through everything that's out there can be overwhelming. There are, for instance, over a thousand agencies that will help provide transportation, indigenous local contact people, and other logistics support for youth groups going on short-term mission trips.

There are also times when it gets a little depressing to think of how much money can be spent in the youth ministry marketplace. Certainly these organizations need to be able to cover their expenses, but the average youth worker has a limited amount of money to spend. Plus, our time is even more limited than our money.

Canned Resources

I've heard youth workers decry the use of so-called canned programs for their youth groups. Though I can sympathize with their desire to not use some cookie-cutter approach, I question using planning time to reinvent the wheel. Even though I write curriculum and activity ideas for public consumption, I use more purchased material with my youth group than original content.

I don't have time to come up with new talks, Bible studies, retreat themes, game nights, and campouts, and still spend time devotionally with God and relationally with kids. I want to be a good steward of my time, which is why I turn to other resources. Though I often add my own flair, I rely on the expertise of others in programming and curriculum resources so that I can spend my energy focused on God, my family, and the kids in my youth group.

Thank God for Technology

Even though computers don't always act the way I'd like them to, and I've had to take time to learn how to use them, computers have proven invaluable to my life and work as the executive editor of *The Journal of Student Ministries* and in my church youth group. What would've taken several hours just a few years ago now takes only a matter of minutes. That frees time for me to do important things in my life like being a husband and father.

When we use products or services that help us cull through scriptures quickly, offer group-building insights and fund-raising ideas, or project images on the wall, we expand our effectiveness in ministry. On the other hand, if we try to use technology to do what God is calling us to do ourselves, we decrease our effectiveness. Youth ministry is relational and always will be. No technology, product, or service can replace you living your calling with the kids God has entrusted to you. If we compare ourselves to ministries who seem to be bigger, flashier, or more technologically advanced, we not only dishonor the ministry to which we've been called, but we run the risk of placing too much reliance on products rather than on God.

Navigating the Industry

Youth ministry is an industry. We need to guard our hearts so that we don't covet the trappings of the industry and forget the heart of ministry.

In *The Journal of Student Ministries (www.journalofstudentministries.com)*, we try to help youth workers stay up to date on things going on in youth culture. We provide information on statistics, quotes, attitudes, and trends, to help you better understand the young people in your care. We provide in-depth articles dealing with topics for adults who work in ministry with young people. And we critically review books, CDs, movies, and other media so you can make informed choices about where best to use your time and money.

Publications like *The Journal*, books like this sourcebook, and resource lists like the one you'll find in the appendix to this book help us sift through the many choices out there and give us ideas about ways we can connect to technology, products, and services that will multiply our efforts and magnify our impact with students. In an effort to be good stewards of our money and our time, we need resources that will decrease the amount of time we spend doing things others have already done. That way, we'll have more time to attend to our relationship with God and our relationships with young people.

Possessing Heaven

by Ben Donley

In this lesson, students will:

✔ Understand the long-term and short-term meaninglessness of material possessions

✔ See the difference between God's expectations and the world's advertising

✔ Recognize the need to simplify in a world dominated by poverty

Stuff you'll need:

❏ TV/DVD player
❏ Veggie Tales: *Madame Blueberry*
❏ DVD or VHS recording of an MTV "Cribs" or VH-1 "The Fabulous Life of…"
❏ Paper, pens, markers
❏ Several magazines with advertisements
❏ Poster board

Memory Verse

Naked a man comes from his mother's womb, and as he comes, so he departs. He takes nothing from his labor that he can carry in his hand. —Ecclesiastes 5:15 (NIV)

Scripture

Matthew 6:19–21

Lesson in a Sentence

Jesus wants us to take our focus off of material possessions and shop in his store for the best buys on things that last and things that matter.

The Big Picture

According to the Bible, we only have one life on this earth. With this fact in mind, we should focus our time on things that are meaningful and eternal. To waste our time on gathering and maintaining material possessions is foolish. Why? Beyond the time factor and the reality of a short life, materialism is a silly focus because possessions break down, take up our space, leave us targeted by thieves, require maintenance, make us dread moving, and do not give us the satisfaction that is promised by their advertising. When we die, we won't be able to take any of it with us anyway. It all stays here.

Even though we know these things, most of us tend to buy in to our culture, to dance along with Madonna and become materialists bent on consumption. In other words, we become lovers of stuff. And because we love stuff, we tend to have a lot of stuff, talk a lot about stuff, shop a lot for stuff and basically make material possessions a major life priority. Mega-malls and Wal-Marts are happy about this and exist because of this. But Jesus is not cool with it.

Christians need to catch a clue about what Jesus wants when he tells us not to spend our lives on such trivial pursuits. He wants us to avoid focusing on material possessions and instead to focus our time, energy and money on doing loving things for God and other people. Jesus wants us to shop in his store for love, wisdom, and faith so that it can be redistributed to the people who need it. He says, "Sell your possessions and give to the poor." When this is done, you will have stored up treasures in heaven that will not ever be stolen and that will never fade.

Focus

Option 1
Watch Something Relevant
VeggieTales: Madame Blueberry
You can use this for any age because it is a profound cartoon, but teens might tune you out if you try to show this without some disclaimer. Preview this DVD and get it to the part just before the "Stuff Mart" rap. Introduce the clip by telling your youth that you have recently gotten into hip-hop and rap music. Mention some real rappers that you have heard of. Then jokingly tell them that you are going to show them a very edgy and controversial clip from an underground artist that most of them haven't heard of—a video that MTV is too afraid to play. This will get their attention. Finally, tell them that you think this artist really has an important message. Ask them to really pay attention to it. Then proceed to show this dumb vegetable rap. They will groan at you, but don't they always? Play as much beyond this rap as you think is necessary to set the stage for the materialism discussion. This clip shows how stupid we are for buying into a materialistic culture.

Pop Culture Materialism Visuals—Get a DVD/VHS recording of an MTV "Cribs" episode or VH-1's "The Fabulous Life of . . ." episode. Choose one that shows some extreme materialism. Show them the clip and ask them to focus on the person's possessions and how the person talks about their possessions. When it is over, simply ask them to tell you what they saw. Let them freely give their own impressions and feelings about the visual.

Option 2
Small Groups and Magazines
Divide your youth into small groups and give each group a stack of appropriate magazines. Tell them to go through the magazines and to tear out five to ten ads about things they want to possess. Have them show the other groups what they found and explain why they want what they tore out.

Option 3
Individuals and Wish Lists

Give each person a piece of paper and a pen. Ask them to take a specific inventory of everything they own. Have them write these things down on the front side of their paper. On the back of their paper, ask them to make a list of all the things that they want. Next to each of these wanted possessions, have them put how much they think it costs. Get them to add these totals up. Once they finish all of this, have them share their lists with two other people.

Discovery

Briefly, discuss these questions:
- If you were to wake up tomorrow and all of your possessions were gone, how would you feel?
- If you were to wake up tomorrow and find that all stores (physical and online) were permanently closed down, how would you feel?
- How much time do you spend either shopping for stuff or thinking about stuff you want? And how important would you say stuff is to you?

Give them five minutes to read Matthew 6:19–21 on their own. Tell them to read it slowly again and again asking the Holy Spirit to teach them about the passage.

When this silent time of reading is over, reread the passage to the group and then ask them to tell you what stood out to them. Use some of their comments to guide your initial discussion about earthly treasures versus heavenly treasures. Use some of the Big Picture information to inform the group and/or ask some of the following questions:
- What do you think Jesus means by earthly treasures? What would be some modern examples of earthly treasures?
- What does Jesus say are some of the problems that accompany earthly treasures? Can you think of any more problems that go along with material possessions?
- What do you think Jesus means by heavenly treasures? What is so good about them?
- How does someone gain heavenly treasures?
- How can someone know if they are too focused on earthly possessions?

Life Application
Break the students into small groups with leaders that can facilitate the following discussion questions:
- What does Jesus want from us? Why would Jesus want this?
- How cool do you think heavenly treasures are?
- How might a shift in focus from earthly possessions to heavenly possessions benefit you? What is hard about this for you?
- If you were to do what Jesus recommends here, what would you have to change?

Hand out poster board and markers to each group. Challenge your students to come up with a good advertisement to promote Jesus' message about focusing on heavenly treasures. Encourage them to use the Matthew verses as well as the memory verse from Ecclesiastes. Allow them to present their ideas to each other.

Making it Personal

Discuss:
- What message does the world want you to hear?
- How can you avoid or limit hearing or seeing this message?
- What do you need to do to shift your focus from the world's advertising to God's advertising?

Option 1

Commit yourself to a month long shopping fast, where you refuse to buy anything beyond the necessities. Tell your youth about your decision, ask for their comments, and then ask them to join you for one week. Have those who commit to this shopping fast keep a journal.

Option 2

Earlier, if you chose Option 2 or 3 from the Focus section, ask the students to bring their torn-out ads or their wish lists up to the cross of Christ during a closing prayer time as a symbol of trading in the world's treasures for heavenly ones.

Possessing Heaven

by Ben Donley

Memory Verse

Naked a man comes from his mother's womb, and as he comes, so he departs. He takes nothing from his labor that he can carry in his hand. —Ecclesiastes 5:15 (NIV)

Scripture

Luke 12:32–33

Lesson in a Sentence

Sell your earthly possessions, help the poor, and God will be pleased.

Focus—JesusBay

Tape a Compassion International child's picture on the wall next to an eBay poster. Ask:
- What is Compassion International?
- What is eBay?
- How are they related?

Let the students tell what they know and guess about the relationship between the two. Confirm their answers and add to them. Make sure that it is established that Compassion International is a group that helps very poor children in other parts of the world and that Ebay is an online auction site where people sell their things to the highest bidder.

You will model what it means to sell your possessions and give to the poor. Either bring out something that you consider to be a treasure or buy something that is somewhat valuable. Place this treasure underneath the eBay poster board and tell the group that you are going to auction this item to the highest bidder. Begin the bidding at 25 cents and run a mini-auction. Let the kids drive up the price, but make sure that you have one plant in the audience who will outbid everyone. (You give the plant the cash to bid with.) Remove the treasure from under the eBay sign and give it to the bidder. Then take the money and put it under the Compassion International sign. Ask: **What just happened?** Let the students comment.

Tell them that this is an example of selling it off for the Kingdom of God. God approves of this kind of act. Tell them that you traded off something pretty cool so that you could get money and give it to the poor—A material possession traded for food, education, and clothes for a little kid that doesn't have even the basics of life.

Discovery

Read Luke 12:32–33.
- What is Jesus asking us to do here? Why?
- How is this different from a garage sale?
- What is difficult about this?
- What do you get in return for selling your possessions and giving to the poor?

Life Application

Look up stories of kids on the Compassion International website and share one of them with your group. Tell your group how much it costs to support a needy child in a foreign country and compare that to several goods or services in America. Ask:
- What if all of us sold even two of our treasures and gave the money to the poor? How would this make a difference in the world?
- What would you have to sell to support one of these poor children?
- Would you be willing to sell some of your possessions do this?

Challenge

Ask each student to prayerfully choose one personal treasure to sell for the sake of the poor. Bring these next week. Sell them and give the money to the poor.

Baptism

by Amy Jacober

In this lesson, students will:
- ✔ Consider Biblical examples of baptism
- ✔ Understand that baptism is modeled and then commanded by Jesus
- ✔ Realize that baptism is neither the beginning nor the end of following Jesus
- ✔ Gain a respect for the event of baptism

Stuff you'll need:
- ❑ Blocks of ice
- ❑ String
- ❑ Buckets
- ❑ Dolls
- ❑ Gelatin, made and set
- ❑ Pool Noodles
- ❑ Toilet plungers
- ❑ Water balloons
- ❑ Rice
- ❑ Paper cups
- ❑ Marbles
- ❑ Squirt guns

Memory Verse

And now, why are you waiting? Arise and be baptized and wash away your sins, calling on the name of the Lord. —Acts 22:16

Scripture

Matthew 3:13–17; Matthew 28:16–20

Lesson in a Sentence

Baptism helps us identify with other believers across denominations and throughout time.

The Big Picture

Baptism is a commonly accepted ordinance within the Christian community. What baptism means is debatable. Rather than focusing on what has not been decided by theologians over the last 2000 years, this lesson will look at what scripture does say and what we can know. Regardless where you stand on the particulars of baptism, it is a part of our Christian heritage. We join in a strong history with hundreds of thousands identifying with Jesus and other Christians through baptism.

Focus

Summer Water Wars

In the peak of the heat, create a night to remember. Feel free to add or adjust any of the following games. The point is simply to get wet and have lots of fun!

Divide into teams and have members of each team sign up for the games. Assign points to each game, the more the better.

Ice Hold

Freeze several blocks of ice ahead of time. Ask for as many volunteers as you have blocks of ice. The object of the game is to see who can hold the ice the longest. Feel free to have them hang onto the ice while playing the other games.

Take The Plunge

This is a large scale, wet rendition of the old ball in the cup game. Before the night begins, get four plungers and tie a string at least the length of the plunger to the spot where the stick and plunger meet. Next fill four water balloons. Tie the water balloons to the end of the string. Ask for four volunteers, the first to catch the water balloon in the plunger without breaking it, wins. You may want extra water balloons on hand for more than one round.

Water Balloon Toss

Have every person get a partner. Have the pairs line up in two lines facing one another. Give each pair a water balloon. At hand shaking distance, have one person pass the balloon to their partner. Both take a step back. Have one partner toss it to the next, and both take a step back. This continues until pairs drop off as their balloons break. Continue play to see who can be the furthest apart tossing the balloon without breaking it.

Quicksand

This is a relay game with at least six players from each team. Go to a dollar store and pick up a bucket and a cheap *Barbie* or *Ken* style doll per team. Fill the bucket with rice. You now get to fulfill childhood dreams: dismember the doll and bury her or him in the rice. Set up a relay where a single member runs from one end of your area to the bucket. They must dig in the bucket and grab a part. The first team to have six members run down, grab all six parts and reassemble their doll wins.

Watch it Wiggle

Have at least five bowls of gelatin made ahead of time. Place a marble in the bottom of each bowl. Ask for five volunteers. The first to fish out the marble wins. The catch, they must fish out the marble with their toes!

Over/Under

Have each team line up front to back. At the front of the line, fill a bucket with water. At the back of the line, give the last team member a large cup. Play a game of over under. Use either a sponge dipped in the bucket or a small paper cup and pass it down the line alternating going over the head and then between the legs all the way back to the large cup. The first team to fill their cup wins.

Super Soaker Showdown

Tell your students ahead of time to bring their best water gun. Feel free to have an all out brawl. There is no winner or loser; this is just for fun.

Noodle Jousting

Get at least two pool noodles (those long foam floaty things that come out every summer at swimming pools). Ask for two volunteers. The object of the game is to hit your partner without being hit. You will need to keep a close eye, but this is a fun and easy game.

Discovery

It's going to be a tough to get your students settled down, but you can do it. Begin by asking your students about every time that water is mentioned or in scripture. What they say is irrelevant, this is simply to transition from wild wet games to a more focused time looking at scripture.

Water is mentioned many times in many ways throughout scripture. One of the most important is baptism.

Ask half to look at Matthew 3:13–17 and the other half to look at Matthew 28:16–20. Give the following questions to the group that has Matthew 3:13–17:
- Was Jesus forced to be baptized?
- Why did John say what he did to his cousin Jesus?
- Why did Jesus respond the way he did?
- What can you learn about baptism from verse 16?
- How are we to understand the voice that says, "This is My beloved Son"?

Give the following questions to the group that has Matthew 28:16–20:
- What were the disciples like in verse 17?
- What did Jesus say had been given to Him?
- Two major things are told to happen in verse 19, what are they?
- What does Jesus say to do in verse 20?
- What does Jesus promise in verse 20?

Ask each group to share what they learned about baptism from their passages. Read Matthew 3:13–17 aloud so both groups will have heard it. When this group is done, read Matthew 28:16–20 aloud and give the second group time to share.

Life Application

Notice that in Matthew 3:14–15 John tries to tell Jesus that it is he (John) who should be baptized by Jesus. But Jesus says He (Jesus) should be baptized to fulfill all righteousness. Here Jesus models baptism. In Matthew 28:16–20, Jesus commands His followers to go and baptize others. A major point to note, Jesus does not say to just be baptized, He says to make disciples and baptize them. Baptism is not a magic spell. It takes both following Jesus for life and the act of baptism to obey the commandment in this passage.

- What do you think about baptism today?
- How does your church view baptism?
- In what other areas have you seen Jesus both model and command?

Making it Personal

If your church offers baptism regularly, tell your students about this. Invite them to the pre-baptism classes so they will better understand baptism and how your particular church carries this out.

Songs

"So Long Self" and "Bring on the Rain" by Mercy Me on *Coming Up to Breathe*

Baptism

by Amy Jacober

Memory Verse

And now, why are you waiting? Arise and be baptized and wash away your sins, calling on the name of the Lord. —Acts 22:16

Scripture

Acts 2:36–42

Lesson in a Sentence

Baptism helps us identify with other believers across denominations and throughout time.

Focus

Put together a power point slide show of pictures of water. Use raging rivers, still waters, the ocean, rain, etc. These can easily be found in a search engine using the phrase "pictures of rivers," "pictures of rain" etc. Create a show long enough to last the entirety of the song "So Long Self" by Mercy Me found on *Coming Up to Breathe.* If you or your students do not have this CD, choose another appropriate song about turning from self to God. Present the slide show and music at the beginning of your time together.

• What do we know of water?
• How can this relate to the song we just heard?

Water is known for cleansing, both literally and figuratively. The topic of the week is baptism. Baptism is not a magic act that immediately fixes all struggles and guarantees a life in obedience to God. It is, however, an expression of change; of turning from what you once were to a new life.

Discovery

Read Acts 2:36–42. This passage is very simple, very straightforward.

• Why were the people asking what they should now do?
• Had they known or had any experiences with God before?

TEACHER'S NOTE

This passage is from Peter's sermon at Pentecost. He and the apostles were being mocked, questioned, and accused of being drunk. Peter reminds them of the miracles they have already seen. He reminds them of what was prophesied and what David said long ago. He reminds them that they have already had an experience with God. Peter's job was to help them recognize what was already occurring around them. The response was their decision.

Life Application

We all do wrong things. We have all also seen God at work in and around us and missed Him for looking for something else.
- In what ways have you seen God this past week?
- In what times did you wish to see God?

TEACHER'S NOTE

This may be a very new way of thinking for some of your students. We don't often talking about seeing God. You may need to explain that this is a metaphor for in what ways or places have you known something could not have happened without God. It may be a sister not arguing with parents or feeling calm taking a test. Not to mention those daily miracles like waking up and being able to breathe. If you need to prime the pump, help your students out by giving an example or two from your life.

Our relationship with God begins long before most of us realize. He has loved you since knitting you in your mother's womb. He has known every hair on your head from the day you were born.
- The passage talks about needing to repent. What does *repent* mean?
- Does repentance save you?

The answer to this question is, "No." Throughout our lives we must draw nearer to God but it is not what saves. Many students get this wrong. They think if they repent and are good people then they are saved. They give up on salvation if they feel like they cannot be good enough.
- How does baptism fit into all of this?
- Do you think baptism is necessary?
- What happens after baptism?

Baptism is important because Jesus finds it to be important. That is reason enough. When baptized, we are living out our obedience to Christ. When baptized we are also identifying with the death, burial, and resurrection of Jesus.

Baptism is also not the end. Some people stick around church just long enough to be baptized.

Talk about what it takes to follow Jesus for life. Baptism is important but it is one event on the journey of following Jesus for life.

The Lord's Supper

by Sharon Koh

In this lesson, students will:

✔ Recognize that it is good to remember the death and resurrection of Jesus Christ on a regular basis.

✔ Be able to connect this remembrance with how we relate to one another and treat each other.

Stuff you'll need

❏ Bread

Memory Verse

For he himself is our peace, who has made the two one and has destroyed the barrier, the dividing wall of hostility, by abolishing in his flesh the law with its commandments and regulations. His purpose was to create in himself one new man out of the two, thus making peace, and in this one body to reconcile both of them to God through the cross, by which he put to death their hostility. —Ephesians 2:14–16 (NIV)

Scripture

1 Corinthians 11:23–26

Lesson in a sentence

When we partake of the Lord's Supper, we remember how much it cost Jesus to offer His body and blood for our redemption and reconciliation.

The Big Picture

To overlook the costliness of Jesus Christ's death and resurrection is to cheapen His precious sacrifice.

Focus and Discovery

This demonstration illustrates the purpose of the Lord's Supper. The second part will take considerably more time than the first part.

Hand everybody small portions of bread and juice and instruct them not to eat or drink yet. Then, send them to different corners of the room or out of the room to be alone and tell them to eat the bread and drink the juice by themselves. Tell them to take ten minutes alone to think about what the death and resurrection of Jesus means in their own lives.

When students come back together, ask them to get into a large circle. Take the bread and read 1 Corinthians 11:23–26. Pray and give thanks for the bread, and then break the bread and pass it around the circle. When each person receives a piece of the bread, have him or her share one thing that they are grateful to Jesus for. Again, pass the cups of juice around the circle. This time, when each person receives the cup, have him or her share one thing they are grateful they do not have to live with in their lives because of Jesus (sins, fears, etc.). You will find that the second exercise takes much more time and is far more meaningful than the first.

Take the time to thank Jesus for the things that are shared. Make it a point to highlight that none of the things celebrated and shared would be possible without the death and resurrection of the Lord Jesus Christ.

Life Application

Ask students to talk about which exercise was easier for them. Then, ask them which exercise made it easier for them to remember and celebrate the gifts that Jesus offers us through His death and resurrection. Highlight the importance of remembering Jesus' sacrifice and gift on a regular basis. However, it is also important to point out that the group had more things to be grateful for when they got together and shared their points of gratitude. This is an illustration of the Christian life. First, it is important to remember who gave us the gift of life. It is also important to notice that the remembrance is to be done in community. It is easier (and more fun!) to remember the Lord we love together.

TEACHER'S NOTE:

This is a hands-on lesson and is designed to help you make the point illustratively while incorporating scriptural study. So, take your time to make the point, but make sure the students are paying attention when you are reading from 1 Corinthians.

The Lord's Supper

by Sharon Koh

Memory Verse

While they were eating, Jesus took bread, gave thanks and broke it, and gave it to his disciples, saying, "Take it; this is my body." Then he took the cup, gave thanks and offered it to them, and they all drank from it. "This is my blood of the covenant, which is poured out for many," he said to them. —Mark 14:22–24 (NIV)

Scripture

Mark 14:12–26

Lesson in a Sentence

When we partake of the Lord's Supper, we remember the events of the evening of the first Lord's Supper.

Focus

Play the scene from the movie *The Passion of the Christ* in which the Lord's Supper is depicted. Ask students to imagine that they were at the table during that very meal.

Discovery

Read Mark 14:12–26 together. Ask students how they would feel if they were present at the Lord's Supper and did not know about the events about to take place. Then, ask the students to talk about how they feel about the Lord's Supper now that they do know about Judas's betrayal, Peter's denial, and Jesus' death and resurrection. Then, read Mark 14:25 again. What did Jesus promise those gathered around Him at the table? How does this impact the way that we live our lives?

Too Mini Loves

by David Upchurch

In this lesson, students will:
- ✔ Learn about Solomon's achievements and failures
- ✔ Know how to daily trust God
- ✔ Keep a God-perspective about their life and things.

Stuff you'll need:
- ❑ Paper and pens
- ❑ Scissors

Memory Verse

Teach me Your way, O Lord; I will walk in Your truth; Unite my heart to fear Your name.
—Psalm 86:11 (NIV)

Scripture

1 Kings 3:1–3; 11:1–6

Lesson in a Sentence

The devotion of the heart guides life's journey more than the knowledge of the brain.

The Big Picture

We often know what is right and how to do it but we just don't do it because the focus of our heart is on something else. Think about all of the things with which Solomon had been blessed. Solomon had a dad who was a great example, a man after God's heart. Solomon prayed for wisdom and received it plus wealth and power. He had witnessed a manifestation of God's presence that blew him away at the temple dedication (1 Kings 8:10–11; 2 Chronicles 7:1–6). Yet, at the end of his life, his choices and way of thinking left him far away from God.

We can learn from one of the wisest men in history by learning from his mistakes. Solomon lived the good life and did many things right. The world remembers him for his proverbs and decisions on important matters. However, all of that wisdom did not get from his brain to his heart—some of the very life lessons he taught he had not learned. We need to remember that our heart holds our life's focus. One's focus can be directed at money, stuff, power, or relationships, ourselves, friends, or any type of good thing. We need to go to God and refocus our heart so that things and stuff don't divide our attention and get our heart off of God's path.

Focus

Keep in step with the leader. Choose a student to be a leader and have six to twelve people line up behind him or her in a single file line. Instruct the leader to lead the group around the room in any kind of locomotion they choose—skipping, hopping, walking around and through the chairs, etc. Tell those in line to do their best to follow and to place their feet in the footsteps of the person in front of them. Then, let them begin. Watch to see how the group does and how hard the leader tries to make it. Also, listen for encouragement, discouragement, and giving up. After several minutes, have everyone sit down for a debriefing. Talk about keeping one's eyes on the leader, watching footsteps versus knowing where they were going, and not giving up when the steps didn't exactly line up because you were staying close and there was someone behind you.

Discovery

Read through verses 1–3. Notice the word in the NIV—*alliances*—What does the king of God's people need that the King of Egypt can provide? That alliance implies a lack of trust in God on the part of Solomon. God had promised peace and provision for his reign. Solomon had God's word in the covenant of 1 Kings 9:3–9.

In verse 3 Solomon is walking with God but there is competition. The exception started small by simply burning incense. This worship began to compete with worship of God. An inward battle became fiercer as hundreds of wives and their practices were added to Solomon's life. What was once an exception became the rule. Solomon seems to be trying to cover all of the religious bases by worship of other gods and goddesses, hoping life would go right.

What about the palace? Is it wrong to build a plush palace? This was an amazing house (see 1 King 7:1–12; 10:14–29). Can you love and serve God and have a big house?

In 1 Kings 11:1–6 we see a big transition word, "*however.*" One has to know that whatever is going to follow this word isn't going to be good. Solomon had many outward signs of success—tons of gold, horses and chariots, houses, worldwide status, and leadership of many people—yet success is very different in the eyes of God. Why did God say not to marry foreign wives? Instead of growing wise in old age Solomon's heart wandered off into foreign places (v. 4). Full devotion and commitment became a thing for others not the king. He "did not follow completely." Notice what kept him from following completely. Solomon could have considered the many marriages to be little things but they eventually caused his ruin.

Who were the gods he worshiped? Ashtoreth was the goddess of fertility, which is important in cultures that are based on agriculture and its fertile soil. Worship of her is a distrust of God who created the earth, sun and moon, plants and animals and seasons. Worship of Molech involved child sacrifice, and God strictly warned them about the consequences of this kind of worship (Leviticus 18:21).

Finally, God sums up Solomon's life. In verse 6, God's eyes are the only ones that matter and he controls eternity. He looks at the heart. David, Solomon's father, had been a great king but one who was also an adulterer and murderer. Still the comment on his life is that he followed the Lord.

Activity

To get the kids thinking about trusting their lives to God it is important to block out other plans. Have the students cut out ads from magazines and newspaper that proclaim the message, "You need this to _____." If you or a student can TiVO or record some commercials during some shows geared to students and examine their message that "these are the cool clothes, or bands, or places, etc."

Life Application

God has a plan for your life and it centers on you being abundantly alive. The cross sets us free from the guilt and shame of sin and frees us to live without fear. Trust God in all areas of life and you will be blessed more than Solomon.

Personal Application

What kinds of alliances do we make? "I'll be your friend if . . ." "I'll just try it once if . . ." "No one will get hurt . . ." "No one will know."
- Do you have some exceptions in your relationship with God?
- Do you tell God, "You can't pick my dating relationships."
- Why is it that "love" or a relationship causes us to do things we normally wouldn't?
- What does God desire for your future? What is there around your life that could keep you from enjoying his promise?

Too Mini Loves

by David Upchurch

Memory Verse

Teach me Your way, O Lord; I will walk in Your truth; Unite my heart to fear Your name.
—Psalm 86:11 (NIV)

Scripture

1 Peter 3:15, 16

Lesson in a Sentence

The devotion of the heart guides life's journey more than knowledge of the mind.

Discovery

Read the two verses above. Peter reminds us of the importance of the heart. He urges believers to set Jesus apart as Lord in the center of their being. As Lord of our hearts Jesus Christ, through the Spirit, guides us. In turn our thoughts, words and actions become more like His. All choices and decisions are evaluated through Him. Questions like, "Whom do I make friends with?" "Do I gossip about that person?" "Do I watch that movie?" "Do I go to that party?" etc., are countered by "How will I glorify Christ?" Anything less compromises our Christian life. If we elevate things, people or thoughts they can become idols, false gods that bring little satisfaction. When we start thinking "What do they think about me?" "If I just had a car, they would accept me," "I have to drink to be cool," frustration will rule our lives.

Peter's goal was to remind the believers of the importance of living differently than this. Under the lordship of Jesus our lives are markedly different than that which the world offers us. People see how you live and wonder about why you live that way. The answer is Jesus Christ. Generally, those who ask about your life are searching for something to live for. You can lead them to a relationship with Christ. This is something you'll never forget.

As you glorify Jesus with your life you'll be delight in the Lord. Living for God's glory transforms your life. You see God at work everywhere. Your prayer life enlarges as you see God attracting those around you. Your life becomes one of worship.

Activity

Have the students write each of the categories of their lives (school, home, entertainment, dating, job, church, clothes, car, hobbies, homework, God, etc.) on a piece of paper. Create a simple puzzle using these categories as the pieces by taping them on a dry erase board or a wall. This helps students see that God often has one piece of their life often stuck over in a corner.

To illustrate how God wants to be their Lord, take a marker and write G-O-D big enough so that some part of the letters touch every piece of the puzzle. Remind them God has a purpose for each of those areas of their lives and desires to be Lord over them all.

Connections

- Psalm 37:4—Delight in the Lord
- Matthew 6:24—Serving two masters
- Luke 16:13—Serving two masters
- John 16:5-15—The Holy Spirit's work
- Roman 12:1-2—The renewing of the mind

The Pursuit of You

by Chuck Hunt

In this lesson, students will:
- ✔ Be introduced to the pursuit of God
- ✔ Be given an opportunity to pursue someone.
- ✔ Have an opportunity of pursue God.

Stuff you'll need:
- ❏ Balloons

Memory Verse

But the hour is coming, and now is, when the true worshipers will worship the Father in spirit and truth; for the Father is seeking such to worship Him. —John 4:23

Scripture

Matthew 18:10

Lesson in a Sentence

God desires to have an intimate relationship with you.

The Big Picture

God desires that followers know and love that they are known and loved. He would have us understand the love between the Father and the Son (Matt. 11:25–30). The cry of God's heart is that we receive His compassion. This compassion is not based on our pain, our lack of faith, or our ability to show up at church. God pursues us always, where we are and how we are.

Focus

Option 1: Balloon Stomp

Pass out balloons and a two-foot piece of string to each of your students and leaders. Have them tie the string around their leg, inflate the balloon, and tie the blown-up balloon to the other end of the string. Ask for a volunteer. When they raise their hand go over and pop their balloon by stomping on it. Tell them they are *it* and need to stomp on another person's balloon. Then that person is *it* as well and joins in stomping every one's balloon until there is one person left. That person wins.

Option 2: Sardines

Before the meeting, designate a leader to slip away and hide somewhere in the church. Start the meeting as you normally would and then in the middle of the welcome say, "We are missing someone and cannot continue until we find that person." The point is that when someone finds that person they are to hide with them. The first five or ten people to hide will get a prize. Once the leader gives away all the prizes, then the game is over and all of the students return to the meeting room.

Discovery

Before the meeting get a few of your students to bring their mp3 players. Break your students into groups of no more than eight. Have the groups read through today's scripture and answer some questions together. For example:
  • According to v. 10, what is Jesus concerned about?
  • Who are the little ones in the kingdom?
  • Do you see yourself as the lost sheep? Do you think most Christians today recognize this? Why or why not?
  • How faithfully should a church pursue lost ones? Do we do this? Why or why not?

After the students answer the questions, ask them to find a song that is on one of the mp3 players that may be like what Jesus is saying in today's verse. Have each group play each song through a speaker so that everyone can hear. (This will help you to see how your students understand the lesson.)

Life Application

One of the issues that have an effect on our students is loneliness. Reassure your students that God to cares for them and loves them so much that He pursues them. Students need to understand God loves them where they are and not where they think they should be.

Making it Personal
Option 1
Pass out another round of balloons and have the students blow them up. Have your leaders walk around the room and give them each a pin. The instruction this time will be for the students to see the balloon as the struggle, pain, or need that they have been hiding from Jesus. Give them a few moments of silence. When they are ready to be found, have them lift their balloon in the air. When a leader sees this , have them go over pray with the student and pop the balloon.

Option 2
Play the opposite of the Sardines game. Send out all of the students to hide. The leader who started the game of hiding is 'it'. The rules are the same—the first ten people to be found win a prize.

   Note: The point is not actually to play the game but to bring to light the reality that if we know that something good awaits us if we are found, why would we hide?

Connections
Jonah; Moses; John 17; Matthew 11:25–30

Quotable Quotes
God is near to you now—nearer to you than you are to yourself. —A. W. Tozer

The answer is out there, Neo, and its looking for you, and it will find you if you want it to. —Trinity in "The Matrix"

The Father gives you as a gift to Himself. —Brennan Manning

The Pursuit of You

by Chuck Hunt

Memory Verse

But the hour is coming, and now is, when the true worshipers will worship the Father in spirit and truth; for the Father is seeking such to worship Him. —John 4:23

Scripture

Matthew 18:10–14

Lesson in a Sentence

Jesus is calling us to be pursuers as well as pursued.

The Big Picture

God pursues us through Jesus Christ. Through Jesus, we know the Father (Matt. 11:25–30). Because of this, tell others that they are pursued as well.

In this lesson, students will:

✔ Be given the opportunity to think of someone other than themselves
✔ Be given the opportunity to care for someone other than themselves

Focus

Option 1

Since this is the beginning of the school year, put together a list of students with whom you have lost touch (this is a great opportunity to clean up your student list). Put your students into groups of four and hand out paper and markers. Divide the list between the groups and have them write a message saying that the absent person is missed and loved, include a calendar of your meetings and have them address the envelope.

Option 2

Tell students and parents that you are going on a scavenger hunt for people. The group that returns with their person first, wins. Send them out with 1 John 4:7–12. Give them an address, directions, and a phone number. Here is the catch they have to love, not bribe the person.

Discovery

When the students are done with the activity, begin a discussion that centers on Matthew 18. Allow the students to visualize what it is like to be pursued by friends and then by God.

Life Application

This is interwoven in the exercises. The point is that God pursues more relentlessly and persistently than your best friend.

Making it Personal

Option 1—Invite the students to follow up on the letters that they wrote.

Option 2—Invite the group to take the student out for lunch outside of the group time.

What Does the Lord Require of You?

by Amy Jacober

In this lesson, students will:
- ✔ Understand salvation is by grace through faith alone
- ✔ Look at several common myths regarding salvation and what the Bible has to say about each one
- ✔ Realize there is nothing they can do in their own strength to earn salvation
- ✔ Practice telling others about salvation

Stuff you'l need:
- ❑ Two large sheets of paper cut into strips
- ❑ Painters blue masking tape
- ❑ Each of the myths in the discovery section pre-printed on paper

Memory Verse

He has told you, O mortal, what is good; and what does the Lord require of you but to do justice, and to love kindness, and to walk humbly with your God? —Micah 6:8

Scripture

Matthew 10:32–33	Romans 10:13
John 3:16	Galatians 2:15–21
Romans 3:23	Ephesians 2:8–9
Romans 5:8	1 Timothy 2:3–4
Romans 6:23	James 2:19
Romans 10:9–10	

Lesson in a Sentence

Salvation is the most precious gift we can ever receive.

The Big Picture

Salvation is not always the most popular of topics. By its very nature, the blessing of salvation is just a thought away from the harsh reality of being lost. Even for those who are churched or claim to be Christians, the idea of salvation can be difficult. It means that they are not in control. It means that they cannot earn their way to heaven. It means that some will never make it to heaven. God is more often considered an all-loving, soft, warm, kind old man rather than the Almighty Creator of the universe whose plan includes salvation from sin.

There are many misconceptions surrounding salvation and all that it entails. While the many traditions understand salvation in different ways, this lesson will not create division or controversy. Talk with your pastor about this to avoid any confusion. This lesson simply looks at scripture and asks a few questions.

Focus

Show a clip from the movie *Walk the Line*. This movie is about the life of Johnny Cash. Throughout the film are scenes about his being a Christian and his upbringing in the church. Show the clip when he is talking about salvation and says he can save himself.

Show a second clip from *Amistad*. Set the stage for your students: The *Amistad* was a ship carrying people who had been ripped from their homes in Africa to be slaves America. The scene is the one in the bottom of the boat where language is an issue and the gospel is shown in pictures.

Ask your students how they get their ideas about salvation. In small groups have your students brainstorm everything they have heard about salvation, true or not, valid or not, whether they personally believe it or not. Write all of this on a dry-erase board. Some students will feel like they need to only say "church" answers that can leave some questions unasked. You will then have a false sense of security regarding your students understanding. So, help the students to open up about this matter.

Discovery

Let your students know that they are going to look at some of the myths surrounding salvation. Ahead of time, type-up the following list. Cut the list into strips and pass these out to small groups. It is fine for them to have more than one. If your group is large, have more than one small group look up the same passage.

Myth
It is not necessary to openly be a Christian in this world. —Matthew 10:32-33

Myth
God only loves some people. —John 3:16

Myth
I need to get saved repeatedly. —John 3:16

Myth
It is possible to be too bad a person for God to love you. —Romans 3:23

Myth

God only loves good people who have their lives together. —Romans 5:8

Myth

Sin doesn't have any real consequences. —Romans 6:23

Myth

We must earn our salvation. —Romans 6:23

Myth

Faith in God is a private affair that should not be communicated out loud.
—Romans 10:9–10

Myth

God loves and will therefore save everyone automatically. —Romans 10:13

Myth

Being a Christian is about following rules. —Galatians 2:15–21

Myth

We can work our way to salvation. —Ephesians 2:8–9

Myth

God only wants to have a relationship with certain people. —1 Timothy 2:3–4

Myth

It is enough to believe God exists, you don't have to follow Him. —James 2:19

TEACHER'S NOTE

This is a good night to have a concordance or other materials with you. While your students are looking up these passages and addressing the myth presented, you may need such resources to consider the perspectives they have offered. Be certain you have at least one leader if not two not assigned to each group to work on this.

After a few minutes go over each myth and what your students learned in each passage. Take your time. Some will be very cut and dried. Others may open up new questions. This is not a race. Take time to talk through each one and its tangents. Don't forget to address any of the major ideas surrounding salvation from your own list on the board.

Life Application

- According to what you have just heard, who needs salvation?
- Why do we as a society so resist the love that God has for us?
- Why do individuals resist the love God desires to pour on us?

Making it Personal

This is going to take patience and prep work but the result is well worth it.

A large sheet of butcher paper will be the easiest to use for this, though you could substitute poster board if you need to. Follow these steps:

Like making a woven placemat, cut two sheets of paper into strips. One sheet of paper is to be cut from left to right and the other sheet from top to bottom.

Weave a giant mat and tape the edges with painter's tape that won't rip the paper when you remove it. Draw on this woven mat a picture of the cross on a hill or, if someone is a fairly good artist, draw a picture of the face of Christ. The drawing is better if the lines are simple and broad but you will need lines on several strips of paper (at least one for every person present).

Number the strips across the top and down one side so that you can re-create the picture after taking apart the weaving.

Take apart the weaving.

Pass out the strips of paper being certain that there is a line from the drawing on each.

Give a few moments to your students, perhaps playing a song in the background. Ask them to consider their relationship with God. Have them write a few words on the line on their strip of paper telling where they would like to be in their life with the Lord or what they need to give to God.

After a few moments, gather the strips of paper back.

Follow the numbers on the tops and sides and re-weave your paper. The picture will reform with slightly thicker lines as the lines are now made of words.

TEACHER'S NOTE

You may want to consider an invitation to salvation at this time. Don't belabor the point, but ask if anyone wants to hear more about what it is to follow Jesus. Be certain you are prepared to lead someone to the Lord and that your leaders are prepared. The Holy Spirit does the saving but this can make some people nervous if they've never done it before.

Close in prayer thanking God for His wonderful gift of salvation.

Songs

"I surrender all" by Matt Papa

"Promise of a lifetime" by Kutlass on *Hearts of the Innocent*

What Does the Lord Require of You?

by Amy Jacober

Memory Verse

He has told you, O mortal, what is good; and what does the Lord require of you but to do justice, and to love kindness, and to walk humbly with your God? —Micah 6:8

Scripture

John 4:7–30

Lesson in a Sentence

Salvation is the most precious gift we can ever receive.

Focus

Ask for four volunteers. Tell each they will be in a whistling contest and to choose a song that the group will try to guess the title. Just before they begin, hand each person six saltine crackers and tell them to put all of the crackers in their mouth at the same time before proceeding. Give them a chance to try and whistle. If you have a student who can do it, give him or her another two crackers.

Offer water to each whistler.

Most of us have been thirsty. Has anyone in your group ever been thirsty and not been able to get a drink? What would they do for water at that time?

Discovery

Read John 4:7–30 out loud. You can either ask for volunteers or arrange this ahead of time. You will need three readers: Jesus, a narrator, and the woman. The passage makes it clear who reads when.

After the reading, break the students up into groups of four each. Ask each group to re-read the passage and come up with one sentence to convey the message they think is being presented.

Share these sentences out loud with the other groups.

Application

Does this passage have anything to do with our lives today? Most of us are never so thirsty that we are desperate for water. There are drinking fountains, sinks, water hoses, and other ways to get water almost anywhere. This passage however is not just about water.

- How does this passage relate to all of the scripture and myths from the last lesson?
- What else can we learn from the woman at the well?

This is a great time for your students to get to know you or one of your leaders a little better. Have one of your leaders share their testimony of when and how they came to know the Lord. Talk of what it meant to finally understand and accept Jesus as the living water.

Service Option

Water is vital for life. While you are talking of living water in this lesson, actual water is certainly a part of the discussion. When we enter into a relationship with Christ, we realize that we are not isolated in this world. Consider ways of giving that would help others around the world to have both living and regular water. Check out World Vision's web site for ways of getting clean, safe drinking water to those in need around the world. If you are feeling ambitious, consider leading your church in a campaign to help fund the digging a well for a community in need.

Intimacy with God in Prayer

by Matthew Freeman

In this lesson, students will:
- ✔ Understand the immense love of God for us that He would prepare the heavens to hear our prayers.
- ✔ Understand that God does not merely listen from on high, but causes physical changes in the world in response to them.
- ✔ Come to a deeper reverence and respect for the gift of prayer and the effect our prayers have in this world.

Memory Verse

Hear my prayer, O God; Give ear to the words of my mouth. —Psalm 54:2

Scripture

Revelation 8:1–5

Lesson in a Sentence

God cares about our prayers and responds to them.

The Big Picture

This passage demonstrates that God cares about our prayers. He is willing to silence the heavens to hear them. He cares so much about them that He preps for holy warfare before we even pray and responds mightily to the prayers. The prayers themselves are mixed with incense from the alter in this passage, signifying that one does not need to worry about the eloquence of a prayer. To them are added whatever is necessary to make them pleasing to the Almighty God.

Focus

Option 1—for Small Youth Groups

Have everyone gather in in a circle. Make sure everyone can see each other. Go around the room and have each person tell their high point and low point for the week—their Hi/Lo.

After everyone has said their Hi/Lo ask them if they have prayed to God about both their highs and lows. Start them in prayer and then give them a few minutes to silently thank God for the good things this week and pray about the bad things. Close in prayer and have them gather back into one group for the lesson.

Option 2—for Larger Groups

Have everyone break up into small groups. Make sure everyone can see each other. Then encourage each person tell their high point and low point for the week—their Hi/Lo. After everyone has said their Hi/Lo, ask them if they have prayed to God about both their highs and lows. Start them in prayer and then give them a few minutes to silently thank God for the good things this week and pray about the bad things. Close in prayer and have them gather back into one group for the lesson.

Lesson

In this passage, we enter in to the throne room of God. It is a magnificent and frightening experience. To help them get a sense of what it would be like to be thrust into the throne room of God, encourage them to close their eyes and help them see in their minds what this experience would be like. The following is formed from images in Isaiah 6:1-4 and Revelation 4:1–11:

> Imagine seeing the Glorious God Almighty of infinite size and scope; A consuming presence, full of majesty and terrible power; Peals of thunder rolling forth from His presence, high and lifted up on His magnificent throne. His very presence shakes the foundations of the temple and His power extends like the train of a robe, filling all of the heavens and the earth!

> Above fly seraphim. These are creatures of fire with six wings. In a show of humility, two wings cover their face, two wings cover their body, and two wings fly declaring the holiness of God!

> Before Him are the twenty-four elders on their thrones, crowned with golden crowns of mighty power. But in the awe, they fall before Him in complete submission, casting down their crowns at his feet!

Discovery

This section is designed in a Q & A format to help the group discover these truths through analyzing the text. Answers are provided to some of the questions; however, these are not the only correct answers. This passage is rich with imagery that allows for multiple possibilities.

Have someone read Revelation 8:1—"When He opened the seventh seal, there was silence in heaven for about half an hour."

Teacher's Note
Scrolls with seals were common in the Greco-Roman world. This kind of sealed scroll was used for things such as law documents, contracts, and wills. Often the seals would be broken when whatever was in the document was about to be put into effect. This scroll is first introduced in Revelation 5:1-7. Jesus is also spoken of in this passage as a slain lamb. This may suggest that the author wanted the imagery here to represent a will that was now about to take effect, due to the sacrifice of Jesus for all mankind. However, that is of no consequence to the central theme of this lesson.

Q. As scary as all of the peals of thunder and earthquakes are in this view of heaven, can you imagine the spine tingling chill when everything falls silent?

Q. What exactly is He silencing here?
A. The rightful praise of His own name!

Have someone read Revelation 8:2—"And I saw the seven angels who stand before God, and to them were given seven trumpets."

Teacher's Note
Jewish tradition of this time understood there to be seven archangels. This verse is probably a reference to the seven archangels.

Q. How powerful would you have to be to be able to stand in the presence of God?

Q. How did God create the universe?
A. By speaking it into existence. Sound is often associated with announcements and movements of military and sovereign power.

Q. The seven chief angels are given seven trumpets. What are they preparing for?
A. Warfare.

Have someone read Revelation 8:3–4—"Then another angel, having a golden censer, came and stood at the altar. He was given much incense, that he should offer it with the prayers of all the saints upon the golden altar which was before the throne. And the smoke of the incense, with the prayers of the saints, ascended before God from the angel's hand."

Q. What was the occasion for God to silence heaven and prepare His greatest angels for warfare?
A. Our prayers.

Q. What happens to the prayers before they ascend before God?
A. They are mixed with incense from the altar. They are made sweet smelling or pleasing to God.

Q. What does that tell us about how to pray?
A. We don't have to worry how eloquent our prayers are. We can just talk to God and they will be made pleasing before Him.

Q. So far, we see our prayers ascending before God. Is it enough for Him to just hear them? What if He never responded to them? Would it be worth praying?

Have someone read Revelation 8:5—"Then the angel took the censer, filled it with fire from the altar, and threw it to the earth. And there were noises, thunderings, lightnings, and an earthquake."

Q. Do the hosts of heaven only listen to these prayers or do they also act?

Q. How exactly do they act?
A. They take holy fire from the altar and throw it to the earth, causing terrifying results. In essence, they respond in a holy, but explosive manner.

Q. So, does God merely hear our prayers?
A. No, He also acts in response to them in extreme ways.

Teacher's Note
The sounding of the seven trumpets, which rocks all of creation, follows this passage!

Q. Did God take action before or after the prayers came up to Him?
A. Both.

Q. What did God do before the prayers were sent to Him?
A. He silenced heaven and prepared his greatest angels for great response.

Q. What happened after the prayers were sent to Him?
A. They were responded to in an exceptional manner.

Q. If God is willing to silence heaven, prep for war, and respond to our prayers, what should that mean for our prayer lives?

Life Application
Encourage them to share a time when they prayed and God acted mightily in response.

Making it Personal
Encourage them to take a few minutes at the end of each day this week to look back on their day and pray for at least two things that happened which may require prayer.

Quotable Quotes

To be a Christian without prayer is no more possible than to be alive without breathing.
—Martin Luther King, Jr.

Looking ahead this week

Next week is See You At The Pole (SYATP). This is a student-initiated time to pray for schools, community, and country. By now, you should have been talking about this with your students. It's still not too late! All it takes is a little conversation and meeting before school to pray. As you do this, you will be joining thousands of other teenagers all across this country and even around the world! Check out their website at *www.syatp.com.*

Intimacy with God in Prayer

by Matthew Freeman

Memory Verse

Hear my prayer, O God; Give ear to the words of my mouth. —Psalm 54:2

Scripture

Philippians 4:6–7

Lesson in a Sentence

Do not worry about your life, but rather pray and God will give you the peace of Christ.

Focus

Repeat the Hi/Lo exercise from the previous lesson. This time, have someone else pray for the person, instead of the person praying for him or herself. This will help to encourage the group to pray for the needs of other people.

Discovery

This week we were reminded of how much God cares about our prayers and how powerfully they are answered. Therefore, since we know that God stoops low to hear our prayers, and responds mightily to them, let us be at peace in knowing that God has our back and, instead of worrying, we should pray to Him in all we do.

Read Philippians 4:6–7 as a group. Re-read this passage in groups of three or four. Instruct each group to put in their own words what they think this passage is saying.

Life Application

Why do we get so anxious about life since scripture tells us not to? Talk about the realities of anxiety in their daily lives. Have them write down three things they worry about and then take some time for silent prayer, encouraging them to take those things to God. Afterwards have them tear up and toss the paper away, resting in the peace of Christ to respond to their needs.

Quotable Quotes

No one is a firmer believer in the power of prayer than the devil; not that he practices it, but he suffers from it. —Guy H. King

Get Rich and Die Trying

by Ben Donley

In this lesson, students will:
- ✔ Understand the costs of living for and loving god-money
- ✔ Realize what God wants them to pursue
- ✔ Learn what generosity and contentment means

Stuff you'll need:
- ❏ Song and lyrics sheets: "Head like a Hole" by Nine Inch Nails
- ❏ Song and lyrics sheets: "Such a Rush" by Coldplay
- ❏ Picture of 50 Cent's *Get Rich Or Die Tryin'* CD cover
- ❏ An eating clip from the Fear Factor television show
- ❏ Two quarters wrapped into a little box
- ❏ A disgusting homemade juice concoction poured into two glasses. (An example ingredient list: Wheat grass, sardines, tapioca pudding, pickle juice, crushed dog biscuits, and carbonated water.)
- ❏ Pens and paper
- ❏ Monopoly money

Memory Verse

No one can serve two masters. Either he will hate the one and love the other, or he will be devoted to the one and despise the other. You cannot serve both God and Money.
—Matthew 6:24 (NIV)

Scripture

1 Timothy 6: 8–11

Lesson in a Sentence

The love and pursuit of so-called god-money leads people away from the real God and towards destruction.

The Big Picture

It is one thing to have money and it is another to love money. Certainly, money is needed to pay for shelter, transportation, food, and everything else. But just because it has become a necessary piece of life does not mean that we should order our lives around getting more of it. In other words, our end goal in life should not be about getting rich. The Bible says in effect that life was not given to us so that we could waste it on pursuing stacks of green paper. Life was given to us so that we might chase after righteousness, godliness, faith, love, endurance, and gentleness.

Is this true? Yes. Do people live like it is true? No.

We live in a capitalist system that trains us to get as much money as we possibly can. Our culture teaches us that money gets you power, access, possessions, and security. The lack of money gets you stress and a dead-end life. The majority of us want the former and not the latter and so most of us devote ourselves to the god of money (god-money). And the more we want what money promises, the more time, energy and compromise we will give as sacrifice to this god.

Here is how it works for many people: If god-money wants us to move for a better job, we will move. If god-money wants us to give up family time for overtime at work, we work. If god-money tells us that we cannot afford to pay taxes, we lie and cheat to hold on to the green. If god-money tells us that we need to make more, then we do whatever it takes to make more, even if it means doing evil that crushes other people's lives. god-money turns our bottom lines into bank statements and turns us away from what the real God of the universe desires. Both God and god-money want everything that we have. Who are you going to trust?

I suggest that we get smart, read 1 Timothy 6, do what God suggests and ignore 50 Cent's world that advises us to get rich or die trying. Can we afford to ignore god-money? Yes, its advice is only worth as much as the value of Fiddy's name and listening to it will cause spiritual loss.

TEACHER'S NOTE

You can download the individual songs and/or the lyrics from a legal site online, if you don't own them already. As well, you can use the Internet to get the 50 Cent picture and the song lyrics. Check with your students to see if you can borrow their CD if they have it.

Focus

Option 1—Quarters

Tell the youth that you are going to show them a picture of a famous person and that you want them to tell you who the person is and what the name of their CD is. Tell them that they cannot just yell out—they have to raise their hand. The first one to raise their hand and get both answers correct, wins a prize.

When you are ready, hold up the 50 Cent picture and cover up the artist's name and CD title. Ask: Who is this? And what is the name of the CD? (Correct answers: 50 Cent and "Get Rich Or Die Tryin".) Call on the first person to raise their hand. Give the winner the wrapped gift of 2 quarters—have them open it and tell you what it is. It is of course, fifty cents, which will make the youth think you are ultra-cheesy.

Ask as few or as many of the following questions as you like: What do you think the name of this CD means? What message is 50 Cent trying to send about life's purpose? If someone took 50 Cent seriously, what might his or her life look like?

Option 2—Fear Factor

Show your group a five-minute clip from the TV show "Fear Factor" in which the participants eat some very nasty things. Ask: What is the main motivation for going on this show? What are they playing for? Let them respond. Say: People are motivated by money. It makes them do things that they would not normally do.

Now, bring out the two glasses of disgusting homemade juice and tell what the ingredients are. Ask: How about you? Would anyone volunteer to drink this stuff or will I have to motivate you with money? What about for five dollars? For ten dollars? For twenty dollars? Allow these volunteers to compete for the monetary prize. Whoever finishes their juice first, wins the money. If possible, present it to them in an airsickness bag. (If you only have one volunteer, then you be the other brave competitor. If there are no youth volunteers, then you grab one of your helpers and go up against them for the cash prize.)

Discovery

Say: Tonight we are going to talk about what the Bible says about the dangers of seeking money and getting rich. Read 1 Timothy 6:8–11, break into small groups and have them discuss the following questions:
- What happens to people who want to get rich?
- How might someone who wants to get rich be tempted? Get trapped? Give in to foolish desires?
- How does the love of money act as the root of all kinds of evil? What does it mean to be the root of something? What kinds of evil grow out of this love of money. What are people willing to do to get money?
- What is the relationship between loving money and being a Christian?
- According to these verses, what should a person who follows God do with their time? What does it mean to flee? What does it mean to "pursue"?

Life Application

Say: Money is important in our world. Without it, life is incredibly hard. Ask: What do we need money for? (Take responses) Say: Just because money allows us to buy shelter, food, transportation, clothes, and deodorant, does not mean that it is the most important thing in the world. And it does not mean that we should spend our lives trying to get as much of it as we can. Ask the following questions:
- Why do you think people want to get rich?
- What does having a lot of money get you in this world?
- How do people get rich?
- Who are some rich people that you can think of? Do you think they are happy or sad? What leads you to believe that? Does money buy happiness?

Optional

Tell the youth a story about someone you have heard about who attained riches and was still terribly unhappy. There are many stories like this. Check out VH-1's "Behind the Music" or read the biographies of Hollywood stars and professional athletes. In these stories, you can often find the theme of seeking and finding riches followed by bouts of depression, substance abuse, and sometimes suicide.

Ask: What does this story tell you about the pursuit of riches?

Making it Personal

Say: God wants us to pursue one set of things while our culture tells us that the proper pursuit is money. If you pursue the things of God, it is going to mean you might suffer in the money department. If you pursue money, it is going to mean you might suffer in the God department.
- Which pursuit are you going to dedicate yourself to?
- How important is it for you to become rich? To become godly?
- What are practical ways that you can gain righteousness, godliness, faith, love, endurance, and gentleness? If you had these things, how would they benefit you?

Give them each a monopoly money dollar and have them write the memory verse on it. Tell them to keep it in their wallet as a reminder of this lesson. Close in prayer.

Get Rich and Die Trying

by Ben Donley

Memory Verse

No one can serve two masters. Either he will hate the one and love the other, or he will be devoted to the one and despise the other. You cannot serve both God and Money. —Matthew 6:24 (NIV)

Scripture

Matthew 6:24

Lesson in a Sentence

The love and pursuit of god-money leads people away from the real God and towards destruction.

Focus

Pop Songs

Say: We have been looking at what the Bible says about money. Tonight we are going to look at/interpret what some rich non-Christians have to say about it. Tell your group you are going to play them two songs that deal with the issue of money. Hand out pens and the lyrics sheets for both Nine Inch Nails' "Head Like A Hole" and Coldplay's "Such A Rush." Ask the group to follow along with the songs and to write what they think the artists are saying about money. Play the songs back to back.

Have the youth share any insights or interpretations. Ask: Why do you think that the NIN song keeps saying, "god-money?" What does god-money do to its followers and how does the singer respond? What is Coldplay's attitude towards getting rich/going after money?

Discovery

Read Matthew 6:24. Say: This verse, like the Nine Inch Nails song, says that money is like a god (god-money) and also like a master. It says that God and god-money are in competition for worship. The Coldplay song simply critiques rushing around to get money. Coldplay tells us that money might act like a master or a god that wants to be sought after, but that it really equals nothing.

Ask: How is money like a god? How do people worship god-money? How is god-money like a master? What are some examples of people obeying god-money? What are some radical things that people do for money? How do people get caught up the rush for money?

Give some of the examples from the Big Picture to fill in any answer gaps and then break them into small groups so that they can discuss the following questions:
- Why can't you serve two masters?
- What does it look like to serve God?
- What does it look like to serve money?
- What does it mean to be devoted to something? To despise something?

Life Application

Tell your group a story of when you either bowed down to god-money and allowed it to be your master or a story of when you refused to give it control. Or you can share with them about how you personally express devotion to God as your only master and how that has made a positive difference in your life.

Give the group an opportunity to respond similar examples from their lives.

Ask them to write down on a sheet of paper the following statement: "God is my master, not money." Then challenge them to take some of their money this week, tape it to this sheet and to give it away to a poor person or to a non-profit that serves the poor as a gesture of devotion to God.

Extra Extra!

See You At the Pole is this week. Don't forget to remind your students!

Identity in Christ

by Justin Little

In this lesson, students will:

- ✔ Memorize 1 John 3:1
- ✔ Discuss in small groups several ways we can be tempted to doubt our identity
- ✔ Be encouraged to pray against temptation using the memory verse

Stuff you'll need:

- ❑ Enough blindfolds, index cards, and pens for each member of the group.
- ❑ *The Lion King* DVD or VHS
- ❑ A large, open space

Memory Verse

Behold what manner of love the Father has bestowed on us, that we should be called children of God! Therefore, the world does not know us, because it did not know Him. —1 John 3:1

Scripture

Ephesians 1:3–14

Lesson in a Sentence

We have been given so much in Christ. We are blessed with every spiritual blessing, we have been adopted as children of God, and we have been sealed with the Holy Spirit.

The Big Picture

The mystery of our faith is that Christ dwells in us, and we are in Him. Therefore, in God's mercy, He has made us free "that we should be holy and without blame before Him in love" (Eph. 1:4). The trouble is that Christians easily forget who Christ is and in turn forget who they are. Christ was tempted three times in the wilderness and He resisted in faith (Matt. 4:5–11). We too are called to resist the devil (James 4:7), humble ourselves before God and believe that we are His purified children, free to worship and adore Him forever.

Focus

Play a clip from *The Lion King*—The scene that begins with Simba chasing Rafiki through the jungle climaxes with the dead Mufasa showing up in the clouds to talk with Simba and ends when Simba decides to return to Pride Rock. This scene is about 3/4 of the way through the movie. Start the clip in the middle of Simba chasing Rafiki, and end it while Simba is running through the desert back to Pride Rock.

After prayer, use the paragraph under "The Big Picture" (above) to introduce this lesson.

Discovery

Have the kids stand around the room blindfolded. Tell them to be silent throughout the activity.

Have two volunteers walk throughout the room telling the kids lies about their identity. For example, "You're worthless," "God doesn't love you," "You've messed up too much," "You're helpless," "Why would God waste time loving you?" etc. These "liars" represent the devil and the temptations he uses. Have the "liars" speak very convincingly, as friends.

Have two volunteers walk throughout the room at the same time, telling the kids the truth about their identity in Christ—"God loves you completely," "You are a forgiven child of God," "God has made you clean and worthy of His love," etc. The "truth-tellers" represent God's Holy Spirit. Have them speak in a loving tone, putting their hand on the shoulder of each student as they speak. They should speak softly and clearly and make sure the kids can hear them. For example, "Hey, pay attention to me, and I'll tell you who God has made you to be," or "Listen closely, because God has given me something to tell you."

After the activity, have the students get into small groups with one volunteer to lead the discussion.

Life Application

In the small groups, have the kids talk about how they were feeling and what they were thinking during the activity. Have the kids each come up with one lie that they or their peers have to face on a daily basis. For example, "You are only as good as your grades," "Only the popular kids matter," "God doesn't really love you because you aren't a good Christian," "God doesn't care about how you live your life," etc.

Pass out the note cards and pens and have them write the lies on the cards, drawing pictures or writing poems if they want to. Go around the circle and have each kid share their card. Then, have someone in the group read 1 John 3:1 out loud, and ask the group the following questions:

- As a child of God, what does it mean to me when I fail a test at school, get in a fight with my parents, or when someone hurts me?
- How should I treat other Christians since they are God's children?
- What about non-Christians? Does God want them to be His children too?

• What about the poor? Are they any different from the rich? How should we treat the rich and poor since we know that God loves them as much as He loves us?

Making it Personal

After the discussion, give the kids ideas of ways to serve their church and community. Explain to them how acts of love are the most effective communicators of the gospel of Jesus Christ. Then close the meeting with praise and worship.

Explain to the kids that they worship God as a response to what He has done for them—He made them His children. Tell them that volunteers will be available for prayer or they can pray with each other if they are struggling to believe that they are children of God. Encourage them to pray for friends and family who don't know that God wants them to be His children too.

Identity in Christ

by Justin Little

Memory Verse

How great is the love the Father has lavished on us, that we should be called children of God! And that is what we are! The reason the world does not know us is that it did not know him. —1 John 3:1

Scripture

Isaiah 62:1–5

Lesson in a Sentence

Do you know how much God has done for you? In Christ, He has given you a new name, He has made you a "crown of splendor", and He delights and rejoices over you.

Stuff you'll need:

- ❏ *The Return of the King* DVD or VHS
- ❏ Paper, pens, and colored pencils

Focus

Movie Clip

The Return of the King—the scene where King Aragorn bows to the four hobbits during the post-war celebration at Minas Tirith.

Discovery

Have the kids write a story, a song or a poem, draw a picture, or come up with a skit that shows how God has made us His children—princes and princesses of the King of Kings. They can work together or on their own for this. If they are willing, have the kids present their work to the group.

Life Application

Ask the kids questions about what being a prince or princess of God means for their daily lives.

- What decisions should they be making?
- How should they treat their parents?
- How should they do their homework, their chores, or treat their siblings?
- Should they be thankful to God every day?

Close in prayer.

Show and Tell—Applied Discipleship

by Ben Donley

Check out the Great Commission (Matt. 28:18–20). I did a while back and it forced me to rethink the way I do ministry. Right there at the end of it, Jesus makes it quite clear that he wants us to make disciples. That's right, you and I make disciples. Not entertained consumer-youth with good snowboarding trips and satisfied parents. Not Pharisee-like youth who burn Britney Spears CDs, denounce MySpace and get special awards for avoiding pregnancy and beer. Not clichéd youth who are equipped with pithy bumper-sticker Christianity and Republican platform shoes.

Nope. That's not the Great Commission.

Jesus wants disciples and he wants us to make them for him. Cool. So, what do we do with this?

Well, before we can make one, we first need to know what a Christian disciple is. Christian disciples have committed themselves not only to Jesus as Savior, but also to Jesus as Lord. Christian disciples are dedicated followers of Christ who, with the help of the Holy Spirit, attempt to put Jesus' words into practice and live up to the Biblical expectation to do what Jesus did. Simply put, Christian disciples are imitators of Jesus who might get mistaken for their Master.

Now that we have this definition established, how can we leaders help make such persons? In other words, how can we develop a population of sold-out disciples, radicals who do not conform to the world but who instead transform whatever community they enter?

I have a few ideas:

Idea #1—Tell Your Youth the Truth about Jesus

Let your kids know what Christianity really is—Explain the expectations—Reveal the high costs of discipleship—Remove the sugar coating—Warn them like Jesus warned his disciples—Sit them down like Morpheus did with Neo and explain the difficulty of the red pill versus the ease of the blue pill—Better yet, have them stare at a cross for a day or two and see if they are interested in carrying such heavy spiritual luggage through the airport of life—Basically, tell them that following Jesus happens on a narrow road and requires everything they have.

Why be so honest?

Jesus was honest with his followers. He did not wait a while before he told them how hard it was going to be. He just told it like it was. Shouldn't we do the same?

I believe that youth are sick of being fine-printed. They do not want some soft version of the truth. They prefer the whole of it, as it is, magnified for their discomfort. The kids I know don't appreciate being told that it's all a salvation game and then later find out that it's really a soldier's battle. You have to tell them straight up. And the ones who see it all as it really is and who still commit are the ones who can be trained.

Now you might think this honesty will shrink your ministry. In sheer numbers it probably will for a while. But, while attendance and parental happiness might suffer for a time, impact and ministry will increase. So, tell them the truth, ask for volunteers in this radical journey and begin training them.

Idea #2—Train Them Using Jesus' Model of Applied Discipleship

When you start training your students, do not just tell them how to imitate Jesus, *show* them how to imitate Jesus. In other words, do not sit around in a comfortable house with chips and dips, study the Greek versions of what Jesus said and did and then send your youth out week after week with the hope that they try Christianity out in their high school.

No. No. Bad Pastor.

Explaining it just teaches them how to explain it. This is not the goal. Jesus wants them to actually do it. And you are going to have to be the one who gets them started. That's right, you are the one who will have to take these Jesus-followers out of their upper rooms and into the real world. You are the one who is going to show them how it is done and then ask them to repeat what they have just seen. You are modeling Christianity.

Generally, this can be done by looking over scripture, determining what areas of action Jesus holds close to his heart, and then creatively acting on them. But let's get specific, shall we?

Specific supermodel examples:
Jesus wants us to feed the hungry, clothe the naked and overall care for the poor.

There is no better way to embed this command than to take your group into a setting where they can do mercy. There are lots of options for this. Two simple ideas: you can head for a homeless shelter to feed, clean, and spend the night. Or, even better you can take them to meet a homeless person and show them how to love someone who is needy. Talk about Matthew 25, Isaiah 58, and the struggle of poverty as you do these field trips. Ask your youth to try and put themselves in the shoes of the people they meet and to imagine that everyone they meet is Jesus.

Jesus wants us to be witnesses to a lost world.

First I recommend that you help these disciples know how to have an encounter with God so that they can witness about a Being they have personally experienced. Second, you should take them to a spot where you have been a regular for a while—a place where non-Christians hang out where you have become known. Let your group see how you have built loving and trusting relationships with unbelievers. Let them see that it is possible to be a Jesus-follower and in relationship with non-Jesus followers. Explain to them how this relational foundation is key to being an effective witness. Maybe even engage someone you know in a spiritual interview. Ask them lots of questions and let them share their God-thoughts, struggles and questions. After a while, your group can choose their own regular spot and know how to witness relationally because they saw you do it.

Jesus wants us to be filled with the Holy Spirit and be spiritually formed.

This is not a call to be a PTL Club charismatic, but you'd better model spiritual full-ness. Fruits of the Spirit need to be popping out of your apple tree. Gifts of the Spirit should be plentiful under your Christmas tree. And the manifestations of the Spirit should be apparent as you engage in spiritual warfare. Take your youth out to deliver and heal. Let them use their faith and the authority that has been given to them to impact those who are spiritually poor. To form them spiritually, lead them in praise, meditation, confession, thanksgiving, intercession and scripture prayer. Show them how to deepen their relationship with the Father and the Son through the Holy Spirit. This is not popcorn prayer time, it is real seeking and finding that will benefit them for life.

I am being long-winded—let me just make two more points and I will leave you with the the Gospels as a better guide.

Jesus wants us to take care of widows and orphans.

Gather your students and get yourselves to a nursing home and an orphanage and figure out what it looks like to care for the cast-aside. Relocation to where these popu-lations are will do wonders for application possibilities.

Jesus wants us to sell off our possessions, give to the poor, and live simply.

Yes, you be the first to sell some of your treasures and adopt some Compassion International kids. Show them that material goods are not that important and let them see what it means to trade stuff for poverty aid.

Is anyone still reading?

I could go on and on, but I won't. I am not being paid by the word and you are not morons. Let me sum this up: Relocate your youth to the outside world. Help them learn to read, simply obey, and apply their faith. Struggle with them as they do their Christianity. It is train and do—on the job discipleship—show and tell. I suggest meet-ing inside once a week and then taking Jesus' words outside the next week. Show them that faith is practical and not theoretical. This will save them a lot of seminary money later.

A Personal Story:

When I was younger and had the guts to do this kind of discipleship, the group shrank some. But the people who bought into applied discipleship became actual followers whom God used to change lives. There were healings, deliverances, salvations, and about seventy-five percent of those involved went on to become full-time ministers. When word got out about this, others in the city decided to join us. They too wanted to be like Jesus and they needed someone to show them and not tell them.

Now it is your turn to be that model. It is a challenge, but it is fun and it is your job.

Dealing with Dishonesty

by Amy Jacober

In this lesson, students will:
- ✔ Consider the consequences of lying
- ✔ Discuss the problems of living honestly
- ✔ Consider why those who are dishonest often win and how to handle this
- ✔ Thank God for clear directions on this subject
- ✔ Seek God's help to live in this radical way

Stuff you'll need:
- ❏ Skit copied and practiced beforehand
- ❏ *Win a Date with Tad Hamilton* video or DVD

Memory Verse
A false witness will not go unpunished, and he who speaks lies will not escape.
—Proverbs 19:5

Scripture
1 Kings 21:1–24
2 Kings 9:1–13, 30–37

Lesson in a Sentence
God is not messing around when He says we are to be honest.

The Big Picture
Honesty seems to be a relative term today. It is optional by the world's standards. Copying papers from the internet is professed to be research. Kissing someone other than the person you are dating is "no big deal." Taking steroids or drugs to achieve the look you want is masked as supplementing what God gave you. Manipulating circumstances for your own advantage is considered being wise and resourceful. We see falsehood in movies, and on TV, hear it in songs, have it glorified by the celebrities in our country, and we see it lived every day.

Living in the truth is completely counter-cultural. In fact, it may be so difficult at first that many slips will occur. It goes against the grain of what the world expects of you because you are playing by different rules. That said, this is not an optional way of living. God is clear, we are not to lie; not even a little bit. In this issue, we must choose whom we will serve. Being totally honest means that you may miss out on some things because lies often win in the short run. Truthfulness is a difficult lifestyle. Still, invite your students to live so that truth reigns supreme.

Focus

Option 1—Dishonesty Skit
by Jacqueline Eleanor Foreman

In a School Hallway

Elizabeth—(Entering; Some friends are present.) Hey you guys guess what I discovered about myself today?!

Victoria—That sleeping with your blanket is no longer cool… It is so Kindergarten!

Friends (Laugh at the joke)

Elizabeth—Ha, ha, ha. Not funny. What I found out was how smart I really am. You know our English teacher Mrs. Spencer? Well, she told us to read "The Taming of the Shrew" by William Shakespeare, and you know how good I am with words? I remembered that I saw the movie "10 Things I Hate About You." So, what I did was put together what I remembered about the movie and some of the information she has been teaching about how Shakespeare writes. I even found all this stuff on the Internet. That made that five-page paper she wanted so easy, and I didn't even read Shakespeare's play! And could you believe it I received an A on that paper.

Samantha—(Sarcastically) Wow! I wish I could have discovered something that unique about myself.

Friends Snicker

Elizabeth—Well I just wanted to tell you how smart and clever I am. I still amaze myself. Talk to you guys at lunch have fun in math. (walks away)

Later, in Math Class

Katherine—Hey, you guys, what do you think about what Elizabeth said on how smart she is? Doesn't it seem like she's just a big cheater and not really smart? Talk about deceitful!

Victoria—Are you kidding?! I say if you can get away with it, go for it! I wish I had the guts to be that smart.

Samantha—I don't care what you say, eventually this will catch up with her and probably in a way that she won't even realize. Not to mention that she's really great in English. There is no reason for her to not be able to read a book and do a great job on that assignment.

Katherine—I think we should tell her at lunch that we don't think what she did was smart. It makes us all look bad when she's supposedly the smartest girl in our class but gets there by cheating, lying, or even making up her answers. I know she's going to be ticked but if we really are her friends, we can't let her think this is OK.

The End

Option 2

Show a clip from *Win a Date with Tad Hamilton*. At the very end of the movie, Tad (the Hollywood star) confesses to Rosie (a small town girl who won a date with him) that he had been dishonest with her. She realizes that the long time friend back home, while not famous, was a much better catch than the deceitful Hollywood hunk. Begin viewing the clip where Rosie is getting out of the cab and run to the end of the movie.

Discovery

Dishonesty is all around us. One of the best-known stories of deceit is found in 1 and 2 Kings. This is the reason why no one names a daughter Jezebel today.

Read 1 Kings 21:1–24 aloud. As you read, ask these questions:
- Who was Ahab?
- Who was Jezebel?
- What did Ahab want?
- How did Jezebel arrange to get it?
- Who was Elijah?
- What message did he bring?
- What was supposed to happen to Ahab and Jezebel? Why?

In groups of three or four have your students read 2 Kings 9:1–13, 30–37.
- A new man is anointed as King, who was he?
- What was he to do to Ahab's house?
- What did Jezebel try to do upon hearing he was coming and at the arrival of Jehu?
- What finally happened to Jezebel?

TEACHER'S NOTE:

The name *Jezebel* has become an epithet typically hurled at a woman. The name connotes a person who is morally unrestrained or shameless. Jezebel used any means to get what she wanted. One might say she was willing to go to any length to help those she loved, which can seem honorable. God did not find her actions honorable regardless of the motivation behind them.

Lead a discussion about well-known people who are shameless in their pursuit of what they want. We needn't look far in our world today to find such examples. Don't forget to remind your students to not talk about people they know at school to avoid this from being a big gossip session.

Life Application

In the same groups, come up with arguments for and against this statement: "Lying should never be allowed".

Discuss

- How are Christians supposed to make it in a world where the unwritten rules almost demand lying at times yet, God tells us it is not acceptable?
- What consequences do you really think come with lying?
- Do you think that eventually the consequences will come?
- How do you handle being lied to?

Have each person write on a strip of paper a way or time they think lying is OK. Use those strips of paper to create a paper chain and place this in a central location in your meeting room.

Making it Personal

- What part of this lesson hit home for you?
- Consider what dishonesty means to you. Why is being honest a struggle for some people?
- In what areas of life do you struggle to be honest?

Share with the group in this way: The burden of dishonesty is much stronger than this paper chain we made tonight. God gives us the strength and courage to live honestly but we must choose to take it. Philippians 4:13 says, "I can do all things through Christ." This includes being honest. We most often talk of the encouragement and blessings that God offers. These are true. Equally true is God's disgust with that which is not holy.

Memory Verse Activity

Dismantle the chain one link at a time and staple another strip to it with the memory verse. Hand a link out to each student and ask him or her to pray for the person who wrote on the link. They don't need to know the details, in fact the struggle written on the link may not be theirs, but God knows. Encourage them to read and re-read the memory verse, committing it to memory as a reality check for what God thinks of dishonesty.

Song

"Well Meaning Fiction" by Main Stay on *Well Meaning Fiction*

Dealing with Dishonesty

by Amy Jacober

Memory Verse

A false witness will not go unpunished, and he who speaks lies will not escape.
—Proverbs 19:5

Scripture

Romans 12:9–21

Lesson in a Sentence

God is not messing around when He says we are to be honest.

Focus

For this activity, use the following examples and add your own, typed-up in a worksheet to distribute to your students. Tell your students they have five to ten minutes to get as many of these answered as possible; put the initials of each person who responds next to their answer; each person may answer no more than two questions at a time. The catch is this: Instruct three or four students to lie on every single question they are asked. They don't need to be consistent, just believable. If their own best friend is asking the questions, instruct him or her to respond with "you already know the answer to that question, ask me another question".

- How well do you know [name of person]?
- What is your favorite color?
- Where were you born?
- How many brothers and sisters do you have?
- What do you want to be when you grow up?
- What really disgusts you?
- What is your favorite childhood memory?
- What scares you?
- What food do you never want to taste?
- Where in the world would you visit if money were no object?
- Do you sing in the shower? If yes, what songs?
- If you could have a super power, what would it be?
- What is your favorite ice cream flavor?
- Who in your family are you the most like?
- What part of yourself would you change?
- If someone famous were going to play you in a movie, whom would you choose?
- Would you rather be president or vice president of the United States?

- How many continents do you think there are?
- With what country is Samoa associated?
- If you could be famous for one talent, what would it be?
- If you were a vegetable, what would it be?
- Who do you admire?
- What is your favorite Bible story?
- What is your favorite worship song or hymn?
- What is your favorite movie?

Call time and ask who has the most questions answered. Offer a prize to the person with the highest count. Movie passes, a CD, or gift certificate are always good. Just before you give the prize, tell your students you have one more thing to cover.

Ask your liars to come to the front. Tell the group that each of these people lied for every answer they gave. Give their initials and if they answered a question on someone's sheet, that question does not count. This should change the winner. Give the prize to the new winner. For some people this is hard to do because it is so unfair, but that is the point.

Ask if anyone is annoyed? Anyone feel cheated or betrayed? Why? This was just a game. How do they feel when they find out they have been deceived in real life?

Discovery

Romans 12:9–21

Dealing with dishonesty and those who hurt us is hard. Unfortunately, God does not accept that as a reason nor an excuse for hurting others.

Check out Romans 12:9-21. This reads like one big long list of what to do when life doesn't work out as we had hoped. It admonishes us to honor the Lord even when we have been wronged.

In pairs, read through this passage. Give each pair a sheet of paper and a pen. On one side of the paper, have each pair write what they think is easy or possible in this passage and what in this passage is just not going to happen—beyond what is humanly possible.

Life Application

What the heck do we do with a passage like this?

Divide your group in half. Give one half the position of arguing why we are to live our lives just as this passage says, no questions asked. Why there is no compromise and indeed this is what God meant, literally. Give the other half the position of arguing that this was not really what God intended. When it is possible, when it is comfortable, these are good guidelines but not always necessary. Let them know that if they need to promote deceit or refer to other scriptures out of context to prove their point that it is fine.

Which group was made a more solid argument? How do we handle the issues that were brought up?

Before you end, read back over the passage with the entire group ensuring them that this is what God meant. With His help, we can handle those who hurt us and attack them in the same way.

TEACHER'S NOTE

For some of your students this may be more difficult than others. Some have been deeply wounded by those who were supposed to care for them. Some feel abandoned and lost. Do not negate these feelings. They will need to work through them. This lesson can offer an alternative to their simply being hurt and victimized. It does not mean the anger and hurt will go away instantly but it can be the beginning to a more healthy way of handling difficult issues.

What Was I Made to Do?

by Sharon Koh

In this lesson, students will:
- ✔ Have the opportunity to reframe their understanding of work
- ✔ Embrace work as useful and wonderful activity
- ✔ Offer their work to God

Memory Verse

Whatever you do, work at it with all your heart, as working for the Lord, not for men.
—Colossians 3:23

Scripture

Genesis 1:26–31; Genesis 2:15–16

Lesson in a Sentence

From the moment we were placed in the garden humankind was to work and given the mandate to "be fruitful and increase in number; fill the earth and subdue it."

The Big Picture

Many of us see work as an unpleasant activity: We go to school so that we can get good jobs that help us make money. If we didn't need money, we wouldn't work. We think we would prefer a lazy aimless existence. However, upon taking another look at the creation story, it becomes evident that work was part of God's plan for humankind's very existence. God created humankind in His own image and immediately asked them to be fruitful. It seems that a huge part of our existence is tied into our ability to work. Adam's fall away from God made work an unpleasant thing (Genesis 3:17-19).

Focus

This lesson will offer an interesting opportunity to consider what life would be like with no work. Around the world, many people desire the opportunity to work and that opportunity is not available to them. Many developing nations do not have the economy to support proper employment rates, and so people who were created to work languish by the wayside. Depending on the maturity of your group and the resources available, this lesson can include a field trip to tour a local rescue mission or homeless shelter. If this is too difficult to arrange, perhaps a video from such a shelter would suffice to expose students life without work.

After the exposure described above, gather students together to talk about what they saw and how they felt. There may be quite a range of observations and feelings, so allow students plenty of time to reflect on what may have been an overwhelming experience. If issues like poverty or injustice arise, let the students have the time to discuss their thoughts. However, as the conversation draws to a close, guide it so that students consider life without work. Offer them the opportunity to discover that many people would like to work and are unable to do so.

Discovery

Reframe the concept of work as a positive one. In many ways, work is something that needs to be reclaimed. Students see parents and other adults complaining about work. A popular bumper sticker reads, "I owe, I owe, so off to work I go!" Thus, society communicates an ethos of distaste for work. The present lesson is an attempt to reclaim the biblical and godly purposes of work—it brings satisfaction and purpose. We were made to work.

Have students make a list of all the activities that they are involved in that constitute work—chores, homework, physical activity, relationships, etc. Have them share with one another what positive thing they would miss in life if this activity were to cease—a clean living space, a proper education, a body that functions well, the opportunity to have and be a friend, etc.

Life Application
Review the memory verse, Colossians 3:23, and have students prayerfully thank God for the opportunity to work.

Additional Resources
Ephesians 4:28

Bakke, Dennis W. Joy at Work. *http://www.dennisbakke.com*. There are some excellent video downloads available at this website that youth leaders could view before the lesson. He essentially makes this lesson's point about work and God's purposes for work.

Work How Should I Apply Myself?

by Sharon Koh

Memory Verse
And we pray this in order that you may live a life worthy of the Lord and may please him in every way: bearing fruit in every good work, growing in the knowledge of God.
—Colossians 1:10

Scripture
Romans 12:1–2

Lesson in a Sentence
We must live our lives unto God as living sacrifices offered up in worship.

Focus
Split into three teams and have each team create a list of the top ten jobs they would not want to have. Give five minutes or so and then have each team share with the group. Offer a prize to the team with the best list of bad jobs.

Ask: Why do we not want these jobs? Are they necessary to life? Does anyone else find it odd that many so-called good jobs are actually not needed but the bad jobs are? We need garbage collectors, sewer workers, harvesters, etc. What we don't need are party planners, sun tanners, doggie day spa workers, or cell phone decorators.

God doesn't want us to be miserable in our work, but what does it mean to be truly called and serve Him in all you do (Colossians 3:23)?

Discovery
Read Romans 12:1–2 with students and ask the following questions:
- What is the motivation for offering oneself as a living sacrifice? (God's mercy)
- Are sacrifices typically alive or dead? (In the Old Testament, they were dead.)
- So, why is it strange to read about a living sacrifice?
- How does this impact our understanding of how we work?

Application
Have students revisit their earlier lists of all their activities that constitute work. This time, ask them to consider how each thing on their list might be a spiritual act of worship. This is an abstract question, so allow students some time to reflect on how the things they do might be offered to God.

Sexuality and the Body

by Christine Kern

In this lesson, students will:

✔ Recognize sexuality as God's gift, so sexuality is good
✔ Plan for ways to keep their hearts, minds, and bodies pure
✔ If they're struggling, be reunited with God and others through repentance

Stuff you'll need:

❑ Large sheet of paper, poster board, or a whiteboard
❑ Markers

OR

❑ Popular magazines
❑ Poster board
❑ Scissors
❑ Glue sticks
❑ Markers

Memory Verse

Since you have purified your souls in obeying the truth through the Spirit in sincere love of the brethren, love one another fervently with a pure heart. —1 Peter 1:22

Scripture

1 Corinthians 6:13b–20, 1 Peter 1:22, Hebrews 13:4

Lesson in a Sentence

God wants us to be sexually pure not because sexuality is bad, but because it's good and powerful enough to unite two people into one.

The Big Picture

God created the body, sexuality, and marriage, so sex is good. It's only negative when one uses another person sexually outside of a complete commitment to them. Using others or allowing others to use you abuses God's gift of the body.

Planning to keep sexuality pure will help you when you are tempted. If you have sinned the past or are struggling with sexuality, don't hide from God because of shame. Go to him for help and share your struggles with a Christian you trust.

Focus

Option 1—The Excuses Game

If you think your group is mature enough, list reasons or excuses that people will give to pressure someone into sexual involvement. Start them out with a few:

- We're going to be together forever anyway, so it's OK if we start now.
- Marriage is just a piece of paper; what matters is that we're committed to each other.
- This doesn't count as real sex.
- You've already gone this far, which does count as sex, so you have to go the rest of the way.
- You're not a virgin, so it doesn't make any difference if you have sex now. You're a hypocrite.
- Are you a freak? What if it's like ten years until you get married?
- I'll leave you if you won't.

Let the students add other excuses if they want to, then for each excuse or group of similar excuses have students come up with two sets of answers—biblical answers and answers worded in contemporary ways.

The point of this exercise is to prepare the students with a ready answer for the challenges that might come in their dating life. By thinking through it when they're not emotionally and physically involved, they have a better chance of intentionally aligning their actions with their faith.

Option 2—Portrayals of Sexuality Collage

Give each group of students several contemporary magazines, Christian and non-Christian. Have them cut out pictures demonstrating aspects of sexuality that do and do not fit with a godly respect for the body. Your students may discover how many times sexuality is used to sell something, and how seldom any healthy, godly sexuality between married people is depicted.

Discovery

Romans 6:11–22, 1 Thessalonians 4:3–8. Read the Romans passage, ask the following questions:

- According to this passage, are people who are sinning sexually free?
- Who is free?
- How can you be free if you're limiting yourself?

After reading the passage in Thessalonians, note verse 6 then move onto the next section.

Life Application

Divide the group into two groups and have each group list as many people as possible who are taken advantage of in a hypothetical act of sexual immorality and tell how this takes advantage of them. (Ideas: the person involved, their future spouse, etc.) You might even bring up issues of pornography—how does looking at a picture of someone hurt anyone?

George MacDonald, in his novel *The Tutor's First Love,* has a scene where the tutor has found his young student pulling a puppy's tail. He asked the student whether Jesus would have pulled the puppy's tail, and the boy said, "No." Then he asked why Jesus wouldn't have done it. The boy guessed, "Because it was wrong?" But the tutor disagreed. He said that Jesus wouldn't pull the puppy's tail not because pulling the tail was wrong but because He loved the puppy.

After telling this story, have the students go back over the list and suggest actions that would instead show love to the other person. Also, have them suggest actions for someone who feels stuck in sexual sin, such as going to a trusted older Christian, etc.

Making it Personal

Ask your students to spend a moment asking God to show them an area of their sexuality in which they could have freedom in Him:

- In his or her thought life?
- In wanting to use other people for pleasure instead of to love them?
- In trying to show love without respect for Christian limits for their bodies?
- In thinking of sexuality as bad instead of as God's gift?

Challenge them to pray silently, committing that part of their lives to God. At the end, pray for the students that they would appreciate the gift of their sexuality and accept the struggles of resisting sexual acts that allow another person to be used instead of loved.

Connections

Hebrews 4:15 is great memory verse. It says that Christ faced every temptation we face, but without sinning.

Sexuality and the Body

by Christine Kern

Memory Verse

Since you have purified your souls in obeying the truth through the Spirit in sincere love of the brethren, love one another fervently with a pure heart. —1 Peter 1:22

Scripture

Ephesians 5:28–33, 1 John 1:9

Lesson in a Sentence

Sin separates; Christ unites. Sex is a union that is so loving it mirrors Christ's union with the church.

Stuff you'll need:

❏ Super Glue (Use care with this!)
❏ Various objects to glue together—especially some that are harmed when they're ripped back apart. Try to include objects that will look funny when glued together: an old tennis shoe to an fruit, a plant leaf to a piece of paper.

Focus

Let the students choose which things should be glued together. After the glue has dried, have students try to rip apart the things that are glued together.

Make the point that God wants us united—glued—to himself, and that similarly, godly sexuality glues together a husband and wife. But that sin separates us. Sexual sin is to allow bonding where it doesn't belong and leads to destruction.

Discovery

Ask students to look for examples of separation and union in the Ephesians passage. Before they read 1 John 1:9, ask what Christians should do when they've sinned. Have them read the verse, and discuss how the idea of separation and coming together work with forgiveness.

Life Application

Think of Adam and Eve in the garden, once they'd eaten from the one tree: who was the one who could help them? God. But that's whom they hid from. The name for this is shame. If shame keeps us from going back to God, then we're losing out twice in a row, first by causing the separation in our relationship, then by staying in it.

Songs

"Create in Me a Clean Heart" by Keith Green

Stand up for What You Believe In

by Joe Usher and Amy Jacober

In this lesson, students will:
- ✔ Have an understanding that they are in a battle with the evil one and his forces
- ✔ Understand what the full armor consists of and how they put it on daily
- ✔ Believe that they are chosen by God to be a warrior for God and His purposes

Stuff you'll need:
- ❏ Foam balls
- ❏ Toy or costume armor
- ❏ Dry erase board and markers
- ❏ Dog tags

Memory Verse
Put on the whole armor of God, that you may be able to stand against the schemes of the devil. —Ephesians 6:11

Scripture
Ephesians 6:10–18

Lesson in a Sentence
When we live out our faith in Jesus we put on the full armor of God because we're in a battle with the spiritual forces of evil in the heavenly places.

The Big Picture
If you are a Christian then you are in a battle. You are initiated in this battle by the blood of the Lamb. The way to succeed in this battle against the evil one is to put on the armor that is our defense against the forces of evil. This sounds like Star Wars, I know, but don't be deceived by the devil that you are not a warrior for the kingdom in a battle for souls.

Focus

Option 1

Have as many foam balls as possible though there is no set amount required. Divide your group into at least two teams. Divide the room into as many sections as there are teams and give each team the same number of foam balls. Be certain you have clearly defined areas with each team having their own section. Have each person sit on the floor in his or her section. They may not move from the position they are in so they will want to be strategic in where each team member sits. When you say, "Go," have each team roll or throw the foam balls to the other sections. At the end the team with the least amount of balls in their section wins. Ask:

- Do you ever feel like you are fighting off things that just keep coming back at you?
- What helped the winning team win?
- What made it hard for the losing teams?
- What could have made it easier for your team?

Option 2

Check out a thrift store or even the costume closet of your church. Create a costume with the five pieces of armor mentioned in the passage. You could even make most of these with a little cardboard, aluminum foil, and imagination.

Create a mock fashion show. Feel free to make this either set as a biblical period fashion show complete with tunics, etc. Or, for an even more surprising turn, have it set in modern day with the exception of an armored soldier. The more you play this up the better. Music, a runway and an announcer explaining each fashion will lend to the impact.

Discovery

Break into groups of four. On a dry erase board have written the following: breastplate, foot coverings, shield, helmet, sword. If you are artistic, draw a soldier and label each piece of armor. Tell the students to discuss what they think each piece of armor did for the soldier. What would the battle be like for a soldier not having one or more of these pieces of armor?

Have each group read Ephesians 6:10–18. According to this passage, what is each piece of armor to do? Ask volunteers to explain what each piece of armor is to do and write this next to the armor on the dry erase board.

Looking back at the armor, point out that four of the five pieces are defensive and one is offensive—the sword. What does it mean to have an offensive weapon? What does it mean that the sword is the Word of God?

Life Application

- Do you really think we are in a battle with the devil?
- Assuming for just a moment that you can accept that we are in a battle with the devil, what is the problem with going into the battle missing one or more of the pieces of armor?
- When you fight the fight for the Lord, why do you need all the armor to fight?
- What do you think of being enlisted in a battle rather than volunteering?
- Is it a privilege or a burden to be in this kind of battle?
- How does this impact the way you view the world and your life?
- What does God tell us to do? (We are to put on the "full armor".) Is this enough or do we need more?
- How can Christians help one another in this battle?
- What practical things can Christians do to prepare for and stay in shape in the midst of battle?

Write the answers to these questions on the dry erase board for all to see.

Making it Personal

Ask your students what kinds of things they go up against every day. Things like temptations to lie, steal, treat others poorly, fight with their parents, be angry with an absentee father, materialism, etc. The devil is scheming against us in these ways.

Stress the importance of God's word being the offensive weapon. We need to be drenched in God's Word so we can combat the lies the evil one throws at us.

Have each student choose at least one place where they know they struggle every day and a practical way to prepare for and stay in shape in that battle. Exchange e-mails or myspace.com accounts with the person on your right and left. Each person is to send a reminder and ask the other how he or she is doing on his or her armor that week.

Memory Verse Activity

Go online or to a surplus army store and purchase blank dog tags. While you don't want to go overboard on the military theme, the reality is that this passage is about a battle. We don't wear suits of armor anymore but we do still battle in this world. Dog tags are for identification. They let others know who you are and are considered important on the battle field. Give each student a dog tag and chain. Read and re-read Ephesians 6:11. Write the verse on the dog tag and have each student take it home.

Songs

"Time to Pray" by Grits on 7

Spiritual Warfare—Standing up for What You Believe In

by Joe Usher and Amy Jacober

Memory Verse

Put on the whole armor of God, that you may be able to stand against the schemes of the devil. —Ephesians 6:11

Scripture

2 Corinthians 10:3–6

Lesson in a Sentence

Our warfare is powerful because God is empowering us for the battle against the lies that humans generate against Christ and Christianity.

TEACHER'S NOTE

Since this is Halloween, it is possible many of your churches are hosting harvest festivals. As this day is handled in different ways by different denominations, consult with your pastor as to the best way to address this holiday. The following lesson may be made much more focused on Halloween or taught as is depending on what best suits your needs.

Focus

Show a clip from *When a Stranger Calls*. This movie is about a young woman who, after getting in trouble for her cell phone bill, must babysit instead of going to the big bonfire at school. While babysitting in an amazing house, the phone calls begin. She makes many unwise moves opening doors and answering the phone. She scares herself again and again. By the time she gets used to the phone calls and lets down her guard, she discovers there really is a stranger calling and he is inside of the house.

Choose any number of clips early in the movie where the phone rings and the babysitter answers and then calls the police. Ask:

- Is there anything good about being scared?
- How many of you have ever been in a scary situation? What was it? How did you handle it?
- Have any of you ever gotten used to something only to find out that you should have been scared afterwards?

Discovery

Before you begin, set up a game of Jenga in a central location.

Read 2 Corinthians 10:3–6 out loud. Ask your students to say back to you in their own words what was just read. What does Paul mean by his being timid and bold? (Paul is saying that he does not want to come down hard on the Corinthians, he would rather be gentle and timid but if he has to, he will. Think about a parent who doesn't want to punish their child but if you back talk, watch out! It's not like you didn't know it was coming; you were warned.)

- What does this scripture mean when it says we do not fight with the same weapons of the world?
- What are strongholds?
- What does it mean to take captive every thought and make it obedient to Christ?

Application

Srongholds are everywhere! Ask your students to make a list of strongholds that they see in the world. If they need a little help to begin the process offer your own examples or use the following: poverty, child abuse, friends betraying others, divorce, illness, etc.

For each stronghold listed, tell your students that you must have at least one weapon to battle this. Point to the Jenga you have set up. This Jenga represents the strongholds in our world. It will take a lot more than going to church on Sunday to break this down. Ask your students to list of ways to fight strongholds. With each item said, pull out a piece of the Jenga. Eventually, this will topple though work to pull out as many pieces as possible before this happens.

Hand each person a piece of the Jenga game and a marker. Write the memory verse on the wood and have each person take it home.

Service to God's Greatest Generation

by Dennis Okholm

Someone once said, "The church is always one generation away from extinction." There are times when I worked with kids in the church that I wished the extinction would be immediate! It can be a thankless task—bagging the debris after a raucous lock-in or fielding a phone call from an irate parent who is going to report you to the elders for mentioning the "m" word in your sex talk to the seniors.

The glamour you once associated with being a youth minister may have dimmed. Why spend your life serving kids in the church when you could be making some significant bucks in the real world without having to stay up all night babysitting adolescents or listening to complaints?

You do it because you want to be great in God's kingdom!

In Mark 10:35–45, James and John ask Jesus if they can be the greatest in his kingdom. Jesus doesn't answer by condemning them for their desire to be great. Instead, he changes the definition of greatness: If you want to be great in God's kingdom you have to be a table waiter. In fact, if you want to be the greatest, you have to bus the tables.

Jesus didn't just teach this, he played the role himself. In his gospel, John tells us that when Jesus knew that he had all power and authority from the Father, he washed the disciples' feet with a towel (John 13:3–5). When did you last notice the bus boy in the restaurant? If you did, were you thinking, "Wow! That guy's got power and authority!" Probably not, because we've bought a bill of goods from our culture that defines greatness in terms of the degrees we've earned, the assets in our bank account, the list of books we've published, the number of kids we can count in our youth group.

When my daughter was in high school I gave her a postcard I had purchased at the Martin Luther King Jr. memorial in Atlanta. It pleased me that she taped it up on her wall. In part, King wrote: "Everybody can be great because anybody can serve. You don't have to have a college degree to serve. You don't have to make your subject and your verb agree to serve. You don't have to know the second theory of thermodynamics to serve. You only need a heart full of grace. A soul generated by love."

James 1:27 says that "true religion" consists in serving orphans and widows in their distress. Those folks are the powerless. They're the ones from whom you'll probably receive nothing in return—not even applause. But they're the ones whose tables you need to bus if you want to be great in the kingdom. And that's why we keep investing in the kids (in their distress). Those investments are treasures that don't rust or get moth eaten. The only treasures we can take with us are our investments in the lives of others.

Be encouraged by Paul's reminder: "Therefore, my beloved, be steadfast, immovable, always excelling in the work of the Lord, because you know that in the Lord your labor is not in vain" (1 Cor. 15:58). Perhaps we can help the church's next generation to become God's greatest generation. In the relay race of the generations they carry the fires of the past, not the ashes dropped along the way. Theirs is the flame that remains ignited by the Spirit of God.

Defend the Oppressed

by Ben Donley

In this lesson, students will:
- ✔ Understand that God is a defender of the oppressed.
- ✔ Realize that they are expected to stand up against oppression.
- ✔ Learn about the value of all people.
- ✔ Choose a group of oppressed people they want to become more familiar with.

Stuff you'll need:
- ❑ Blank sheets of paper
- ❑ Markers and pens
- ❑ Big piece of butcher paper
- ❑ A paper bag filled with corporate symbols from companies that are known for sweatshop abuses (Nike's Swoosh, The Yellow Dot from Wal-Mart, Ralph Lauren's Polo player, Guess' Triangle, etc.)
- ❑ Pictures of poor and oppressed people from around the world (include names and basic information). Have enough for each of your students.

Memory Verse
Then the King will reply, "I tell you the truth, whatever you did for one of the least of these brothers of mine, you did for me." —Matthew 25:40 (NIV)

Scripture
Psalm 10 and Isaiah 58:6–12

Lesson in a Sentence
God defends the oppressed and expects His followers to do the same.

The Big Picture
The world is filled up with oppressors and the oppressed. Oppressors are people, who for the sake of money or power push the oppressed down, preventing them from achieving full humanity. Oppressors thrive on injustice to gain higher levels of wealth and position. You can find them oppressing in sweatshops, in the slave trades, in corporate and political boardrooms and anywhere else that policies and practices are used to submerge other people and to widen the gap between the haves and have-nots. Oppressors want more and think they deserve more and so they do whatever it takes to get more even if that means ignoring basic human rights. As a result, the poor get poorer, the weak get weaker, and people that God made forget that they are made in His image.

The oppressed are those who are victimized by the oppressor. Who will speak up for these voiceless people? Who will help these helpless? Who will bring justice? Who will remove these yokes of oppression? God is clear that his followers are the ones who must speak up, help, bring justice, and take off the heavy burdens.

Focus

A Sweatshop Story

Define the terms *oppressor* and *oppressed* using the information given in The Big Picture above. Take out your corporate bag and tell the group that you are going to take out symbols one at a time and have them guess which company they belong to. If they guess right, they get a small prize. Then, remove a symbol and have them shout out answers. After the right guess is made, ask the entire group to tell you a few things that they think of when they think of this company (slogans, celebrity endorsers, etc. The Swoosh symbol: Nike™—Just do it—Michael Jordan—Tiger Woods, etc.) Do this with all of the symbols.

Say: Every one of these companies has something in common. Ask: Do you know what it is? Let them make a few guesses. Tell your group to pay attention to the story and see if they can figure out what links the corporations to one another.

Read the following story: Once upon a time, a very poor young woman goes to work at a factory early in the morning. For sixteen hours, seven days a week, she works as hard as she can with very little break. If she makes mistakes or talks with her fellow workers, she will be yelled at and probably even beaten by her boss. If she gets hurt in her work's unsafe conditions and cannot continue, she will be fired. The room she works in is dark, hot and has poor lighting. These conditions can lead to serious health problems but she is not allowed to complain. Sometimes when she needs to go to the bathroom, she is not allowed to. In fact, her overall freedom is limited. She gets paid less than two dollars a day (15–40 cents an hour) to make shirts and shoes. Multinational corporations ultimately sell the shirts and shoes that she helps to make for as much as $125.00 per item. These multinational corporations make billions of dollars a year off of the hard work and sweat of young women like this one.

Tell the youth that this story is common. Explain that many people in the world today have to deal with these types of conditions to survive. Ask:
- How would you feel if this were your life?
- What bothers you about this story?
- What is unjust?
- Is this young woman oppressed?
- Who are her oppressors?
- Why do you think corporations would use sweatshops to develop their products?

Emphasize to them that corporations get rich because they use this kind of sweatshop labor. Tell them that use of oppressive sweatshop labor is what links these companies together. Ask:
- Did you know this about these companies?
- Why should it matter to Christians?

• What do you think should be done about this kind of oppression?

Say: Sweatshop oppression is only one form of oppression in the world today. We will mention others later in the meeting.

Discovery

Tell your group that you are going to read a biblical description of an oppressor. Read Psalm 10 and ask the following questions:
• According to these verses, what is the mindset of an oppressor?
• How do oppressors think about God and about others?
• What are they interested in?
• Who are their victims and how do they suffer?
• What does the writer here want God to do about the oppressor?
• What does God do about it?
• How do you think God feels about those who oppress others?

Break the students into smaller groups. Have them read Isaiah 58:6–12 and then answer the following questions:
• What does God expect his followers to do about injustice and oppression?
• What does God want his followers to spend their time doing for the poor and needy?
• What good things will happen because of doing these things?

Life Application

Say: Here are a few facts that we should all remember.
• There is a lot of oppression and injustice in the world and in your community today.
• God hates injustice and oppression.
• God reaches out to those people who are being oppressed and defends them.
• God brings down oppression and injustice.
• God expects Christians to hate injustice and oppression, to defend the oppressed and to do what is necessary to get rid of oppression and injustice.

Tell the small groups to:
• List some examples of oppression and injustice in the world/in their community today. (Hunger, Sweatshops, Homelessness, Unjust imprisonments, Slavery (sexual and worker-based) etc.)
• Pick one area of oppression as their focus.
• Discuss ways that they, the church and their youth group can reach out/help/defend their chosen oppressed group.
• Discuss ways that they, the church and their youth group can bring this oppression down.

If there is time, have each group share a little about what they discussed.

Making it Personal

Bring your group back together and have them sit down on the floor in a circle. Pass out the 'oppressed peoples' pictures with some pens and have them write down their memory verse on the back. Ask them to take this picture home, hang it somewhere that they will see it often, and pray for their person as often as they see them. You might suggest that they pray the following: "God bring justice to _____ today. Set them free from their oppressors and give me a compassionate heart for all those in need."

Defenders of Jesus

by Ben Donley

Memory Verse

Then the King will reply, "I tell you the truth, whatever you did for one of the least of these brothers of mine, you did for me." —Matthew 25:40 (NIV)

Scripture

Job 24: 2–24

Lesson in a Sentence

God defends the oppressed and expects His followers to do the same.

Focus

Option 1—Shocking Stats

Hand out pieces of paper and pens to your group. Tell them that you are going to read them a few facts about world oppression and injustice and that you want them to try and picture what you are saying. Tell them that you want them to respond to each fact by writing whatever comes to their minds.

Read each of the facts twice and slow enough so that they can write a response. Feel free to research your own facts an statistics and use them instead of those listed below.

- About 24,000 people die every day from hunger or hunger-related causes. Three-fourths of these deaths are children under the age of five.
- It is estimated that one billion people in the world lack adequate housing, including 100 million who are homeless.
- Depending on whose definition you use, there is anywhere from 3 million to 100 million people being held as slaves in the world today.

Encourage some of them to share their reactions. Ask: Why do you think these things occur in our world?

Option 2—Society Creation Exercise

This exercise is based on a thought experiment created by political philosopher, John Rawls. Break your youth up into small groups. Name each group as a different letter – A Group, B Group, C Group, D Group, etc. (Make sure and post each group's name near them so that the other groups can see.) For each group, come up with a different identity page that tells them about their group's specific economic class, talents, abilities, ethnicity, gender, religion, or belief system. (For example, Group A might be upper class white males who are good at playing golf, who believe that money is god and who think that women should stay at home and take care of children. Group B might be ultra lower class Asian women who are good at dancing salsa, who believe that everything Jesus said is true and who think that everyone should be equal.) Tell the groups that they are going to be responsible for setting up rules for a new world that they will all live in. They can make up any rules that they want for this new world – but they must take their identity and the other groups into account. They should decide which groups will do what sort of work, how money will be distributed, who is in power and how that is decided, etc.

Let them take ten minutes for this and then have each group share what they came up with. Write down their ideas on the butcher paper. Make a mark next to any of the ideas or rules that might be oppressive to another group.

After each group explains their new world rules, ask if anybody from the other groups has any problems with their suggestions. Ask: How would your group like to live in this group's world?

TEACHER'S NOTE

This exercise can go several ways. If it all goes as planned, some groups will make rules that give their identity grouping an advantage. This advantage might oppress another group and cause discontent that should be discussed. If your youth group is abnormal and completely full of unselfish people who all decide to make rules that will promote a checks and balances equality, where every other group has access to money and power, then simply commend them and discuss the value of the oppression-less society they created. Ask:

- What does this exercise teach?
- What kind of rules would your group have made if you did not know what your identity was going to be until after the rules were made and you stepped onto the planet?

Discovery

Read Job 24:2–24 and then ask the following questions:

- What are the actions of the oppressors in these verses? How do their actions affect other people in negative ways?
- How do these verses make you feel?
- Does God see what is going on? How does He respond? Why does He wait?

Life Application

Say: As followers of Jesus, we have a responsibility to know about the injustice that is going on in the world and then to do something about it.

- How much did you know about oppression and injustice before this group's meeting?

- How can you get to know more about oppressors and the oppressed?
- Where is this sort of oppression happening? What can be done about it? How might you use your life to do something about it?

If you were being severely oppressed in some other country, and you could send a message for help to this youth group, what would you say? What would you want this youth group to do about it? Do you think they would? Why or why not?

Say: It is by the grace of God that most of us were born into non-oppressive situations. This week, try to imagine what it could have been like for you if you had been born into unjust situations. Then, be thankful for your blessings and be willing to do something with your life to show God's love/mercy to those being oppressed right now. Open the time up for them to pray out loud about these issues.

Identity and the Children of God

by Chuck Hunt

In this lesson, students will:
- ✔ Begin to explore their racial identity and that of others.
- ✔ Become aware of their racial prejudices.
- ✔ Understand a biblical precedent for equality in light of Christ.

Stuff you'll need:
- ❏ *Do the Right Thing* video or DVD
- ❏ Set of special cards
- ❏ Dr. Seuss's book *The Sneetches*

Memory Verse
There is neither Jew nor Greek, there is neither slave nor free, there is neither male nor female; for you are all one in Christ Jesus. —Galatians 3:28

Scripture
Galatians 3:26–29

Lesson in a Sentence
Your racial identity is not as important as your identity as a child of God.

The Big Picture
No matter who you are or where you come from you are affected by race and its effect in society. In much of our society, we are defined by race and the cultural identity that comes with it. We live, go to school, work with those who are like us generally. These things are bound by geography but they are also bound by race. This does not only exist between members of different races but within racial delineations as well. Blacks are prejudiced against other blacks, whites against other whites, etc. Not only has society suffered because of prejudice, the church has as well.

It has been said that the playing field is level at the foot of the cross. That may be true in the eyes of God, but it is not true in the eyes of people. We are God's children through faith in Christ Jesus (Gal. 3:26) and none is given greater rights or responsibility based on their human racial identity. We need to understand and begin to live in our identity as children of God, not our racial identity.

Focus

Option 1

In *Do the Right Thing,* is a clip where the actors have short monologues that quickly go through derogatory statements. The clip begins with Spike Lee saying, "Dago, garlic-breath, guinea, pizza-slingin', spaghetti-bendin'." This clip has plenty of power and will get your students attention. More important, it will set the tone for a serious discussion of race. After the clip, give students an opportunity to reflect on:

If they have heard those words

If they have said those words

What they believe was the effect on the person to whom those words were directed.

You may need to help them know where their thoughts are by asking what words made them laugh and what words made them mad, if only silently. Note: This clip uses strong language, screen it for appropriateness.

Option 2

Divide your group into small groups of no more than eight. Give to each group a set of five cards. The Cards: One card in each set of five has one of the following statements printed on it—*Strongly Agree, Agree, Not Sure, Disagree,* and *Strongly Disagree.* These cards can be used for future difficult topics so you may want to make them high quality. Write a list of statements, not questions, which deal with race or you can use the list below. Put one statement on the board at a time or say them one at a time giving the students time to respond between each of them. The group must come to a consensus about their opinion. Though you may have a leader in the group to observe and help discussion. It is important that the leader keep his or her opinions about the statement quiet. This option is designed to give students the freedom to state their opinion; say whatever they think without correction or intimidation. If you listen, you will learn a lot about what your students think.

Statements:

Racism is a problem of the past

All people are created equal

All people are treated equal

I have never been apart of racism

Racism hurts whites as well as people of color.

I am a racist.

Option 3

Find a copy of the Dr. Seuss story *The Sneetches.* Read the story as a melodrama and get a few students to act out the story as you read it. When you are done reading the story get the students to talk about where they see prejudice happening in the world, country, school, and family.

Discovery

Separate your students into groups of no more than eight with a leader. Give each group an ethnic identity. (i.e.—Black middle-class and sheltered, Mexican immigrant, White on welfare, American Indian on a reservation) You can use existing stereotypes or mix up the stereotypes to keep them thinking. Have the group read Galatians 3:26-29 as if they were that group of people. Give them some time to think about what those verses mean to them. Then have the students explain their ideas to the rest of the group.

Talk about what it means to be in the family of God and that faith in Christ makes it so. Talk about the fact that faith in Christ is the only thing that levels the playing field and that in Christ we are a new creation (Gal. 6:15-16, 2 Cor. 5:14-20). One of the important pieces in this new creation is the ministry of reconciliation.

Life Application

We can never completely separate ourselves from our ethnic or social identity. God would not want that. God does want us to see ourselves as heirs in his kingdom. Our perception is important because the more we see ourselves as members of God's kingdom the more we become aware of responsibilities of the kingdom. We are to be humble and compassionate without regard for race. Our prejudices keep us from being all that God is created us to be.

Making it Personal

Encourage your students to have a conversation with someone who they would normally be prejudiced against so they may understand more about who they are. That person does not need to know why.

Remind the students of the Focus and ask if there is a way to respond differently because of Galatians 3:28.

Option 1

Ask your students to write down their response to the clip as a child of God.

Option 2

Ask students to rejoin their opinion groups and go through the statements on race and respond as a child of God.

Option 3

Ask students to talk about how they should respond if they see prejudice going on around them.

Quotable Quotes

Perhaps travel cannot prevent bigotry, but by demonstrating that all peoples cry, laugh, eat, worry, and die, it can introduce the idea that if we try to understand each other we may even become friends. —Maya Angelou

Web Connect

Blue Eyes—*http://www.newsreel.org/guides/blueeyed.htm, http://www.janeelliott.com/*
Color of Fear—*http://www.viewingrace.org/index.php*
Milgram Experiment—*http://www.new-life.net/milgram.htm*

Service Options

The next time your church does a service project, team up with another group of different ethnic and social background than your own. Go together to a neutral site to do the service project. Afterwards, discuss what it was like to work together.

Still a Struggle

by Chuck Hunt

Memory Verse

There is neither Jew nor Greek, there is neither slave nor free, there is neither male nor female; for you are all one in Christ Jesus. —Galatians 3:28

Scripture

James 2:1–10

Lesson in a Sentence

Your racial identity is not as important as your identity as a child of God.

Focus

Have students compete in a relay or another of their favorite group games with one team having a clear advantage because of rules, opportunity, strength, or favoritism. You will soon see that the students given advantage will play harder and continue to enjoy their winnings. The disadvantaged group will begin to complain. Do not explain why the rules are the way they are. Tell them that is just the way it is. This group will begin to get discouraged and quit. Stop the game before it gets too bad. Continue to keep the groups separated for the rest of the night. At certain points in the evening toss out candy or give preferential treatment to the team that wins.

Discovery

Have the students who won the game sit in the preferred place in the room. The students who lost can sit wherever else is left. Begin to give a talk about James 2:1-10. This verse is about favoritism based on possession. The remedy is that we love one another. The lesson is obvious and it should be short. Once it becomes obvious move on to the application.

Application

Make students compete in a different relay or another of their favorite group games with one team having a clear advantage because of rules, opportunity, strength, or favoritism.

You will hopefully soon see that the students given advantage will give up some of their advantage or play a little easier. You may allow them to request a rule change or play by the rules with less enthusiasm. The disadvantaged group will begin to complain again if this doesn't happen.

If the students given advantage do not respond in a way that reflects James 2:8, "love your neighbor," stop the game, sit down, and give the discovery lesson again. Keep repeating until they get it.

The point is this. Even though you have set rules that give students an advantage when they live by the law of love everyone wins. As it applies to race, it speaks to the fact that though laws may dictate a disadvantage for underprivileged people the people of advantage have the power to change laws and circumstances for those without a voice.

Connections

The story in Acts 10 reflects God's understanding of equality as it applies to the gift of God and the Spirit. The story of the Samaritan Woman in John 4 also speaks to how Jesus views the gift of God.

Life in the Land of Plenty

by Amy Jacober

In this lesson, students will:
- ✔ Learn of the strong stance taken by Daniel and his friends
- ✔ Be encouraged to pay attention to their food choices
- ✔ Learn of the struggles with nutrition in America and around the world

Stuff you'll need:
- ❑ Pictures from magazines of all shapes of people
- ❑ Tape or glue
- ❑ Construction paper
- ❑ Tables
- ❑ Tablecloths, plates, napkins, and eating utensils
- ❑ Table decorations
- ❑ Current world food statistics
- ❑ Movie—*Supersize Me*
- ❑ Plain bread or cooked rice

Memory Verse

Therefore, whether you eat or drink, or whatever you do, do all to the glory of God.
—1 Corinthians 10:31

Scripture

Daniel 1:1–21

Lesson in a Sentence

By caring for your body, you honor God.

The Big Picture

We live in a land of plenty. Discussions and reports about diet simply cannot be escaped. But we still don't get it. People suffer eating disorders on both ends of the spectrum? anorexia, bulimia, and obesity. Struggles with body image are real. During the adolescent years, they can be overwhelming. This lesson is not meant to chastise anyone. It is about God's concern with our health. We are blessed to have abundant food available, yet we take this for granted. Diabetes is a public health issue. Malnutrition still occurs in spite of the availability of nutritional foods. Life in the Land of Plenty requires discipline, which is advocated in scripture.

Focus

Dinner and a Movie

Have tables set up with paper tablecloths, plates, napkins, forks, and, if you are feeling ambitious, decorations as if you are about to offer a meal. Collect current world food statistics and set these on the tables. Check out Bread for the World, a Christian organization focused on ending hunger: *www.bread.org*. As your students assemble, give each a half glass of water and a plate of plain rice or bread. When they complain, point out the facts on the table.

Show a clip from *Supersize Me.* The basic premise for the film is that a man eats only food from McDonald's for a month and supersizes his meals when asked. Choose a clip toward the end of the film in which he talks of feeling ill. Clearly, he has gained weight.

After the clip, ask your students what they think of the experience.
- What have they learned about eating in America and around the world?
- What would they think if this was all they got to eat today?
- What about everyday?
- What foods and nutrition would you miss?
- What foods would you miss but not need?

Discovery

Group your students in groups of three to four. Have each group read Daniel 1:1-21.
- What happened in this passage?
- What did Daniel and his friends decide about food?
- What foods were being offered to them?
- What did they choose to eat instead?
- How did they compare to the others?

Life Application

Daniel and his friends decided to go vegetarian for a season. They didn't die, they didn't even get weak. Do you think this was through divine intervention or simply that they didn't need all the rich foods?

Distribute pens and ask each group to write on the paper tablecloths what they typically eat in a week. Include meals and snack foods. Using the scripture passage and what has been learned in and during the "meal" discuss what has been learned about food.
- It's Thanksgiving week. Is there a chance anyone will overeat?
- Did you realize this is not even an option in most countries?
- Many of us complain about the food choices we have. How can we learn to be thankful for what we have?
- What factors do we use typically to choose food? Nutrition? Taste? Convenience?

Read some of those world food facts that are on the tables.
- Where do we fit in with these facts?

- What food is needed to sustain life?
- Do you think overeating is as much of a problem as undereating?
- How might we address either issue?
- What does food have to do with Christianity?
- How do you think God views food?

Food is a blessing from God. We live in a world where food is found at every turn. How do we, like Daniel and his friends, learn to make better food choices?

Making it Personal

Discuss with your group one of your poor food choices. This doesn't need to be earth-shattering but if it's cookies every day after school or downing an entire bag of potato chips in one sitting, something needs to change. You may be eating healthily, but there is always room for improvement.

Close in prayer asking God to help us to be thankful for what we have while realizing many in this world do not have enough to eat. Pray that we would develop a heart of gratitude. Pray also that we will develop healthy food habits.

TEACHER'S NOTE

Don't send your students on a guilt trip. Describe our world in which health issues surrounding food are increasingly common; in which nutrition and health issues result from both a lack of food and an abundance of food. For many of our students, lack of food is not the issue. Eating the right foods is the issue. Just like Daniel, proper diet is a conscious choice. Just because certain foods are in front of them does not mean they are the best for them.

Life in the Land of Plenty

by Amy Jacober

Service Option

Since tomorrow is Thanksgiving, there are many ways for your group to serve. It may be at a food pantry, the Salvation Army, a homeless shelter, or other non-profit agency. Your church may be delivering food to families in need this season. In some way, choose a way for your students to experience serving others.

Don't Be Led by the Sheep

by Eric Shamp

In this lesson, students will:

✔ Know that they cannot control God
✔ Learn that bargaining will not make God do things
✔ Seek ways to give up control to God

Memory Verse

"For whoever wants to save his life will lose it, but whoever loses his life for me will find it." —Matthew 16:25

Scripture

Acts 17:22–34

Lesson in a Sentence

One of the main differences between our God and those of other religions is that no matter what we do, we cannot control the actions of God.

Focus

Option 1

Give each person a chance to answer this question: What do you have complete control over in your life?

Option 2—Cross the River on Pontoons

Stuff you'll need for this game:

❏ 8 2-in. x 6-in. x 12-foot pieces of wood
❏ Screws
❏ Nylon straps

Instructions for setting up the pontoons:

• Cut Nylon straps into 40 8-inch strips
• Screw the strips down onto each piece of wood as foot holders at 2-foot intervals
• Each 2-in. x 4-in. should have 5 nylon-strip foot holders

Instructions for the game:

The group splits into four teams of five people each and then cross an imagined forty-foot wide river using their pontoons. They must have one foot in a foot holder on one pontoon and the other on the second pontoon. If they fall down, they drown and have to start over. They must work together and have faith in each other in order to get across the river successfully. The first team to get across wins.

TEACHER'S NOTE

If there are more than twenty people in your class, have multiple races so that everybody can join in.

Discovery

TEACHER'S NOTE

Pick one or two people to read Acts 17:22–29. Go verse-by-verse and discuss the following points to foster dialogue between the students.

Verse 22—Introduce Paul. Where is he? Why was he there? What is the Areopagus? (A place where Athenian philosophers could debate issues of philosophy and religion.)

Verses 23—Why have an altar to an unknown God? (They wanted to cover all their bases.) 600 years before this time, a terrible epidemic hit Athens and they released a flock of black and white sheep into the city in an attempt to alleviate the epidemic. Wherever a sheep lay down, it was killed and sacrificed to the God of the nearest temple. The belief was that the epidemic came because some god was angry. If they could appease the god, then the epidemic would go away. If the sheep did not lay down near a known temple, they were sacrificed to an unknown God so they would appease every god, not just the ones they knew of.

In effect, the sheep decided why the people worshipped a god. Not only were these gods false, they were being worshipped because of the random actions of the sheep.

Verse 24—What is the difference between their gods and ours? (God made everything and cannot be controlled by our work.) No matter how majestic our churches may be, God is not going to act favorably because we built him a better house than the one down the street.

Verse 25—What is the difference between their gods and ours? (We did not make God. God made us.) The Athenians believed that their gods ate the food they prepared for them. They left it in the temples overnight and threw away what was left in the morning. If they did not fix their gods some food, they feared the gods would become angry and cause bad things to happen. This means the Athenians thought they had a direct control over their gods and that their gods needed their sustenance.

Why then did the Jews offer food sacrifices to God? What's the difference between them and the Athenians? (God didn't need Israel's sacrifices, he wanted the Jews to trust that he would make up for what they lost by sacrificing to him.)

Verse 26—God is behind history. He is in control of what is happening. He determines when a nation rises and falls. Why did this resonate with the Athenians? (They sacrificed to their idols in hopes of controlling them. They thought if they were nice enough, built a good enough temple, and fixed good enough food, the gods would preserve them.)

Verse 27—God is behind the rise and fall of nations, but he has also placed us where we are now. We exist for a reason. What is that reason? (So that we may search for God and find him.) God has made us in such a way that we instinctively long for and grope after Him even ignorance and darkness. Do you agree with this statement? Why? What do you see in other people that confirms it? (People are into spirituality like Wicca, black magic, astrology, and meditation; they try to satisfy themselves with material things.)

What does the image of groping for God bring to mind? (People in ignorance and darkness with no control over what they find.)

Verse 28—We live, move and exist in God. Therefore, when we give up our attempts to control our lives and our God, our relationship with God will grow.

Verse 29—Since we are his offspring we shouldn't think of God as a sculpture we can make. We do not make God just as we do not make our own fathers. Your dad and mom made you and brought you up. It is not the other way around.

God knows and loves you and desires an intimate relationship with you. You must give up control of your life and not let the sheep make your decisions.

Life Application
Follow up with these questions:
- Why do we want to be in control of our lives?
- What does the world teach us about being in control of our lives?

Making it Personal
Name one thing you think you control that you must give to God.
- What are some other control issues in your life?
- How can you give these to God? (Pray.)
- What are issues you don't try to control?

Song
"Blessed Be the Name"
"Come Thou Fount of Every Blessing"

Lose Your Life
So God Can Use It

by Eric Shamp

Memory Verse

For whoever wants to save his life will lose it, but whoever loses his life for me will find it. —Matthew 16:25

Scripture

Genesis 12:1-8

Focus

Option 1

Tell a story of a time you have lost something important like keys to your car, a birth certificate, or a homework assignment. Tell of the anguish and struggle you went through and the impact it had not only on you but also on others. A story from your life will always have impact.

Ask your students to share their own stories. What are the craziest things they have lost? What are the most important?

Option 2

Go through the church's found box one item at a time and try to identify the owner of the item and when it may have been lost. Ask why these items are so easy to forget? What do the students have that they would never want to lose?

Discovery

Read Genesis 12:1–8. "The Call of Abraham"
Talking about how Abraham gave up control of his life and everything he owned to follow God.
   • What did Abraham have to leave behind?
   • What made it possible for Abraham to leave behind all of his stuff? (His love for God was greater than his love for his stuff. He trusted in God more than he trusted in himself.)
   • How would you feel if you were told to give everything up?
   • What, exactly, would this look like for you?
   • What would be the hardest thing to give up?

Have a pastor or adult volunteer share about how God has taken them through the different stages in their life. Ask them to share how God was able to use them when they gave up control of something.

Life Application

Split up into small groups and talk about the future:

- Do you think you can follow God without giving everything up?
- What does this mean?
- Are you willing to give up everything to follow God?
- What are the areas in which God is calling you to step out of their comfort zone?

Consistency and Presence in Youth Ministry

by Terry Linhart, Ph.D.

When I was in high school there was an evangelistic para-church youth ministry that I didn't care for very much. It wasn't that they were bad, it was just that I didn't understand relational evangelism. I resembled a Pharisee—legalism ruled the day. However, a leader of that youth ministry named Bill had a tremendous impact on my life despite the fact that I never went to any of their meetings. His goal wasn't to get students to his programs, but rather to be a presence in the community, ministering to those around no matter where they were.

Because of Bill's influence on my life, I attempted to model many of the attributes that I saw in him when I entered youth ministry. Now, some twenty years later, many of the things he did have proven to be the most powerful practices for youth workers, paid or volunteer.

Consistency

It is difficult to overstate this as a necessity for adults involved in youth ministries. The old adage is, "90% of life is just showing up." This might be an exaggeration in terms of ministry since it fails to account for the role of the Holy Spirit. However, I have seen many problems in youth ministries that could have been remedied by an commitment on the part of adult leaders to be a consistent presence in the lives of students. Bill showed up each Tuesday on campus, stood in the same place, and obeyed the guidelines given by the school for visitors who came to the school. He seemed to be ever-present at prominent school events and, when he was around, he was always open for good conversation. My research (Rahn & Linhart, 2000) shows that the presence of an adult as model and mentor is crucial for effective outreach and leadership in students' lives.

Some call this being present in the lives of others, a term that means more than just showing up. It embraces the power that one person's example and presence can have on another. Two leading Christian educators (Issler & Habermans, 1994) note that youth learn primarily through watching others. This means that that ministry doesn't happen only through the words we say, we need to be aware of what students see as we live our lives in front of them.

Grace-full Relationships

Not only was Bill consistent during the cycles of the school year, his approach to students resembled how I thought Jesus Christ would have dealt with students. If students learn primarily through watching adults, and if the presence of an adult is among the most fruitful ministry in the life of a student, then we need to consider the nature of those interactions.

The opposite of this is easily seen in the frantic youth leader who rushes in to a meeting or appointment, barely ready to focus; In the conversations that turn to "when I was in school," or "I know exactly what you're going through." The conversation that turns from the student and his or her life to the adult leader. A minister full of grace mirrors the grace that God has extended to humanity. He was mindful of us (Psalm 8:4). He interrupted history through the grace-full life of Jesus Christ (John 1:14). He calls us to follow Christ as a sweet fragrance for His name's sake in the lives of others (2 Cor. 2:14).

Thought-provoking Teaching Methods

It is amazing, but I still remember the lessons Bill taught. He occasionally was a guest speaker at meetings and retreats I attended. He was not a lecturer. He didn't have canned speeches and great stories, rather he was an ordinary leader who worked hard to understand how adolescents learn and think. He used role playing, discussions, and panel discussions. He captured our imagination with his teaching, not assuming that we wanted to learn (we often came to the meetings just for the donuts). He brought life to the content.

I often see youth leaders using the Bible and presenting their lessons as if their teaching methods don't matter. If we don't put life into our teaching and understand how students interpret the content, then we're not teaching in a way that changes lives (Hendricks, 2003). I'm a college professor and believe in good content, but often our methods fail to deliver good content in helpful ways. I recommend that youth ministry leaders (and college professors) try a new teaching method each month to then evaluate its effectiveness. Like Hendricks says, you may just find the "open sesame" to the hearts of students as they think about God, Jesus Christ, and the Bible in new ways.

"Wherever you are, be all there."

I once heard Chuck Swindoll quote the famous missionary Jim Elliott, "Wherever you are, be all there. Live to the hilt every situation you believe to be the will of God." In an age where we are often anything but present in the lives of others, mastering this quality has far-reaching implications. I often find full-time youth workers living so far in the future that they fail to focus on the current day's opportunities to make a difference in their church, neighborhood, or city. What if each day we let our preoccupations center on how we can be faithful to Christ, family, and others (Matt. 6:34)?

I cannot count the number of times I've reminded myself to "be all there" in a youth ministry situation. To be consistently present in the lives of students with a grace-full like approach provides rich opportunities for fruitful ministry. I've talked to countless college students about their experiences in youth ministries. The most meaningful memories were of godly adults invested in the concerns of youth.

Though I never attended a program that Bill organized, the times we spent together and the example he set for me had enormous impact. His consistency, Christ-likeness, availability, and effective teaching serve as powerful examples of what youth workers can do. When adults enter the lives of adolescents, youth ministry actually begins. May you minister with a renewed commitment to "be all there" in the lives of you students.

Hendricks, H. *Teaching to Change Lives: Seven proven ways to make your teaching come alive.* Sisters: Multnomah Books, 2003.

Issler, K., & Habermans, R. *How We Learn: A Christian teacher's guide to educational psychology.* Grand Rapids: Baker Books, 1994.

Rahn, D., & Linhart, T. *Contagious Faith: Empowering student leaders in evangelism.* Colorado Springs: GROUP Publishing, Inc., 2000.

The Coming of a King

by Amy Jacober

In this lesson, students will:
- ✔ Name several attributes of Jesus
- ✔ Connect scripture with different aspects of Jesus
- ✔ Understand that no single attribute fully describes Jesus
- ✔ Recognize Jesus as the King of kings

Stuff you'll need:
- ❑ Purple party items
- ❑ An advent wreath
- ❑ A purple candle
- ❑ Matches
- ❑ Strips of paper with scriptures
- ❑ Bowl
- ❑ Dry erase board
- ❑ Markers

Memory Verse

I am the Lord, your Holy One, the Creator of Israel, your King. —Isaiah 43:15

Scripture

1 Timothy 6:13-15

Lesson in a Sentence

The coming of the baby Jesus is the coming of a king.

The Big Picture

This is the first Sunday of Advent. The word *advent* simply means "coming." Now, we begin to turn our thoughts and attention toward the birth of Jesus Christ. We want to get a picture of just who was born in that manger. We have the blessing of being alive after He was here on earth, so we should take advantage of this. This is no ordinary baby. This is the creator, redeemer, and sustainer of the universe! Jesus is the King of kings.

Focus

Option 1

It is time to throw a purple party. Bring grape juice; make cupcakes and tint the frosting purple; decorate with purple balloons, streamers, and tablecloths; use whatever you can find that is purple.

Divide into teams of five each. Pass out purple paper and a purple marker to each team. Give each team one minute to create a list of as many purple things as they can. After one minute, go around the room and have each team read their list. If an item is found on more than one list, cross it off all lists. At the end, the team with the most unique items on their list wins the prize of a crown for each member. Or, simply stay with the purple theme and give grape bubble gum.

TEACHER'S NOTE

In biblical times purple was a color associated with royalty. Purple dye was very expensive. Consequently, those with wealth and power could afford it. While Jesus certainly would not have been considered wealthy while here on earth, purple is a fitting color for Him. Ironically, purple was used to mock Him at His trial, little did they know they were properly honoring Him (John 19:2,5).

Option 2

Today is the first Sunday of Advent. Advent means coming or arrival. Each week we will be focusing on the arrival of Jesus as we await and celebrate His birth! The wreath is evergreen to remind us of the everlasting life God offers. It is in a circle to remind us of the eternal nature of His love, there are no beginning and no end to a circle. The first candle is purple to remind us of Jesus as King, purple is the color of royalty. There are several ways to focus the advent season. This year we are looking at Jesus, Joseph, Mary, and the angels. This Sunday we focus on Jesus.

The prophets spoke of a Savior. We look for what the Lord is doing in the world today as well as for His second coming. Have one of your students read Isaiah 9:2,6-7. Isaiah was a prophet full of hope. Light the first candle on your wreath and allow it to burn during the remainder of the lesson. Pray thanking Jesus that He came as a baby we now recognize as a King. He fulfilled that which had been promised, what had been prophesied indeed came to pass.

Discovery

Ask your students if they were to choose one or two words to describe Jesus, what would they be? Write these on a dry erase board.

At this time of year most of us think of Jesus primarily as an infant. Write the following passages on separate strips of paper and place them in a bowl at the front of the room. Have a dry erase board near by. Ask one student at a time to draw a paper and read the passage. After the passage is read, ask for one or two words that describe who

Jesus is according to that passage and write that on the board. Be certain the final four verses are read. These four emphasize His role as King. (Feel free to add more verses.)

- Matthew 4:1–11, Mark 1:2–13—Jesus is tempted
- Matthew 15:1–9—Pharisees rebuked, Jesus as discipliner
- Mark 6:45–52—Jesus walks on water
- Mark 10:13–16—Jesus favors children
- Luke 2:41–50—Jesus disappears from family and visits the temple at age 12
- Luke 4:28–30—Jesus rejected at Nazareth
- Luke 7:36–48—Jesus is anointed by a sinful woman
- Luke 9:43–45—Jesus' death foretold
- Luke 9:51–56—Jesus is rejected by the Samaritans
- Luke 10:25–37—Jesus encourages us to help one another
- John 2:1–11—Jesus performs a miracle, water into wine
- John 4:46–54—Jesus heals
- John 5: 17–47—Jesus asserts His divinity
- John 6:25–59—Jesus is the bread of life
- John 6:60–71—Some of Jesus' followers fall away, Jesus loses friends
- John 8:1–11—Jesus forgives, the adulterous woman
- Isaiah 43:15—Jesus as King
- Matthew 27:37—Jesus as King
- 1 Timothy 6:13–15—Jesus as King
- Revelation 20:6—Jesus as King

Life Application

Jesus is so much more than any one word or phrase! While we most often talk of Him as an infant at this time of year, let us remember who He is entirely.

We ended with Jesus as King of kings. What does this mean for us today? How can we understand this in today's terms? If we were really preparing for the birth of a king, what would we as Christians be doing to get ready?

Making it Personal

- If each of us were preparing for the birth of a king, what would we be doing to get ready?
- Are there areas of your life where you are not allowing Jesus to reign?
- How can you let go and allow the King of kings take His rightful place in every area of your life?

Song

"Yahweh" by U2 on *How to Dismantle an Atomic Bomb*

Advent—The Coming of a King

by Amy Jacober

Memory Verse
I am the Lord, your Holy One, the Creator of Israel, your King. —Isaiah 43:15

Scripture
Luke 24:13-32; Mark 10:45, Matthew 20:28

Lesson in a Sentence
The coming of the baby Jesus is the coming of a king.

Focus

On at least ten separate sheets of paper, create a collage of three pictures cut from magazines that go together and one that does not. You could make this Christmas themed or better yet choose things that are in their world. Enlist one of your students to help, they will always be better at knowing what is current.

Examples:
- Number separate sheets of paper and place one each something like;
- One Tree Hill, the OC, Everwood, and Law and Order
- Usher, Nelly, Kanye West and, Tim McGraw
- Beyonce, Chakira, Madonna, and Jessica Simpson
- The leaning tower of Pisa, London Bridge, the Eiffel Tower, and McDonald's Arches

Break into five teams giving each team a piece of paper and pen to record their answers. Give each team one of the collages and be certain they put the number of the collage with each answer. The object of the game, to get through all ten sheets as quickly as possible while being the most accurate about who or what does not belong in the collage. Give two bonus points to the team that finishes first. Add points for each answer they get correct, take a point away for each one they get wrong.

How is this like Jesus? Last time we were together, we talked about Jesus coming as a king. What do we think of when we imagine a king? Did Jesus fit these? Do you think there were people who missed Him simply because He did not come looking like what they were expecting?

Discovery

Have someone read Luke 24:13–32 out loud. Break into groups of three and ask them to read this story again. After they are finished, ask them to consider the following questions with their group.

- What happened here?
- What were the two men discussing as they walked?
- Who began walking with them?
- What did He ask?
- How did the two men answer?
- What did He teach them as they walked?
- What did they ask Him to do?
- When did they finally recognize Him?

Teacher's Note

The story is a little bit long but it is a story so it should be able to hold their attention. If you know your group struggles to maintain attention, insert questions throughout as the story is read to be certain they are able to pay attention and comprehend. Remember, sitting quietly does not always mean they are with you.

Life Application

This story is all about recognition. If we had a sheet of paper with four pictures, three of which were of men with gold crowns and jewels, expensive clothes and a Rolex, and one man with no gold, wearing a t-shirt; Jesus is the one who does not fit in. While we may not be looking for Jesus to waltz down the street in a purple velvet robe, even today we tend to see Jesus in the wrong ways.

Ask your students to consider:

- If Jesus showed up, would you recognize Him?
- Is it possible that He speaks to us regularly and we miss it?

Wealth, prestige, and power are all associated with royalty. This is the opposite of what Jesus presented while here on earth. How can we begin to see the Holy Spirit at work here and now and not miss His presence?

We talk a lot about wanting to be with Jesus; to follow Jesus. Unfortunately, too many of us are just like those on the road to Emmaus. Check out Mark 10:45 for how Jesus viewed His role as a king while in this world.

- Is this still something you want?
- What would change if all Christians took this to heart?
- What would change if each person in your group would take this to heart?

Service Option

Many people serve others at the time of the holidays. While this is needed, the rest of the year there are needs as well. Consider taking this to heart, Jesus came to serve. It is popular right now to talk of our purpose in this world. If indeed we are to imitate Christ (Ephesians 5:1) then we too have come to serve not to be served. Brainstorm a few ways in which your group can serve in an ongoing project. It may be tutoring at your local grade school. You may consider a monthly visit to a local retirement home for an afternoon of games. You may collect shoes for a mission on the other side of the world. The options are limitless. Set a plan in place and one or two people to be responsible for it so the project won't go by the wayside. Be blessed as you serve and join Jesus in what He came to do.

The Example of Joseph

by Amy Jacober

In this lesson, students will:
- ✔ Be able to identify the noble act of obedience
- ✔ Be encouraged to know that being misunderstood by others does not mean that you are not honoring God
- ✔ Discuss what righteousness means
- ✔ Consider putting others before themselves

Stuff you'll need:
- ❏ *Cheaper by the Dozen* video or DVD
- ❏ Advent wreath
- ❏ Poster board
- ❏ Markers

Memory Verse

In God I have put my trust; I will not be afraid. What can man do to me? —Psalm 56:11

Scripture

Matthew 1:18–25, Isaiah 43:1–7

Lesson in a Sentence

Embrace God's will even when it doesn't make sense.

The Big Picture

No one in his right mind would actually believe that his fiancé did not have sex with another man if she were pregnant. At least no one who had not also heard from an angel. Scripture is clear that Joseph was a righteous man of God. It is no wonder that God chose him to be the earthly father of Jesus. Ironically, the fact that Mary was pregnant while betrothed to Joseph called into question his righteousness. He risked being mocked and misunderstood while honoring God. Joseph is an example of acceptance and love for those the world leaves behind. Even more, obedience to God is costly and difficult. Despite what the world might think, this does not make the obedient one wrong.

Focus

Option 1

Show a clip from *Cheaper by the Dozen,* a movie about a large family and the sacrifices of its father. Show the clip where the father's boss tells him he must choose his job or his family. Begin the clip where Tom is looking at his college yearbook and end when he hugs all his children.

Discuss with your students:
- Have any of you ever thought of the sacrifices your parents made for you?
- Go home tonight and ask your parents what they dreamed of doing or being when they were younger.

Joseph made huge sacrifices to be the father of Jesus. He didn't have to risk his position in life by staying with a woman who was pregnant with a child that was not his.

Option 2

Today is the second Sunday of Advent. This week we turn our focus to Joseph, who models for us a life that honors God. We live in a world where too many fathers are absent. Joseph not only cared for a child that was not his but took care of his new family to the best of his ability.

Have one of your students read Luke 2:1–5 as you light this week's candle and relight last week's candle. Close by thanking God for fathers and the father figures in our lives.

Discovery

Split the class into small groups and have each read Matthew 1:18–25. Make a list of all of the things that happened to Joseph and his responses in these verses. Based on what you read, what kind of man was Joseph?

Now read Matthew 2:13–18. What more do we learn about Joseph in these verses? Here are a few clues:
- Charitable: Matthew 1:19
- Faithful: Matthew 1:24
- Obedient: Matthew 2:13–14

Life Application

Joseph challenges our understanding of what it means to follow God.

Put four poster boards up in easily visible places in the room. On the first is written, "He was righteous even by the standards of his day." On the second is written, "He embraced those rejected by others." On the third is written "He chose to be obedient to God and misunderstood by people." On the fourth is written have written, "He gave up his right to honor God."

Direct each group to read the posters and use them to guide their conversation. How might the sentence on each poster board be applied today? If they need help, you may rephrase by asking, "What does righteousness look like by today's standards?" or, "In what ways are we called to be obedient to God that do not make sense to our friends or family?" One poster may strike a chord more than another with different groups. The point isn't to get through all of the posters, rather, to dive into a deep discussion.

Making it Personal

Choose one of the four sentences on the posters and claim it as your own this season. Talk about this with one or two other people. Ask your students to consider what would have to change in order for them take this seriously?

Share this with a fellow student and pray for one another.

The Example of Joseph

by Amy Jacober

Memory Verse

In God I have put my trust; I will not be afraid. What can man do to me? —Psalm 56:11

Scripture

Luke 1:36-45

Lesson in a Sentence

Embrace God's will even when it doesn't make sense.

Focus

Christmas Carol Gargling! Ask for three to four volunteers. Have each of them choose a partner from those still sitting. The goal of this game is to guess the song your partner sings for you. Before each team has a turn, the person singing must take a drink of water (or eggnog, or whatever you choose) and hold the liquid in his or her mouth. They then gargle the song to their partner. The first to guess the song gets a point. The team with the most points at the end wins! Offer some small prize to your winning team.

Feel free to create your own list of songs:
  "Silent Night"
  "Little Drummer Boy"
  "Oh Holy Night"
  "Come All Ye Faithful"
  "Jingle Bells"
  "Deck the Halls"

Ask the teams what made this difficult? What made it easy? Ever notice that no matter how hard you try sometimes, those around you misunderstand you?

Discovery

Picture a teenage girl who comes to you saying she has never had sex but is pregnant and an older married woman who has never been able to get pregnant but all of a sudden is. Read Luke 1:36–45. This is exactly what has happened here. Mary was young and a virgin and Elizabeth was an older, barren woman.

Life Application

What part of this story is the most difficult for you to believe?

This month the church considers the miracle of the birth of Jesus. The miracles come again and again: Angels speaking, impossible pregnancies, etc. It is hard to believe all that happens in this. While it is unlikely anyone in your group will receive a visit from an angel saying they are about to be the father or mother of the Messiah, miracles still happen.

Both Mary and Joseph had to make decisions surrounding what God was doing in their lives. They could have chosen to follow the rules of the day that made sense to the other people around them *or* they could have chosen to obey God.

- In what places in your lives today does it seem the ways of God are the opposite of what the world calls you to do?
- What do you risk by not buying into the ways of the world and seeking God's ways instead?

An important part of this story is the result of obedience. Joseph and Mary did not just choose to do right and suddenly there was a mansion with servants and flocks of people honoring them. What happened is that, even with God, they had to run for their lives. They fled to Egypt to be obedient.

Many of us expect that following Jesus will make life easier. Spend some time talking about the real struggles that can come when you decide to follow Jesus instead of the world. Spend some time talking of the blessing and privilege that comes with following Jesus.

Beyond Belief

by Amy Jacober

In this lesson, students will:
- ✔ Understand that God truly is the One in control
- ✔ Celebrate the ordinary in the world
- ✔ Recognize Mary's significance
- ✔ Consider their own perspective of what makes someone great

Stuff you'll need:
- ❏ A collection of random items
- ❏ Advent wreath

Memory Verse

Blessed is she who believed, for there will be a fulfillment of those things which were told her from the Lord. —Luke 1:45

Scripture

Luke 1:26–38

Lesson in a Sentence

God often chooses the least likely candidate to carry out His greatest work.

The Big Picture

This story is so familiar it is easy to miss how remarkable Mary is. Here was an average young woman, betrothed, and looking forward to the next season of her life. Nothing in scripture hints at anything but surprise when Mary learned she was to give birth to the Savior of the world. She wasn't posturing or trying to prove her worth. She was who she was and nothing more. So often today, we see those who do amazing things for God as people who have power, prestige, and money. What we don't see are the countless average people whom God chooses everyday to serve, give, and change the world. There could not have been a less likely candidate for greatness in Biblical times than a young woman who was not yet married.

Focus

Option 1

This is a game called "What Is It?" Bring a random assortment of objects. For example: a spatula, broom, Christmas stocking, platter, license plate, etc. Bring in at least twelve items. Give a bell or whistle to two of your leaders assigned as judges. Divide the group into two teams. Give one person in each team one of the items. The game begins as a first person from team A gives an interpretation of the item. If the judge says this is valid, the second person takes their turn. Play continues until one of the players cannot think of a unique use for their item.

For example:
    Player one is given a spatula
    Player two is given an innertube.

    P1: See my new fly swatter
    P2: It is a giant donut
    P1: A conductor's baton
    P2: My yo-yo lost its string
    P1: It's a Backscratcher
    P2: A bloated hula-hoop
    P1: …I can't think of anything!
    P2: A halo

    Player 2 gets the point.

Each member of each team competes. The team with the most points at the end of the game wins. Then ask: Have you ever noticed how even the most ordinary items can be considered in extraordinary ways if seen through the right eyes?

Option 2

Today is the third Sunday of Advent. We have looked at Jesus and Joseph. Another central figure in this event is Mary. It is astonishing that a young woman could be pregnant never having been with a man. It is also astonishing that a woman was mentioned prominently when this story was written. God could have just shown up on earth, fully grown as a man. Instead, he chose to come in the humblest of forms, completely dependent as a baby. Even more, he chose to depend on an average young woman. Wouldn't it have made more sense to choose the wife of Pharaoh, a queen, or any other woman of power?

Read Isaiah 9:6–7 as you light this week's candle. Don't forget to light the last two weeks' candles as well. Close with a prayer of thanks to God for using average people in remarkable of events.

Discovery

Pass out papers with the passage printed on it designating parts for girls and boys to read as follows:

Luke 1:26–38

Narrator: Now in the sixth month the angel Gabriel was sent by God to a city of Galilee named Nazareth, to a virgin betrothed to a man whose name was Joseph, of the house of David. And the virgin's name was Mary. And having come in, the angel said to her,

Boys: "Rejoice, highly favored one, the Lord is with you; blessed are you among women!"

Narrator: But when she saw him, she was troubled at his saying, and considered what manner of greeting this was. Then the angel said to her,

Boys: "Do not be afraid Mary, for you have found favor with God. And behold, you will conceive in your womb and bring forth a Son, and shall call His name Jesus. He will be great, and will be called the Son of Highest; and the Lord God will give Him the throne of His father David. And He will reign over the house of Jacob forever, and of His kingdom there will be no end."

Narrator: Then Mary said to the angel,

Girls: "How can this be, since I do not know a man?"

Narrator: And the angel answered and said to her,

Boys: "The Holy Spirit will come upon you, and the power of the Highest will overshadow you; therefore, also, that Holy One who is to be born will be called the Son of God. Now indeed, Elizabeth your relative has also conceived a son in her old age; and this now the sixth month for her who was called barren. For with God nothing will be impossible."

Narrator: Then Mary said,

Girls: "Behold the maidservant of the Lord! Let it be to me according to your word."

Narrator: And the angel departed from her.

Life Application

What just happened? Spend a few moments in small groups talking about how you might have reacted if this happened to you or someone you know. Share reactions with the entire group. Ask: What did Mary do to deserve this? (She did nothing.)

Let's take the principle of this story. An angel approaches Mary, the betrothed of Joseph. This angel lets her know the Lord wants to do something amazing through her. She was not wealthy nor from a powerful or prestigious family. To the best of our knowledge, she was average.

- How does God use average people today?
- How could you recognize if God was calling you to do something for the kingdom?
- Consider all of the ways God can use teenagers today. What ways could God use your group right now just as you are?

Making it Personal

Have you ever felt like God was calling you to do something? What did that look like? In pairs, talk about a time God was calling you to do something or guiding you along the way. Pray with one another asking God for an unmistakable calling.

Song

"Possibilities" by Sanctus Real on *The Face of Love*

Beyond Belief

by Amy Jacober

Memory Verse

Blessed is she who believed, for there will be a fulfillment of those things which were told her from the Lord. —Luke 1:45

Scripture

Luke 1:39–56; Isaiah 64:8

Lesson in a Sentence

God often chooses the least likely candidate to carry out His greatest work.

Focus

Hand out lumps of clay and ask each person to make the best average item they can. Most likely, they will want more explanation but resist this. Encourage them to be creative and let their imaginations go. Give two to five minutes for them to work. Make a big deal of it as you count down the final moments they have to work. When you call time, and have each person share their creation and why it is unmistakably average. You may want to consider giving an average award for the most average item.

Tell the students, "Each of you began with a lump of clay and in just a few moments it was transformed into an object. What is it about the clay that made it easy to shape? (It is pliable, has no will of its own, etc.)

TEACHER'S NOTE

You can buy clay or make your own. Recipe below:
1 C flour
1/2 C salt
3 Tbsp. oil, vegetable
1 package of Kool-Aid
1/2 C water
Mix together
Place in refrigerator in an airtight container.
Repeat with a new flavor or Kool-Aid for another color.

Discovery

Read Isaiah 64:8. What is your gut reaction at hearing this passage? How does this fit with our individualistic world? Is it comforting or frustrating to think of God as the potter and us as the clay?

Last time, we looked at Mary. An ordinary woman used in extraordinary ways. Her willingness to be used by God—to be shaped in His image—led her to a role of honor. Interestingly, being used by God did not elevate her in the world. She still raised children, cleaned, cooked, and took care of the family. She did not gain great wealth. She did not gain great power or prestige. She was still ordinary but God was lifted up.

Read Luke 1:39–56. Luke 1:46–56 is best read aloud. It is a hymn of thanks and praise.

Teacher's Note

This portion of scripture is known as the Magnificat. Mary praises the Lord for choosing her to be the mother of Jesus and for remembering Israel and His promise to her. It is divided into two parts, personal and corporate. In the first part, vv. 46–49, Mary praises God. Verse 50 is a transition. She acknowledges that God shows mercy on those who fear Him, in that she fears the Lord and acknowledges that this mercy is not for her alone but all those who fear the Lord. In verses 51–53, she reminds God that He will bring down the proud and in verses 54–55 that He remembers His promises and will raise the humble.

Life Application

If not in the will of God, being used by God can simply seem like being used in the negative sense. In the will of God, being like clay in the potters hands allows us to become more than we ever could have before.

Allow your students to recreate their clay into a new shape. What would they like God to do in their lives? Have them symbolically create something to visualize what God could be doing.

After a few moments, pass out paper and pens. Invite each student to write his or her own hymn to God. It can be as simple as pointing out that Mary was praising God for what He chose to do in her life and inviting others to do the same. It can also be more complicated and follow the format outlined in the Teacher's Note above. Let your students be the guides of how simple or complicated this should be.

Note: It is easy to skip the writing of a hymn and have further discussion. There is nothing wrong with discussion but do not neglect the teachable times when you invite your students into a discipline like writing praises to God that has been practiced for thousands of years.

In the Field at Night

by Amy Jacober

In this lesson, students will:
- ✔ Learn what the angels told the shepherds before they ever saw the baby Jesus
- ✔ Be challenged to respond with action when they hear the gospel
- ✔ Understand that praise is the proper response to the gospel's proclamation

Stuff you'll need:
- ❏ *A Charlie Brown Christmas* video or DVD
- ❏ Advent wreath and matches
- ❏ Giant birthday card for Jesus
- ❏ Markers

Memory Verse

For He will give His angels charge concerning you, to guard you in all your ways.
—Psalm 91:11

Scripture

Luke 2:8–20

Lesson in a sentence

The proper response to proclamation is praise!

The Big Picture

I am certain you have never done this, but I have heard of people checking off the activities in a church service, counting down to the end. I have heard of people making to-do lists during the sermon.

Most of us say we love God, but we don't want to hear more about Him than what we picked up in grade school. Unfortunately, our students are the same. Hearing the word of God is anything but boring or irrelevant though we teachers can make it seem so. According to scripture, the proclamation of the good news of Christ results in praising the Lord. Not only was this the response of the shepherds, it should be our response today. Do you get excited to hear about God? Do your students come to church hungry for His Word? Do you really believe God is the creator, redeemer, and sustainer of the world? Isn't about time we live like these things are true and respond as we should?

Focus

Option 1

Show a clip from *A Charlie Brown Christmas*. Use the scene where Linus is reading the Christmas story on stage. Let this be the jumpstart for conversation.

Option 2

This is the final Sunday of Advent. It is the Sunday of Proclamation. Interestingly enough we have been proclaiming the coming of Christmas since before Thanksgiving. Think about the music that began in the malls. When did stores put out Christmas decorations? What about catalogs and wish lists for the holiday? These all began weeks ago! These however are not quite the same as how we tend to think of Christmas being proclaimed in the church. Originally, the news of the birth of Christ came via the angels. We have spent the last three weeks celebrating Jesus and considering Joseph and Mary. Today we look at a visit from an angel.

Read Luke 2:8–20. In the days before Christmas, just like the shepherds, we are told Jesus is on the way. Light each of the candles reminding the group of the symbolism of the advent wreath. Evergreen for everlasting life, purple candles for royalty, a circle shape for eternity, and flames to remind us that Jesus is the light of the world.

Discovery

Ask students to volunteer and create a melodrama from this passage. At a minimum, you need an angel, shepherd, Mary, and Joseph though you can have more than one shepherd. Give them fifteen minutes to read the passage and create their own skit to convey what took place.

Meanwhile, have your students gather round a sheet of butcher paper and give each a marker. Have them create a giant birthday card for Jesus offering praises in the form of messages to Jesus. The chances are that some of your students will think this is lame. This is fine. Often kids feel silly creating something like this. Do your best to keep your students on task and let them enjoy the process. This struggle will come up in later conversation.

When your student volunteers are ready, gather the group to watch the passage acted out. If you need, read the passage either before or after the sketch.

Life Application

Ask:
- What parts of this story stand out to you?
- Sum up the response of the shepherds as you saw in the skit and heard in the scripture.
- Did you notice the first words from the angels were to not be afraid? Why would they need to say that?

When might we need to hear this same prelude to God's messages today?
- What can we learn from the angels' words that we needn't be afraid to hear what God has to say?

- The shepherds wasted no time after hearing from the angels. They listened and were on their way to see the baby Jesus. How quickly do we respond when we hear from God?
- The shepherds did another major thing after hearing from the angels. They praised God. They listened, they acted, and they praised. This is a good pattern to follow today.
- What do you think God is telling us today?
- Does it seem crazy to you to think God might want you to take action immediately?
- Is it possible to be a Christian and stay within our comfort zone?
- Do you think God calls us to move out of our typical world in order to see Him?
- When you hear the gospel or a proclamation about God what is your typical response?

We celebrate sports championships. We throw parties for our own birthdays. We yell and cheer at the New Year.
- What emotions does saying the word *preaching* or *proclaiming* conjure up for you?
- Have you ever been moved to praise God because of hearing His Word? If yes, when? If no, why not?

Making it Personal
You spent some time earlier creating a birthday card for Jesus writing down messages of praise to Him.
- Did any of you feel silly doing this? Why?
- Is it possible that we could get to the place where we do not feel self conscious for praising God?
- Does the thought of the birth of Jesus excite you?
- Do you really understand that Christmas is about the creator of the universe stepping out of heaven because of His love for you?
- If you say you get this, why is it that so much of Christmas is commercialized even for Christians?
- How Christmas again be about what it was be from the beginning? (A celebration of the birth of the King.)
- How can you shift your perspective and make Christmas more about responding in praise to the proclamation of the birth of Jesus?
Consider a birthday gift that honors the Lord.

Invite each student to revisit his or her thoughts about working on the giant card. Go around your group and have each person offer praise to God based not on what He has done but who He is. Remind them that this time of year we celebrate Jesus as an infant. Babies do not do anything for the adults around them. They are dependent and helpless. In a sense, they are useless. Even in His infancy, Jesus was still the King of kings and Lord of lords. How might we praise the baby Jesus?

Songs
"You Are My Joy" by the Dave Crowder Band on *A Collision*

Two Steps Forward . . .

by Amy Jacober

In this lesson, students will:
- ✔ Learn of many of the great heroes of the faith
- ✔ Be encouraged that others have made it through difficulties
- ✔ Understand that following Christ is both joyous and difficult

Stuff you'll need:
- ❑ Construction paper
- ❑ List of verses and references

Memory Verse

No temptation has overtaken you except such as is common to man; but God is faithful, who will not allow you to be tempted beyond what you are able, but with the temptation will also make the way of escape, that you may be able to endure it.
—1 Corinthians 10:13

Scripture

Hebrews 11:1–12:3

Lesson in a Sentence

Looking back can help us move forward.

The Big Picture

It's the end of the year, a close of one chapter and the opening of a new one. It is time to recall how God has been at work in our lives and to take encouragement from those who have gone before, realizing that many of these people have been blessed and many have suffered. Too often, we think following Jesus makes life easy and perfect. God never says this. He does say He will be with you and that something better is coming.

Focus

Option 1

Create a giant game of concentration. On sheets of construction paper, create a deck of cards with matching objects on them. For example, have two sheets with squares, two with circles, two with hearts, two with stars, etc. If you are really creative and have the time, use more elaborate pictures like images you find on the web or digital photos from past youth-group events. The possibilities are endless, just be certain you have two of each. Have at least twenty-one pairs though you can have many more. Turn all of the cards face down in random order on the floor.

Break your group into at least two teams. Players take turns turning over two sheets cards at a time. If they match, the player picks up the pair. If they do not, they are turned back face down. Play alternates between the teams until all the pairs are found.

For more difficult play, the teams they may not communicate using words.

Debrief with your students. How did they know which cards to turn over to make a pair? What made this difficult? What made it easy? Why was it important to pay attention to what happened in the past to get the next pair?

Option 2—Are You Paying Attention?

Divide into pairs. Have each pair face one another. Give them three minutes to study one another, paying attention details. Now, have them turn back to back and change five things about themselves. They might untie a shoe, take off a ring, roll up a sleeve, mess up their hair, whatever. Turn back around, and each person tries to guess what five things have changed.

Ever notice how easily change happens and how little we realize it? Every day, what is present quickly slides to the past. If we do not pay attention, we will not even realize change has occurred.

- Why do you think it is important to know that change has occurred?
- How can what has gone before be useful today?

Discovery

Break into groups. Have each group read Hebrews 11:1–40. What did they observe? This passage references many things from the past. In reading through this, have each group take a section (see below) and look up the cross-references. Give each group a piece of paper. Divide the paper into two columns. In one column, list the person or group of people being referenced. In the other column, write the event or action to which it is referring according to the cross-reference.

Group 1—Hebrews 11:1–6

Verse 3—Genesis 1
Verse 4—Genesis 4:4
Verse 5—Genesis 5:21–24
Verse 6—Hebrews 7:19

Group 2—Hebrews 11:7–11
Verse 7—Genesis 6:13–22
Verse 8—Genesis 12:1–7
Verse 9—Genesis 12:8; 18:1,9
Verse 11—Genesis 17:17–19; 18:11–14; 21:2

Group 3—Hebrews 11:12–16
Verse 12—Genesis 22:17; Romans 4:19
Verse 13—Genesis 23:4; Matthew 13:17
Verse 15—Genesis 24:6-8
Verse 16—Exodus 3:6; 2 Timothy 4:18

Group 4—Hebrews 11:17–20
Verse 17—Genesis 22:1–10
Verse 18—Genesis 21:12
Verse 19—Romans 4:21
Verse 20—Genesis 27:27–29, 39–40

Group 5—Hebrews 11:21–24
Verse 21—Genesis 48:1,8–22
Verse 22—Genesis 50:24–25; Exodus 13:19
Verse 23—Exodus 2:2; 1:16,22
Verse 24—Exodus 2:10–11

Group 6—Hebrews 11:25–28
Verse 25—Hebrews 11:37
Verse 26—Hebrews 13:13; Hebrews 10:35
Verse 27—Exodus 12:50, 51
Verse 28—Exodus 12:21–23

Group 7—Hebrews 11:29–32
Verse 29—Exodus 14:21–31
Verse 30—Joshua 6:12–20
Verse 31—Joshua 2:1, 9–14; 6:22–25
Verse 32—Judges 4–5; 1 Samuel 16:1, 13

Group 8—Hebrews 11:33–36
Verse 33—2 Samuel 7:11; 8:1–3; Daniel 6:22
Verse 34—2 Kings 20:7; Judges 15:8
Verse 35—1 Kings 17:22–23
Verse 36—Jeremiah 20:2; Genesis 39:20

Group 9—Hebrews 11:37–40
Verse 37—2 Chronicles 24:21; 1 Kings 19:10; 2 Kings 1:8
Verse 38—1 Kings 18:4

Have each group share briefly what they learned.

Life Application

Did you realize all of these things happened? We all know many of these stories, but put all together it can be pretty overwhelming!

- Who in your church or tradition's history has played a significant role?
- What can you learn from past missionaries, pastors, writers of songs, etc.?
- How can we relate to this today?
- Does it matter to you that others have gone through struggles before you?
- How might you offer help to others based on what things you have experienced in life?

Read Hebrews 12:1–3 out loud for the entire group.

TEACHER'S NOTE

If you have significant people in your tradition's history, this is a great lesson to introduce them to your students. There are also many historical fiction and biographical books written about missionaries from the past. It's Christmas break and everyone loves a good story! Reading might not be everyone's favorite thing, but you'll never know unless you try. Who knows, you may turn a student on to an entire new way of thinking looking at the lives of Christians from the past!

Making it Personal

Talk about who has gone before you to encourage or teach you about what it means to follow Christ. What about this person has been encouraging? What about this person makes you question things? Has this person ever let you down? What if they did, what does this do to your faith?

Re-read verses 2 and 3. These verses remind us to keep our eyes on Christ. He will never fail nor let you down.

Songs

"Beyond the Walls" by Warren Barfield on *Reach*
"Stand Still" by Mary Mary on *Mary Mary*

Two Steps Forward . . .

by Amy Jacober

Memory Verse

No temptation has overtaken you except such as is common to man; but God is faithful, who will not allow you to be tempted beyond what you are able, but with the temptation will also make the way of escape, that you may be able to endure it.
—1 Corinthians 10:13

Scripture

1 Corinthians 10:1–13

Lesson in a Sentence

Looking back can help us move forward.

Focus

Post around the room several ancient symbols from Christianity. There is not single, special way to draw these. In fact simple stick figure drawing is just fine so do not be intimidated if you are not artistic!

As your students enter, give each a piece of paper and a pencil. Ask them to look at each symbol and decide what they think it means. Offer a small prize to the person who gets the most correct. Examples include:

A Butterfly (resurrection)
A Thistle (the passion)
A Dagger in the Heart (Mary)
A Dove (the Holy Spirit)
A Dove with Olive Branch (peace)
Fish (Christian, ICTHUS, Jesus Christ, God's Son, Savior)
Three Leafed Clover (the Trinity)
Scalloped Shell (Baptism)
Bread and Cup (Lord's Supper)
Lamp (God's word)
Keys (Peter)
Ladder (Crucifixion)
Lion and Lamb (God)
Crown (King of Kings)
Scales (Justice)

These are just a few! If you want more, use a search engine to search for Christian Symbols. You'll be amazed how many pop up! Remember those art classes you took years ago? This is where many of those symbols may be seen today. They can also be found in jewelry and logos all over the world.

Discovery

We are not alone. We are also not the first to seek after Jesus. Read 1 Corinthians 10:1–13.
   • What do we learn from this passage?
   • What does Paul warn for us to consider?
   • How can paying attention to others help us not make the same mistakes they have made?
   • What does 1 Corinthians 10:13 say? How can this help in your daily life?

Life Application
Think back over the last year. In groups, share the following:
   • Where have you seen God at work in your life or the lives of those around you?
   • Where have you questioned God's presence?
   • Where can you see in hindsight that God was working but you were clueless?

Distribute construction paper and markers to each group. Ask each person to draw a symbol of who God has been to them in the past year.

Encourage your students to begin reflecting regularly on where God has taken them. To learn from the past, find encouragement and recognize God's presence.

Memory Verse Activity
Write the memory verse on the back of the paper with the symbol they have drawn. Remind your students that no matter what they go through it is not the first time something like this has happened in the history of the world, and it will not be the last. You will not be given anything you cannot handle as long as you are not trying to handle it on your own.

Appendix: Web Resources for Youth Ministry

Publishers offering curriculum resources

www.abingdon.com

www.augsburgfortress.org

www.Cokesbury.com

www.cookministries.com

www.grouppublishing.com

www.helwys.com

www.lifeway.com

www.standardpub.com

www.studentlife.net

www.thomasnelson.com

www.tyndale.com

www.upperroom.org

www.urbanministries.com

www.wjkbooks.com

www.youthspecialties.com

www.zondervan.com

Games

www.egadideas.com—a directory of indoor and outdoor games

www.funattic.com—games of all sorts, for all age groups

www.ferryhalim.com/original—silly internet games

www.gameskidsplay.net—recreational activities for all ages

www.thesource4ym.com—a huge collection games

www.youthministry.com—games for large and small groups; noncompetitive; illustrate a point.

Human and Social Resources

www.adopting.org—assistance, information, and support for adoption

www.amnesty.org—a group seeking to end human rights violations

www.aspenyouth.com—information about Aspen Youth Ranches, which provide education, treatment, and rehabilitation to at-risk youth

www.behindthelabel.com—information about name brands and the conditions under which the products are made

www.bread.org—Bread for the World—lobbyists to Congress that provide study materials for high school aged students

www.breakawayoutreach.com—a ministry that reaches troubled youth through juvenile justice ministries, sports, and multimedia productions

www.childrensdefense.org—Children's Defense Fund—materials on the needs of American children, in particular the poor

www.faithtrustinstitute.org/index.html—Formerly the Center for the Prevention of Sexual and Domestic Violence, now the FaithTrust Institute—seeks to educate and prevent sexual and domestic violence from a faith perspective

www.esa-online.org—Evangelicals for Social Action—publishers of Bible-based materials on social justice

www.goshen.net/directory/Teens/— numerous links for youth pastors and youth who are struggling with issues such as suicide, drugs and alcohol

www.jmpf.org—John Perkins Foundation—social justice and service

www.mcc.org—Mennonite Central Committee—relief and development agency of the Mennonite and Brethren in Christ churches

www.rainn.org—a confidential 24-hour rape hotline

www.smartlink.net/~tag—Teen Age Grief—insight and information concerning the developmental issues of adolescence and grief *www.stopthetraffik.org*—Stop the Traffik—seeking to raise awareness about human trafficking and the impact on ministry and adolescents worldwide

www.tamethemonster.com—information and practical advice for combating poverty beginning with prayer

www.vpp.com/teenhelp—VPP—a national toll-free hotline designed to assist parents, childcare professionals, and others in finding resources for the treatment of struggling youth

Magazines

www.briomag.com—Brio—a magazine for teenage girls that strives to teach, entertain, and challenge girls while encouraging them to grow in a closer relationship with Christ

www.gp4teens.com—Guideposts for Teens—tackles real issues such as sex, dating, faith, and spirituality

www.theotherjournal.com—An online journal about the intersection of theology and culture

www.pluggedinonline.com—Plugged In—designed to help parents, youth leaders, ministers, and teens to understand and impact the culture that they live in; offers reviews and discussions regarding entertainment and its effects on youth and families

www.relevantmagazine.com—considers God and progressive culture

www.sojo.net—Soujourners—source for Faith, culture, and politics

www.youthspecialties.com—Youthworker Journal—a thematic magazine aimed at youth workers. Practical articles, devotional articles, resources and information regarding thoughts and trends in youth ministry

Missions and Service

www.amor.org—mission agency specializing in trips to northern Mexico

www.apu.edu/iom/mexout—Mexico Outreach—ministry based out of Azusa Pacific University taking high school and young adult groups into northern Mexico for service

www.agrm.org—Association of Gospel Rescue Missions—links to local missions that provide shelter, kitchens, community development, and community centers

www.asphome.org—Appalachia Service Project—ministry that takes groups on week-long mission trips to Kentucky and Tennessee to repair homes for the poor

www.calebproject.org—information and resources for global missions

www.christiansurfers.net—helps students form a Christian organization of surfers; missions in the surfing community

www.compassion.com—Compassion International—relief organization with programs that educate and involve junior and senior high students

www.crm.org—Church Resources Ministries—exists to develop leaders in the church and to provide resources worldwide

www.empoweringlives.org—addresses spiritual and physical needs in struggling countries primarily Africa; outreach and leadership development and child sponsorship opportunities

www.gospelcom.net/csm—Center for Student Missions—customized mission trips to large cities for junior and senior high students

www.habitat.org—Habitat for Humanity—housing for low-income families with many service opportunities

www.joniandfriends.org—one of the only resources for ministry with those with disabilities

www.larche.org, www.larcheusa.org, www.larche.org.uk, www.larchecanada.org— L'Arche—provides communities for those with and without physical or mental Disabilities; Henri Nouwen was associated with the organization

www.newadventures.org—missions organization providing trips for junior and senior high school students

www.oneliferevolution.org—encouraging youth groups to raise awareness regarding the AIDS pandemic

www.servlife.org—seeks to develop and empower indigenous workers in difficult areas

www.worldvision.org—provides relief to third world countries by reaching out to the poor and staying aware of current worldwide events

Music Resources

www.acaza.com—current news on Christian artists

www.ccmcom.com—up-to-date news on today's hottest contemporary Christian musicians *www.christianfestivals.com*—list of Christian festivals and concerts all over the country

www.christianitytoday.com/music/—reviews of new Christian music; interviews with artists

www.cmcentral.com—editorials on music and artists; album and artist reviews; tour dates; MP3 downloads

www.christianradio.com—a list of over 2,000 Christian radio stations and over 500 Christian artists

www.christianrock.net—24-hour radio show broadcast on the internet; two sister stations: *http://www.christianhardrock.net/*; *http://www.christian-hiphop.net/*

www.rockrebel.com/—articles on Christianity and spirituality in secular music

www.wellwatermusic.com—for and about new artists

www.worshiptogether.com—overview of what is hot in Christian music; top ten lists, free song downloads

www.youthfire.com/music/compare.html—Youth Fire—Christian music comparable to the mainstream

Pop Culture

www.christianitytoday.com—detailed reviews on movies and music; discussion questions

www.cmli.org—Christian Media Literacy Institute

www.cpyu.org—Center for Parent and Youth Understanding—comprehensive site; constant updates covering youth culture

www.dickstaub.com—pop culture review from a Christian perspective

www.commonsensemedia.org—media reviews

www.gracehillmedia.com—points of connection between Hollywood and the Christian community

www.hollywoodjesus.com—perspectives of today's pop culture; reviews for today's newest movies, music

www.medialit.org/focus/rel_articles.html—Center for Media Literacy—some faith-based articles on media discernment *www.mrfh.cjb.net*—Screen it Entertainment Reviews—detailed description of what viewers will see (i.e. violence, sex, bad language) in current movies; MPAA ratings

www.planetwisdom.com—reviews of movies and music with insights on culture and faith

www.rollingstone.com—reviews movies and particularly secular music, providing CD reviews, photos, and videos

www.screenit.com—reviews on all sorts of entertainment

www.textweek.com—sermon topics stemming from current and past movies

www.tollbooth.org—reviews of Christian music, concerts, and books

www.wikipedia.org—An open source online encyclopedia

Spiritual Disciplines

www.contemplativeoutreach.org—information and links with other sites and groups interested in exploring the contemplative side of faith

www.labyrinth.co.uk—Jonny Baker—the most commonly known labyrinth among youth workers

www.lectiodevina.org—articles and explanations into the practice of lectio devina

www.sdiworld.org—Spiritual Directors International

www.sfts.edu—San Francisco Theological Seminary—the Youth Ministry and Spirituality Project

www.soulsearching.ie—spirituality from a Christian perspective including art, social justice, prayer, philosophy, music

www.taize.fr—Taize community in France

www.tddm.org—devotionals, poems, stories and chat rooms geared toward teens

T-Shirts etc.

www.mcduck.com—familiar with youth ministry; embroidery and screen printing

www.zazzle.com—create your design and have it printed on multiple variations of shirts; relatively low cost.

Worship Resources

www.audiblefaith.com—downloadable worship music and sheet music in any key

www.ccli.com—comprehensive and valuable informational resources about worship

www.christianguitar.org—Christian guitar resource; over 7,000 songs in tablature; lessons, PowerPoint slides, and message boards

www.heartofworship.com—Bible insights and resources for worship

www.integritymusic.com—worship resources; information on artists, albums

www.maranathamusic.com—resources for worship and worship leaders

www.pastornet.net.au/inside—Inside Out—downloadable contemporary and evangelical worship music for non-commercial use

www.songs4worship.com—worship resources including music, community, freebies

www.worshipmusic.com—music resource with CDs, cassettes, sheet music, videos, software

Youth Activities

www.30hourfamine.org—fights world hunger with the help of youth and churches

www.adventures.org—Adventures in Missions—short-term missions organization; programs for youth, college, and adults

www.bigworld.org—customized short-term mission trips for youth, adults, individuals, groups, church networks, and Christian organizations

www.thejeremiahproject.org—missions trips for junior high youth

www.noahsark.com—Christian whitewater rafting, rock climbing, rappelling in Colorado

www.syatp.org—See You at the Pole—a youth ministry tradition when students gather around the flag pole at school and pray

www.ywam.org—YWAM Urban Ministries—safe and exciting events to communities in need; innovative ministries; living in the community

Youth Pastor—Emergent

www.emergentvillage.com—links for missional Christians across generations *www.emergingchurch.org*—connections point for postmodern thinking churches

www.churchnext.net/index.shtml—Tribal Generation—a loose look at many topics from a Christian perspective

www.theooze.com—bringing all issues them into conversation within a Christian community

Youth Pastor Resources

www.americanapparel.net—a socially responsible resource for plain shirts printed for camp or retreat

www.biblegateway.com—online concordance of many Bible translations

www.buwc.ca/youthline—Youthline—youth ministry resource page with events located primarily in Canada

www.capernaumministries.org—division of Young Life which focuses on ministry for adolescents with special needs

www.crosswalk.com—resources, articles, advice, Bible translations, scriptural commentary

www.discipleshipresources.org/downloads.asp—discipleship downloads from the United Methodist Church

www.family.org—articles for help parents with their growing children and changing families; wisdom for the ups and downs of family life

www.highwayvideo.com—culturally relevant videos for ministry and worship

www.hmconline.org—training sessions for urban youth leaders

www.ileadyouth.com—articles, training, resources; and events

www.notboring.com—Free comics, jokes, e-cards, etc.; updated three times each week

www.nwgs.edu—Northwest Graduate School—accredited school offering a global perspective and experience to theological education; allows the student to remain in ministry while training

www.parentministry.org—articles that help build a stronger family-based ministry; articles for understanding adolescent children

www.persecution.com—updates and prayer requests regarding the persecuted church *www.reach-out.org*—books, articles, Bible studies, illustrations, ideas for training volunteers; insight into leading a successful mission trip

www.teamce.com—Christian Endeavor—philosophy and training for simplified youth ministry

www.uywi.org—training for those working in urban settings

www.yfc.org—Provides current information on youth ministries for youth pastors, youth, and parents.

www.ymwomen.com—networking resource for women in youth ministry; articles; resources; e-mail newsletter

www.younglife.org—information about Young life and its work with today's youth

www.youthbuilders.com—for parents and youth leaders; articles; answered questions

www.youth-ministry.info—information both practical and philosophical; links to everything connected with youth ministry

www.youthpastor.com—articles; games; youth group names; recommended reading; topical music resources.

www.youthspecialties.com/links—thousands of links to websites on leadership, missions, skit ideas, crisis hotlines, much more

www.youthworkers.net—allows youth workers to connect with each other by region. links to nationwide activities for youth